SOURCES, STORIES, AND SONGS

ANTHOLOGY

United States

ADVENTURES IN TIME AND PLACE

- Biographies and Autobiographies
- Diaries and Journals
- Essays
- Fiction and Nonfiction Selections
- Folk Tales and Legends
- Interviews
- Letters
- Newspaper Articles
- Plays
- Poems
- Songs
- Speeches
- Visual Documents

Macmillan McGraw-Hill

New York   Farmington

PROGRAM AUTHORS

Dr. James A. Banks
Professor of Education and Director of the Center for Multicultural Education
University of Washington
Seattle, Washington

Dr. Barry K. Beyer
Professor Emeritus, Graduate School of Education
George Mason University
Fairfax, Virginia

Dr. Gloria Contreras
Professor of Education
University of North Texas
Denton, Texas

Jean Craven
District Coordinator of Curriculum Development
Albuquerque Public Schools
Albuquerque, New Mexico

Dr. Gloria Ladson-Billings
Professor of Education
University of Wisconsin
Madison, Wisconsin

Dr. Mary A. McFarland
Instructional Coordinator of Social Studies, K–12, and Director of Staff Development
Parkway School District
Chesterfield, Missouri

Dr. Walter C. Parker
Professor and Program Chair for Social Studies Education
University of Washington
Seattle, Washington

NATIONAL
GEOGRAPHIC
SOCIETY
Washington, D.C.

Acknowledgments

"Lineage" from FOR MY PEOPLE by Margaret Walker. ©1942 by Yale University Press.

"The Beautiful Dream" from AND IT IS STILL THAT WAY by Byrd Baylor. ©1976 by Byrd Baylor. Published by Trails West Press, Santa Fe, NM.

"The Conquistadors Search for Gold" from THE BROKEN SPEARS: THE AZTEC ACCOUNT OF THE CONQUEST OF MEXICO by Miguel Leon-Portilla. ©1962 by Beacon Press, Boston.

"Faith that Moved a Dump Heap" by Mary McLeod Bethune from WHO, THE MAGAZINE ABOUT PEOPLE, vol. 1, no. 3, June 1941 issue.

Excerpt from CÉSAR CHÁVEZ by Consuelo Rodriguez. ©1991 by Chelsea House Publishers, a division of Main Line Book Co.

"Night Journey" from THE COLLECTED POEMS OF THEODORE ROETHKE by Theodore Roethke. ©1940 by Theodore Roethke.

"Two Views on Women's Rights" from THE BOOK OF ABIGAIL AND JOHN: SELECTED LETTERS OF THE ADAMS FAMILY 1762-1784, L.H. Butterfield, editor, Cambridge, MA: Harvard University Press. ©1975 by the Massachusetts Historical Society.

"Sweet Betsy from Pike" and "Erie Canal" from MUSIC AND YOU, Senior Authors: Barbara & Merrill Staton. ©1991 Macmillan Publishing Company, a division of Macmillan, Inc.

Excerpt from GRASSHOPPER SUMMER by Ann Turner. ©1989 by Ann Turner.

Excerpt from CHARLIE PIPPIN by Candy Dawson Boyd. ©1987 by Candy Dawson Boyd.

"Let America Be America Again" from A NEW SONG by Langston Hughes. ©1938 by Langston Hughes, renewed 1965 by Langston Hughes.

"Life in a Japanese American Relocation Camp" from AND JUSTICE FOR ALL by John Tateishi. ©1984 by John Tateishi.

"Reaching the Americas" from THE LOG OF CHRISTOPHER COLUMBUS, by Robert H. Fuson. ©1987 by Robert H. Fuson. Published by International Marine, an imprint of TAB Books, a Division of McGraw-Hill Inc., Blue Ridge Summit, PA 17294-0850.

"Dust Storm Disaster" Words and Music by Woody Guthrie. TRO ©1960 (renewed) and 1963 (renewed) Ludlow Music, Inc. New York, NY.

"From the Walls of Angel Island" excerpted from ISLAND *Poetry and History of Chinese Immigrants on Angel Island, 1910-1940* edited by Him Mark Lai, Genny Lim, and Judy Yung. ©1980 by the HOC DOI (History of Chinese Detained on Island) Project. Published by University of Washington Press, 1991.

"Don't Fence Me In" (Cole Porter) ©1944 Warner Bros., Inc. (Renewed) All Rights Reserved.

"Save the Earth (It's Not Too Late)" by Professor Rap. ©1990 Professor Rap.

"I Have a Dream" speech by Martin Luther King, Jr. from A TESTAMENT OF HOPE *The Essential Writings of Martin Luther King, Jr.* edited by James Melvin Washington. ©1986 by Coretta Scott King, Executrix of the Estate of Martin Luther King, Jr.

(continued on page 199)

Macmillan/McGraw-Hill

A Division of The McGraw-Hill Companies

Macmillan/McGraw-Hill
1221 Avenue of the Americas
New York, New York 10020

Printed in the United States of America

ISBN 0-02-146667-X / 5

6 7 8 9 079 02 01 00 99 98

TABLE OF *Contents*

= audio cassette

USING PRIMARY SOURCES AND LITERATURE WITH SOCIAL STUDIES

The readings in the *Adventures in Time and Place Anthology* have been carefully selected to enhance Social Studies concepts and to provide enjoyable and worthwhile reading experiences for students. All readers bring to the reading experience their own backgrounds and prior knowledge. Exposing students to a variety of viewpoints while encouraging them to question and ponder what they read will help them to become critical readers and thoughtful citizens.

The readings include **primary sources, secondary sources,** and **literature.** These fall into several categories and include:

- songs
- official documents
- oral histories
- posters
- diaries and journals
- photographs and graphics
- interviews
- political cartoons
- poems
- folk tales
- letters
- autobiographies and biographies
- newspaper articles
- fiction and nonfiction
- personal recollections
- speeches

The readings offer you a unique teaching tool. The following suggestions will help your students use the readings to build and extend their knowledge of social studies as well as to sharpen their analytical skills.

PRIMARY AND SECONDARY SOURCES

A **primary source** is something that comes from the time that is being studied. Primary sources include such things as official documents of the time, diaries and journals, letters, newspaper articles and advertisements, photographs, and oral histories. A **secondary source** is an account of the past written by someone who was not an eyewitness to those events. Remind students of the difference between primary and secondary sources. Point out that primary sources give historians valuable clues from the past because they provide first-hand information about a certain time or event. Primary sources let the reader see how people lived, felt, and thought.

However, primary sources express the view of only one person. Thus, it is important for students to understand the point of view of the writer and to find out all that they can about his or her background to decide whether the writer is credible, or believable. Secondary sources often compare and analyze different points of view and give a broader view of the event, but once again it is important for students to understand the writer's point of view and analyze his or her credentials. Suggest to students that when they read primary and secondary sources, they ask themselves these questions:

- Who created the source?
- Can the writer be believed?
- Does the writer have expert knowledge of the subject?
- Does the writer have a reason to describe the events in a certain way?
- Does the writer have a reputation for being accurate?

When you work with the primary sources in this Anthology, you may wish to encourage students to think about the following as they read some of the various sources:

Diaries and Journals Was the diary or journal originally written to be shared with the public?

Speeches Was the intent of the speech to persuade the audience to adopt a particular point of view or was the speech merely informative?

Newspaper Articles Did the newspaper in which the article appeared have a particular political stance or bias that might have influenced the writer?

Official Documents Are there any words or phrases in the document that you do not understand? If so, what other source can you consult for clarification?

LITERATURE

In Social Studies, literature is used to motivate and instruct. It also plays a large role in assisting students to understand their cultural heritage and the cultural heritage of others. For example, the folk tales included in the *Adventures in Time and Place Anthology* were chosen from a wide range of cultures to offer students a glimpse of the wisdom various cultures deem important to impart. The songs, stories, and poetry of different cultures offer students an opportunity to compare and contrast and hence understand aspects of cultural identity.

Well-written historical fiction can not only give students a chance to observe historical events from the perspective of someone close to their own age, but it can also provide motivation for students to read more about the events described. For example, *Johnny Tremain* by Esther Forbes has long motivated students to learn more about the American Revolution.

USING YOUR *Anthology*

In *United States* you will be reading about many different people, places, and times. This Anthology, or collection of documents created by different people, will make the information in your textbook come to life in a special way. Some of the documents are letters, stories, diaries, songs, poems, and political essays. Others are items you might not have thought of as documents, such as old advertisements, posters, illustrations, photographs, and even a buffalo hide. As you study these documents, you will be able to see, feel, and hear what it was like to live in other times and places. The documents in the Anthology will help you to better understand the story of our country and the people who helped to build it.

INTRODUCTION •
Gives you background information about the selection and tells you what kind of document it is. Is it fiction or nonfiction? Is it a poem or a song? The introduction also gives you information about the author. At the end, the introduction asks you a question to think about as you read the document.

CASSETTE LOGO •
Tells you that the selection appears on the Anthology Cassette

TEXTBOOK LINK •
Tells you which chapter and lesson in your textbook the document is linked to

DEFINITIONS •
Gives you the meanings of difficult words

CONCLUSION •
Provides additional information and asks you to think further about the selection

SOURCE •
Tells you where the selection came from

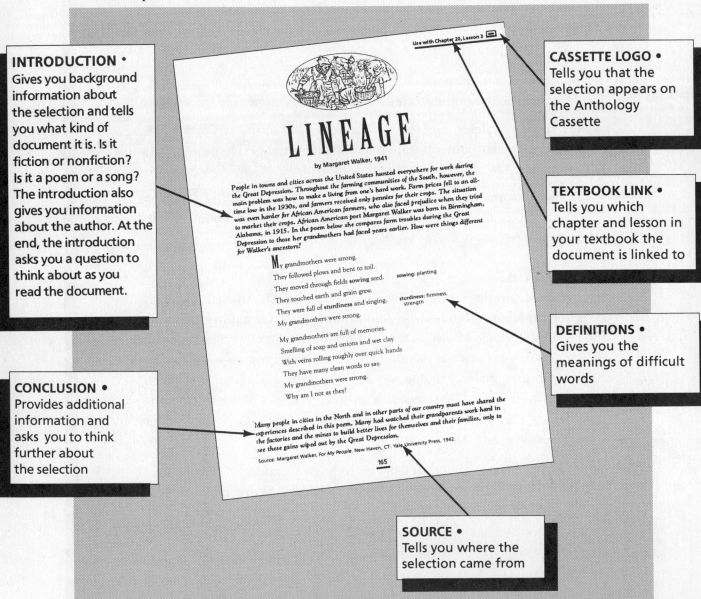

Use with Chapter 20, Lesson 3

LINEAGE

by Margaret Walker, 1941

People in towns and cities across the United States hunted everywhere for work during the Great Depression. Throughout the farming communities of the South, however, the main problem was how to make a living from one's hard work. Farm prices fell to an all-time low in the 1930s, and farmers received only pennies for their crops. The situation was even harder for African American farmers, who also faced prejudice when they tried to market their crops. African American poet Margaret Walker was born in Birmingham, Alabama, in 1915. In the poem below she compares farm troubles during the Great Depression to those her grandmothers had faced years earlier. How were things different for Walker's ancestors?

My grandmothers were strong.
They followed plows and bent to toil.
They moved through fields sowing seed.   sowing: planting
They touched earth and grain grew.
They were full of **sturdiness** and singing.   sturdiness: firmness, strength
My grandmothers were strong.

My grandmothers are full of memories.
Smelling of soap and onions and wet clay
With veins rolling roughly over quick hands
They have many clean words to say.
My grandmothers were strong.
Why am I not as they?

Many people in cities in the North and in other parts of our country must have shared the experiences described in this poem. Many had watched their grandparents work hard in the factories and the mines to build better lives for themselves and their families, only to see these gains wiped out by the Great Depression.

Source: Margaret Walker, *For My People*. New Haven, CT: Yale University Press, 1942.

165

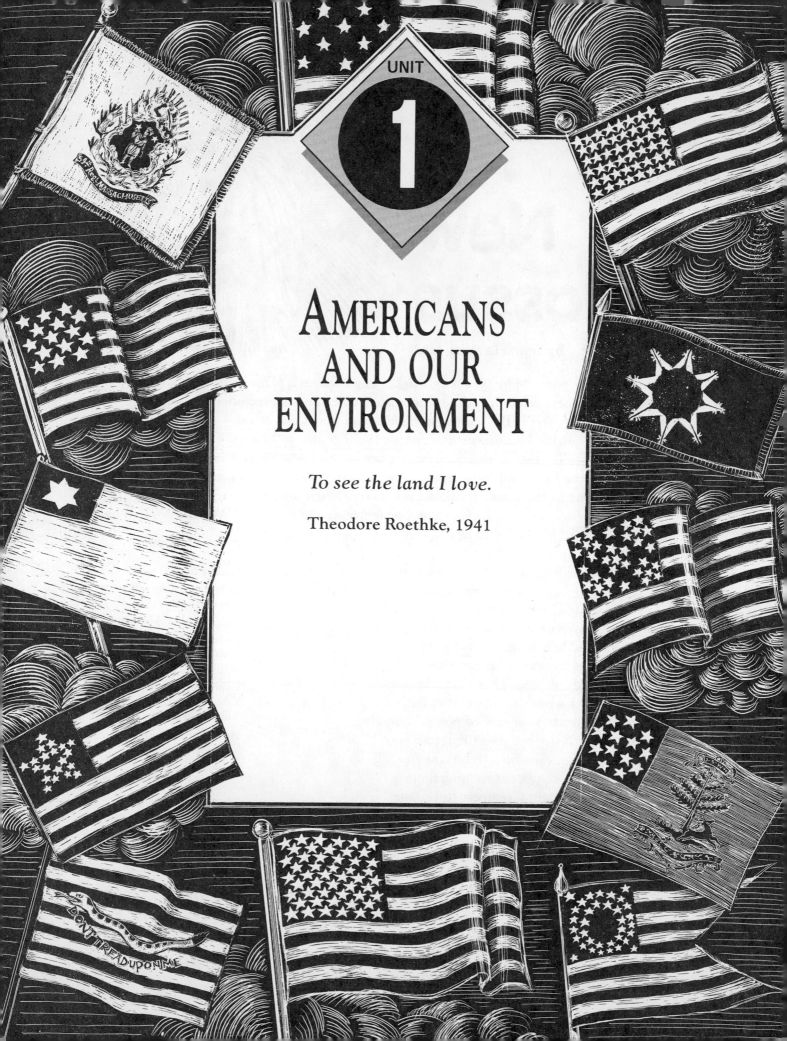

UNIT

1

AMERICANS AND OUR ENVIRONMENT

To see the land I love.

Theodore Roethke, 1941

The New Colossus

by Emma Lazarus, 1883

Emma Lazarus's poem "The New Colossus" is engraved on a plaque inside the Statue of Liberty. The poem celebrates the spirit of acceptance and appreciation of diverse cultures that many feel is the most remarkable thing about our country. "The New Colossus" was written by Lazarus as a tribute to the Statue of Liberty. Designed by Frederic-Auguste Bartholdi, the statue was given to the United States in 1886 by France, as a symbol of the friendship between the two countries. Yet the poem, which is now almost as famous as the statue itself, did not attract much attention until the 1930s, when America became a haven for many people fleeing the horrors of World War II. What might the phrase "Mother of Exiles" mean?

Not like the **brazen** giant of Greek fame,
With conquering limbs astride from land to land;
Here at our sea-washed, sunset gates shall stand
A mighty woman with a torch, whose flame
Is the imprisoned lightning, and her name
Mother of **Exiles**. From her **beacon**-hand
Glows world-wide welcome; her mild eyes command
The **air-bridged harbor** that **twin cities** frame.
"Keep, ancient lands, your **storied pomp**!" cries she
With silent lips. "Give me your tired, your poor,
Your huddled masses yearning to breathe free,
The **wretched refuse** of your **teeming** shore.
Send these, the homeless, **tempest-tost** to me,
I lift my lamp beside the golden door."

brazen: bold

Exiles: people forced to leave their countries

beacon: guiding signal

air-bridged harbor: New York harbor, spanned by the Brooklyn Bridge

twin cities: Brooklyn and Manhattan, which were separate cities at the time

storied pomp: old habits and fancy ways

wretched refuse: unwanted people

teeming: swarming

tempest-tost: battered by storms

The poet compares the Statue of Liberty to the Colossus of Rhodes, a huge monument known as one of the Seven Wonders of the World. The Colossus of Rhodes was built as a symbol of the power of the mighty Greek empire. What does the "new Colossus" stand for? Why does the poet contrast the two statues?

Source: Emily Stipes Watt, ed., *The Poetry of American Women from 1632 to 1945*. Austin: University of Texas Press, 1977.

Save the EARTH
(It's Not Too Late)

by Professor Rap, 1991

In the past 25 years, many Americans have become aware of the dangers of pollution. What can you do to help clean up the environment? A musician living in Michigan named Professor Rap has a few ideas. In 1991 Professor Rap wrote a song called Save the Earth (It's Not Too Late). As you read or sing this song, notice the different types of geographic features and the forms of pollution that he mentions. What are some of Professor Rap's suggestions you can use to help save the Earth?

Just suppose you were a crystal blue lake and
    through bad decisions and mistakes
People filled you with things that don't belong
Now you're not so blue no more, something's wrong
'Cause people won't swim in you (that's right)
And the fish can't live in you
Your shore was once filled with sand
And now it's a garbage can
D'ya see what I'm sayin'?
It's not a game that we're playin' (no more)

(Chorus)
It's not too late
Let's not hesitate
Let us all work together
To protect the earth we treasure

Just imagine you were a beautiful green tree
And the air that's around you made you sick, you see
The kids used to climb in you, you used to give shade
    to someone reading a book on a lazy Saturday
Now the kids can't climb in you, your
    limbs have gone weak
You can't give shade no more, if only you could speak
The birds can't nest in you, do you see
    what I'm sayin'?
We've got to start living right, it's not a
    game we're playing

(Chorus)

3

Now, if we all work together, and get involved
Our environmental problems will one day be solved
No we're not preaching, or blaming you alone
We just want these problems to be better known
Now, no one could ever be too educated
And to those who want to learn, this song is dedicated
So, take it from me, the hip-hop cat
You just can't argue when it comes to facts
Pollution is everywhere and often hides
In factory smokestacks and pesticides
It's time we got serious and lend a hand
With things like not using aerosol cans
The things you can do are debatable
But, it's always good to use **biodegradable**...
Products...to stop the growth of **landfills**
And help clean up the litter on the sides of our hills.
The **ozone layer** protects us from...
harmful rays sent down by the sun
After years of polluting, it's formed a hole
It grows every day over the South Pole
We are only adding to its growing rate
It's been said to be three times the size of the U.S.A.
To me, that's a problem, and to you it should too
It's time we decided what we want to do
It's a real scary fact, yet hardly known
We're **deteriorating** our ozone...
Layer upon layers of garbage sits...
   in landfills...I mean, if it fits
We need to recycle, all of us, and soon
So we can help control our planet's doom
It's as simple as that...ten minutes a day
And help save the next generation on the way

(Chorus)

biodegradable: able to
   be broken down by
   nature
landfills: garbage dumps
ozone layer: layer of air
   high above the earth

deteriorating: breaking
   down

Now, if everybody, from the richest to the poorest...
Helps out...we can save the rain forest
We're losing our trees, one by one
We need the trees to make oxygen
Did you know that? That's what we breathe
I like to breathe! So help out—please!
It's not going to take you that much time
You do your share and I'll do mine
Okay, but, polluted air hurt states like Maine
Where, like in many other places, has **acid rain**
Factory smoke can take some of the blame, (but)
Laws aren't that stiff, and that's a shame
Acid rain is formed from **toxins** in the air...
   falling down in rain drops here and everywhere
Slowly, but surely, these things come back to haunt
Now tell me...is that what you really want?

acid rain: poisonous rain caused by pollution

toxins: poisons

(Chorus)

I am tired of things that make me cough
Like the smell of smoke, or car exhaust
Every day stuff adds up to ruin our planet
It's these things that we all take for granted
Unrecyclable plastic bags add up to a lot
It takes hundreds of years before they rot
And Styrofoam...we see it everyday
When you throw it out, you think it's gone, it never goes away
We've got to get serious, and want to win
So let's stick together through thick and thin
Like stop using aerosol and Styrofoam cups
Believe me, all the little things will soon add up
Be a part...set a goal and pursue it
We're in too deep to "let the other guy do it"
So...to every man, woman, boy and girl
Let's share a goal to make our earth a better world.

(Chorus)

Source: Professor Rap, *Save the Earth (It's Not Too Late)*. Utica, MI: Dalka Studios, 1991.

Night Journey

by Theodore Roethke, 1941

*Seeing the United States from an airplane is very different from seeing the country
from a train. From a plane, mountains, lakes, and valleys look tiny and almost like
toys. Through a train window, however, the geography of the land comes to life—
especially when you take a ride with the poet Theodore Roethke (reth' kē, 1908-1963).
Born in Michigan, Roethke became one of the leading poets in the United States. In
Night Journey, the poem below, Roethke describes a midnight train ride across the
United States. As you read this poem, picture in your mind what Roethke is describing
from his train window. Notice the different types of geographical features he passes.
How do Roethke's words make you feel the land and the train as well as see them?*

Now as the train **bears** west   **bears:** heads

Its rhythm rocks the earth,

And from my **Pullman berth**   **Pullman berth:**
         bed in a railroad car

I stare into the night

While others take their rest.

Bridges of iron lace,

A suddenness of trees,

A lap of mountain mist

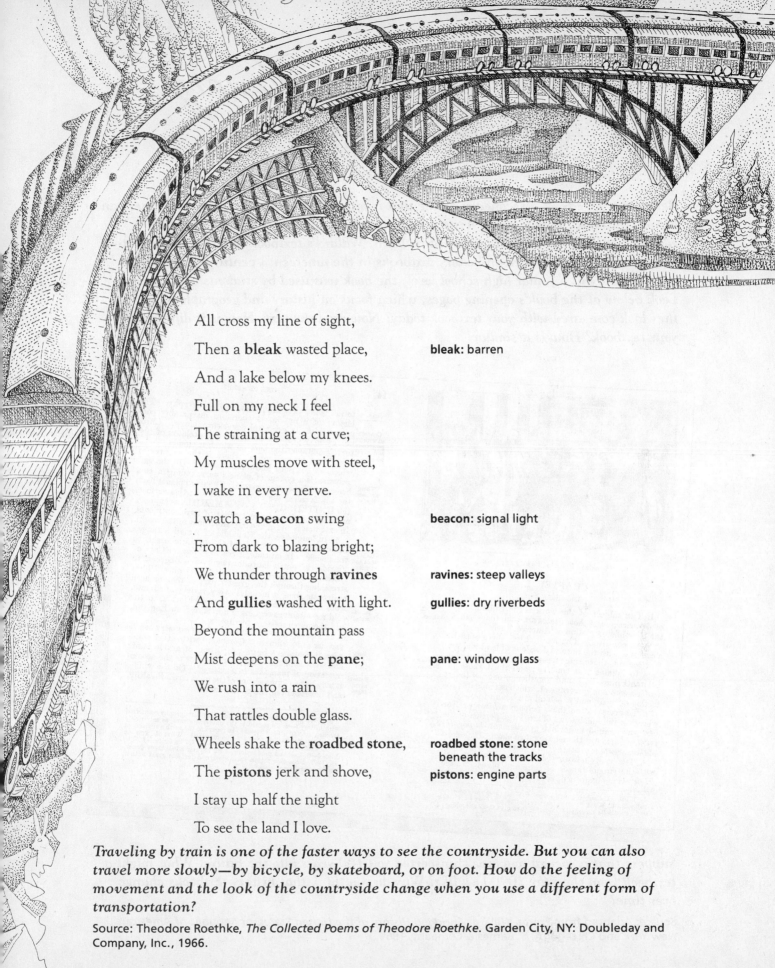

All cross my line of sight,

Then a **bleak** wasted place,   **bleak:** barren

And a lake below my knees.

Full on my neck I feel

The straining at a curve;

My muscles move with steel,

I wake in every nerve.

I watch a **beacon** swing   **beacon:** signal light

From dark to blazing bright;

We thunder through **ravines**   **ravines:** steep valleys

And **gullies** washed with light.   **gullies:** dry riverbeds

Beyond the mountain pass

Mist deepens on the **pane**;   **pane:** window glass

We rush into a rain

That rattles double glass.

Wheels shake the **roadbed stone**,   **roadbed stone:** stone beneath the tracks

The **pistons** jerk and shove,   **pistons:** engine parts

I stay up half the night

To see the land I love.

Traveling by train is one of the faster ways to see the countryside. But you can also travel more slowly—by bicycle, by skateboard, or on foot. How do the feeling of movement and the look of the countryside change when you use a different form of transportation?

Source: Theodore Roethke, *The Collected Poems of Theodore Roethke.* Garden City, NY: Doubleday and Company, Inc., 1966.

An American History Textbook in the 1800s

by Emma Willard, 1869

Below is a page from a secondary source that is often used by fifth graders—an American history textbook. This one was written by Emma Willard (1787–1870), a leading educator of the 1800s. First published in 1828, Willard's textbook was one of the first— and most popular—American history textbooks in the nineteenth century. Although written at about a junior high school level, the book was used by students of all ages. Look below at the book's opening pages, which focus on history and geography. How do they look compared with your textbook today? Now read the text. How is it different from your textbook? How is it similar?

Washington's Inauguration.

CHAPTER I.

Definitions, &c.

1. THE subject of this work is the United States of America; or, as those States are sometimes called, the Republic or Nation of America.

What constitutes a nation? First, there must be a country, with the natural divisions of land and water; second, there must be men, women, and children to inhabit that country; and third, those inhabitants must be bound together in one, by living under a common government, which extends its protection over all, and which all are bound to obey.

2. To every nation there belongs a *history:* For whenever the inhabitants of any large portion of the earth, are united under one government, *important public events* must there have taken place. *The record of these events* constitutes the history of that country.

3. The events of history should always be recorded, with the circumstances of *time* and *place*. To tell *when* events happened, is to give their chronology;

(margin notes: Subject. Its triple division. Any nation's history.)

1. What is the subject of this work? What three parts compose a nation?—2. What constitutes any nation's history? 3. How should events be recorded? What is it to give their chronology?

13

---

14   ONE NATION.

to tell *where* they happened, their geography. The history of a nation, is therefore inseparably connected with its geography and chronology. Chronology may properly be called the skeleton of history, geography the base on which it stands.

4. First, let us inquire, where is the country of which we desire to know the history? In the vast universe, is a system of planets surrounding a sun, hence called the solar system. The third planet from the sun is called the earth. On the earth's surface, the UNITED STATES OF AMERICA occupies a northern portion of the smaller of two continents. In extent, it is one of the largest nations of the world.

5. In longitude, the Republic of America ranges through sixty degrees, from the Atlantic ocean to the Pacific. In latitude, it reaches from the Cape of Florida, in north latitude twenty-five degrees, to British and Russian America in forty-nine. Thus stretching through the greater part of the northern temperate zone, it includes every variety of climate, from the hot unhealthy swamps of Florida, to the cold mountainous regions of northern New England, and the north-western territories.

6. The soil and productions of our country are as various as its climate. Compared with other countries, it contains a large proportion of arable land; and what is of the utmost consequence to the accommodation of man, it is *well watered.* On the whole, it may be pronounced, one of the most fertile, healthy, and desirable regions of the earth.

(margin notes: CHAP. I. Connected with its geography and chronology. Where our country is. Its latitude and longitude. Its climate. Soil. Natural advantages.)

3. Their geography? Are chronology and geography connected with history?—4. In regard to the universe where, as astronomy teaches, are the United States? In regard to the earth's surface, or as respects geography, where is this country? What can you say of its extent?—5. What of its longitude? Of its latitude? Climate?—6. Soil and productions? Its natural advantages generally?—7. Does this region seem designed for one great nation, or for several small ones?

Suppose that a special machine transported you 100 years into the future. What might a textbook from the year 2090 look like? Why do you think that history textbooks change over time?

Source: Adapted from Emma Willard, *Abridged History of the United States, or Republic of America.* New York and Chicago: A. S. Barnes & Company, 1869.

8

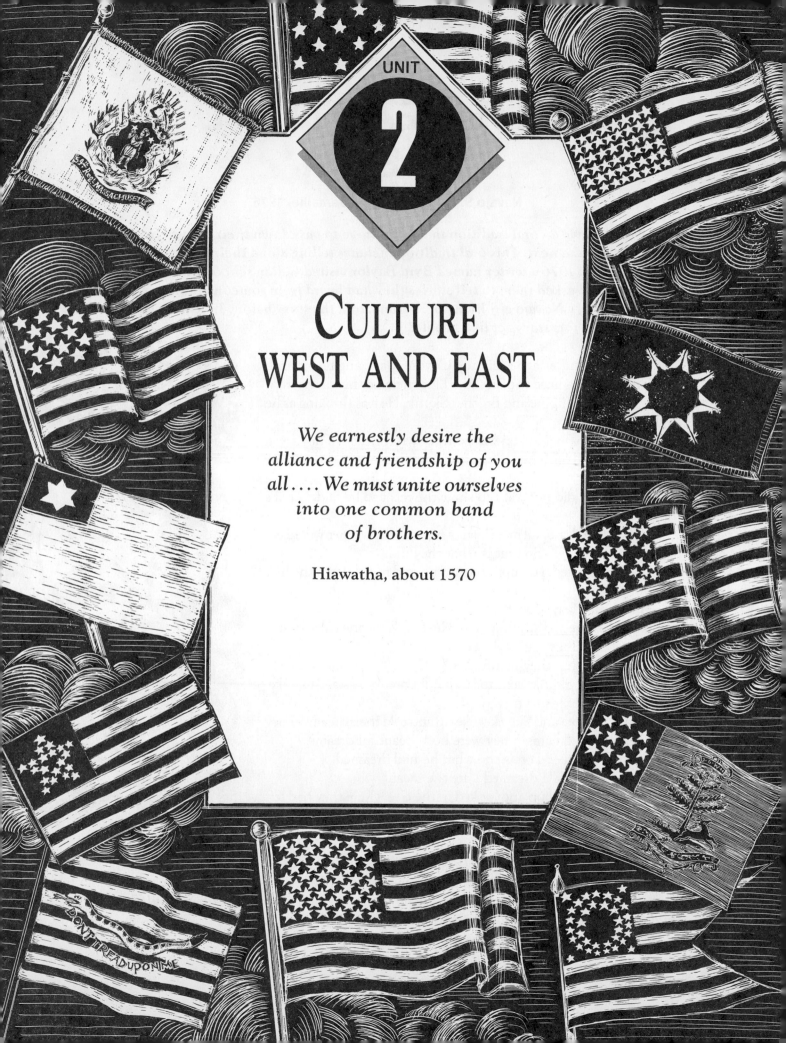

CULTURE WEST AND EAST

We earnestly desire the alliance and friendship of you all.... We must unite ourselves into one common band of brothers.

Hiawatha, about 1570

THE BEAUTIFUL DREAM

Navajo Story Told by Lana Semallie, 1976

The Navajo have an oral tradition that helps them to pass down their culture from one generation to the next. This oral tradition includes telling aloud their stories, legends, and history. In 1976 a writer named Byrd Baylor visited Indian schoolchildren in the Southwest and asked them to tell stories they had heard from someone in their tribes. Lana Semallie, a Navajo girl living in Arizona, told the story below. In which ways do the animals in this story act like people?

Many centuries ago Maii, the Coyote, was hanging around.

Coyote always liked to plan something tricky so this day he went walking with Porcupine and Brother Skunk. He was thinking as he walked along.

Ahead of them a wagon was going down the road. They saw a piece of meat fall off. They all ran for it and they all got there about the same time.

But Coyote did not want to share the meat so he said, "That's not fair."

He suggested they all race down a hill and the winner would eat the meat by himself. So that is what they did.

The race started. Porcupine curled up and rolled down the hill. He won.

"That's not fair," Coyote said.

Coyote suggested another plan. He said, "The one who dreams the most beautiful dream will eat that meat."

So that is what they planned.

Coyote and Skunk went to sleep but Porcupine stayed awake. He had a plan of his own.

Finally Coyote and Skunk woke up and told their dreams. They were both good dreams. They were both beautiful dreams.

Then they asked Porcupine what he had dreamed.

Porcupine said, "I dreamed I ate the meat."

They all jumped up and looked in the tree where they had left the meat. The meat was gone and Porcupine was looking fat.

Coyote is a popular character who appears over and over again in stories of the Navajo and other Southwest Indians. He is usually a funny character who gets into mischief when trying to trick his friends. But no matter how clever Coyote is, he often ends up getting fooled. If you were to write a story about Coyote, what adventures would you make up? What kinds of mischief would you have him getting into?

Source: Byrd Baylor, *And It Is Still That Way.* New York: Charles Scribner's Sons, 1976.

Aztec Poetry from Nahuatl Texts

Retold by Toni de Gerez, 1971

The Aztec civilization dates back to ancient times in what we now call Mexico. By the fifteenth century, the Aztec had conquered many other peoples and created a mighty empire. The Aztec poem below celebrates and mourns the passing of Quetzalcoatl (ket sahl KWAH tul), who was both an Aztec god and an historical person. The real-life Quetzalcoatl lived in the A.D. 900s. He was a priest-king of Tollan, an Aztec city also known as Tula. Quetzalcoatl brought the arts of writing, drawing, metal-working, and pottery-making to the Aztec. He also abolished human sacrifice. The Aztec god Quetzalcoatl was believed to be the god of learning and agriculture. Perhaps the historical and the religious figures are merged in this Aztec poem. Which aspects of Quetzalcoatl seem most important to the speaker of the poem?

Where is the house of **quetzal**
    feathers?
where is the house of turquoise?
where is the house of shells?

in Tollan
in Tollan
    o ay!

but our lord Quetzalcoatl has
    vanished
he has gone to **Tlapallan**
to the red-and-black country
    o ay!

In Tollan they say
there were birds rare and
    beautiful
small birds the color of
    turquoise
birds with green-and-yellow
    feathers
and yellow birds with breasts
    fire-color
    flame-color
and all sang in the name of our
    prince
o **Nactitl**
    o ay!
    o ay!

In Tollan squashes
were round and heavy as drums
    and gold as morning

an ear of corn
was as big as the great tongue
of the **metlatl**
    the yellow corn
    the red corn
    the dark corn
and one ear was all a man could
    carry

amaranth leaves were as big
    as palm fronds
you could climb up on them

and cotton grew on the bushes
in balls of every color
blue and green and red and
    yellow

in Tollan
in Tollan
    o ay!
    o ay!
our lord Quetzalcoatl has
    vanished

quetzal: Central American bird

Tlapallan: historic Aztec city

Nactitl: legendary king of Tollan

metlatl: the stone on which corn and chocolate are ground

amaranth: group of weeds and garden plants grown for their colorful leaves and flowers

Scholars and translators of Aztec poetry say that each poem must be seen as a part of one long poem. Together, they form a large body of literature that tells us what was vital to the Aztec culture. They were also used in religious dances and ceremonies.

Source: Toni de Gerez, *2-Rabbit, 7-Wind: Poems from Ancient Mexico Retold from Nahuatl Texts.* New York: Viking Press, 1971.

A Dakota Winter Count

by Lone Dog, 1801–1870

How do you keep track of past events that have happened in your life? Do you use a calendar or perhaps keep a diary? For hundreds of years the Dakota, who are also known as the Lakota Sioux, used a special kind of calendar to keep track of their history. These calendars were called winter counts because each winter the Dakota gathered together and chose an important event of the past year. An artist then recorded this event by drawing a pictograph, or picture, on the hide of an animal.

During the 1800s a Dakota named Lone Dog, who lived in what is today Montana, recorded in red and black on a buffalo hide most of the winter count shown on the next page. The first pictograph in Lone Dog's winter count dates from the winter of 1800-1801. This pictograph, which is highlighted, shows three short columns of 30 parallel lines. These lines stand for the deaths of 30 Dakota who were killed in battle during the past year. You can read each year of the winter count by following the pictographs in a spiral, counterclockwise. Lone Dog wrote the final pictograph in the winter of 1869-1870.

Here is another example of a pictograph and the story it tells:

1840-1841. Two hands are about to grasp one another. This shaking of hands stood for a peace agreement between the Dakota and the Cheyenne. The hands are different colors to represent two different peoples.

Locate this pictograph in the winter count on the next page. Then study Lone Dog's other pictographs. See if you can figure out their meanings before checking the key on page 14, which explains some of them. How does the winter count show the events and issues that the Dakota considered important? How is Lone Dog a historian of his people?

1801-1802. Spots cover the body of a person. These spots represent blotches caused by smallpox. Many Dakota died of smallpox in this year.

1812-1813. A lasso stands for the first year that the Dakota caught and tamed wild horses.

1817-1818. A building with smoke coming out of its chimney is next to a dead tree, which means that the structure was built with dry wood. During this year a Canadian trader built a store near the Dakota in the valley of the Minnesota River. Can you find other pictographs that show trading stores or forts?

1825-1826. Five circles appear above a line. The circles may represent the heads of people trying to stay above water. The Missouri River overflowed its banks in 1825 and caused a major flood, killing many Dakota.

1833-1834. The moon is surrounded by many falling stars. On November 12, 1833, a great meteor shower fell all over the United States.

1853-1854. A man wearing a hat holds out a striped blanket. The Dakota exchanged many goods this year with traders.

1861-1862. Buffalo tracks appear beside a tepee. Note the cloven, or split, hoofs, characteristic of the buffalo. Food was so plentiful during this year that buffalo seemed to come right up to the Dakota's homes.

1867-1868. A flag stands for a peace conference that Dakota leaders held with officials of the United States government. The two groups met in August 1867 and agreed to a peace treaty during the following year.

Dakota winter counts are one of many written documents that Native Americans made to help preserve their history. If you were to make a winter count of your own life—or that of your school or community or state—what kinds of events might you want to include? Winter counts are one type of historical document that can teach us about the past.

Source: Garrick Mallery, *Picture-Writing of the American Indians.* Washington, D.C., 1893; reprinted New York: Dover Publications, 1972.

Founding of the Iroquois League

by Hiawatha, about 1570

During the 1500s five Native American peoples known as the Iroquois were living in what is today New York State. These five peoples—the Onondaga, the Oneida, the Seneca, the Cayuga, and the Mohawk—fought frequently with each other. Around 1570, however, a Mohawk chief named Hiawatha began to spread a message of peace among the Iroquois. In one powerful speech he urged the five peoples to stop fighting and unite into a peaceful league, or union. Hiawatha's words were passed down by Iroquois families for hundreds of years, a tradition known as oral history. Then, in 1881, an Iroquois chief named Elias Johnson wrote an English version of the speech as it had been told to him. This is the version of Hiawatha's speech that you are about to read. Note the different terms Hiawatha uses to refer to the place where each people believed its creation began. These terms are printed in italics. How does Hiawatha describe the strength of each Iroquois people?

Friends and Brothers: You being members of many tribes, you have come from a great distance; the voice of war has aroused you up; you are afraid . . . [for] your homes, your wives and your children; you tremble for your safety. Believe me, I am with you. My heart beats with your hearts. We are one. We have one common object. We come to promote our common interest, and to determine how this can be best done.

To oppose those **hordes** of northern tribes, singly and alone, would prove certain destruction. We can make no progress in that way. We must unite ourselves into one common band of brothers. We must have but one voice. Many voices makes confusion. We must have one fire, one pipe [of peace] and one war club. This will give us strength. If our warriors are united they can defeat the enemy and drive them from our land; if we do this, we are safe.

hordes: crowds

Onondaga, you are the people sitting under the shadow of the *Great Tree*, whose branches spread far and wide, and whose roots sink deep into the earth. You shall be the first nation, because you are warlike and mighty.

Oneida, and you, the people who recline your bodies against the *Everlasting Stone*, that cannot be moved, shall be the second nation, because you always give good **counsel**.

Seneca, and you, the people who have your **habitation** at the foot of the *Great Mountain*, and are overshadowed by its **crags**, shall be the third nation, because you are all greatly gifted in speech.

Cayuga, you, whose dwelling is in the *Dark Forest*, and whose home is everywhere, shall be the fourth nation, because of your superior cunning in hunting.

Mohawk, and you, the people who live in the open country, and possess much wisdom, shall be the fifth nation, because you understand better the art of raising corn and beans and making cabins.

Great Tree: tree of peace, or white pine

Everlasting Stone: rock near present-day Oneida, New York
counsel: advice
habitation: home
Great Mountain: hill near Canandaigua Lake
crags: steep cliffs
Dark Forest: forest near Cayuga Lake

You five great and powerful nations, with your tribes, must unite and have one common interest, and no **foe** shall disturb or **subdue** you.

foe: enemy
subdue: conquer

And you of the different nations of the south, and you of the west, may place yourselves under our protection, and we will protect you. We earnestly desire the **alliance** and friendship of you all. . . .

alliance: cooperation

If we unite in one band the Great Spirit will smile upon us, and we shall be free, prosperous and happy; but if we shall remain as we are we shall **incur** his displeasure. We shall be enslaved, and perhaps **annihilated** forever.

incur: bring on
annihilated: destroyed

Brothers, these are the words of Hiawatha. Let them sink deep into your hearts. I have done.

Hiawatha's speech helped convince his listeners to put aside their differences and unite. Leaders of the five peoples formed a new government and called themselves the Iroquois League. A sixth people, the Tuscarora, joined the league in 1712. The Iroquois soon became one of the most powerful Native American groups in North America. Benjamin Franklin, a leader in the fight for American freedom from Great Britain in the 1700s, admired the league's strength and system of government. He later urged people in the 13 colonies to consider a similar plan of union.

Source: Elias Johnson (A Native Tuscarora Chief), *Legends, Traditions and Laws, of the Iroquois, or Six Nations, and History of the Tuscarora Indians.* Lockport, NY: Union Printing and Publishing Co., 1881.

HOW RAVEN MADE THE TIDES

Tsimshian Legend Told by Joseph Bruchac, 1991

Having respect for all living things on Earth is important to most Native American peoples. Regarding animals as their brothers and sisters, Native Americans often use them as characters in their stories. Raven is a favorite character in the stories of Native Americans from the Northwest Coast. Although he sometimes uses magic, Raven also uses clever tricks to achieve his goals. His actions often change the lives of people in important ways. In "How Raven Made the Tides," clever Raven outwits the old woman who has held back the ocean's tides. According to this legend, how did Raven's actions help the Native Americans of the Northwest Coast?

A long time ago, the old people say, the tide did not come in or go out.

The ocean would stay very high up on the shore for a long time and the clams and the seaweed and the other good things to eat would be hidden under the deep water. The people were often hungry.

"This is not the way it should be," said Raven. Then he put on his blanket of black feathers and flew along the coast, following the line of the tide. At last he came to the house of a very old woman who was the one who held the **tide-line** in her hand. As long as she held onto it the tide would stay high. Raven walked into the old

tide-line: furthest reach inland of the tide

17

woman's house. There she sat, the tide-line held firmly in her hand. Raven sat down across from her.

"Ah," he said, "those clams were good to eat."

"What clams?" said the old woman.

But Raven did not answer her. Instead he patted his stomach and said, "Ah, it was so easy to pick them up that I have eaten as much as I can eat."

"That can't be so," said the old woman, trying to look past Raven to see out her door, but Raven blocked the entrance. So she stood up and leaned past him to look out. Then Raven pushed her so that she fell through the door, and as she fell he threw dust into her eyes so that she was blinded. She let go of the tide-line then and the tide rushed out, leaving all kinds of clams and crabs and other good things to eat exposed.

Raven went out and began to gather clams. He gathered as much as he could carry and ate until he could eat no more. All along the beach others were gathering the good food and thanking Raven for what he had done. Finally he came back to the place where the old woman still was. "Raven," she said, "I know it is you. Heal my eyes so that I can see again."

"I will heal you," Raven said, "but only if you promise to let go of the tide-line twice a day. The people cannot wait so long to gather food from the beaches."

"I will do it," said the old woman. Then Raven washed out her eyes and she could see again. So it is that the tide comes in and goes out every day because Raven made the old woman let go of the tide-line.

The stories told by Native Americans are often more complicated than, for instance, the animal fables of Aesop. Native American tales can usually be interpreted in more than one way. Although the stories are intended as lessons, listeners of different ages find different meanings in them. What are several varying ways you might describe the character and actions of Raven?

Source: Joseph Bruchac, *Native American Stories.* Golden, CO: Fulcrum Publishing, 1991.

Yeh-hsien

Chinese Folk Tale Retold by Judy Sierra, 1992

Did you know that many of the folk tales we read today were first told thousands of years ago? From China, one of Earth's oldest civilizations, comes the first full version of the Cinderella story to be written down. The tale of Yeh-hsien (YE shen) was originally passed on from one storyteller to the next, in the oral tradition. This tradition preserved a body of literature until it could be written down. It may surprise you to learn that there are several hundred versions of the Cinderella story. While each culture tells the story somewhat differently, the core of the tale is always the same. A poor but good child is mistreated by a cruel family. She is aided by a magical being and is at last rewarded by a prosperous marriage and happiness. The voyages of Zheng He (ZHAHNG huh), a fifteenth-century Chinese explorer, helped to bring new stories to and from China and its neighboring countries. How might you expect the tale of Yeh-hsien to differ from the Cinderella story you know?

Among the people of the south there is a tradition that before the **Ch'in and Han dynasties** there lived a **cave-master** called Wu. People called the place the Wu cave. He had two wives. One wife died. She had a daughter called Yeh-hsien, who from childhood was intelligent and good at making pottery on the wheel. Her father loved her. After some years the father died, and she was ill-treated by her stepmother, who would always order her to collect firewood in dangerous places and draw water from deep pools. Once Yeh-hsien caught a fish about two inches long, with red fins and golden eyes. She put it into a bowl of water. It grew bigger every day, and after she had changed the bowl several times, she could find no bowl big enough for it, so she threw it back into the pond. Whatever food was left over from meals she put into the water to feed it. When Yeh-hsien came to the pond, the fish always swam up and rested its head on the bank, but when anyone else came, it would not come out.

Ch'in and Han dynasties: ruling families of China from 226 B.C. to A.D. 220

cave-master: wise man who lived in a cave

The stepmother watched for the fish, but it did not once appear. So she tricked the girl, saying, "Haven't you worked hard! I am going to give you a new dress." She then made the girl change out of her tattered clothing. Afterwards she sent her to get water from a spring that was very far away. The stepmother put on Yeh-hsien's clothes, hid a sharp knife up her sleeve, and went to the pond. She called to the fish. The fish at once put its head out, and she chopped it off and killed it. The fish was now more than ten feet long. She cooked it, and when she served it up, it tasted twice as good as an ordinary fish. She hid the bones under the dung-hill.

The next day, when the girl came to the pond, no fish appeared. The girl ran out into the fields, howling with grief. Suddenly there appeared a man with his hair loose over his shoulders, dressed in coarse clothes. He descended from the sky, and he consoled her, saying, "Don't cry so! Your stepmother has killed the fish and its bones are under the dung-heap. Go back, take the fish's bones and hide them in your room. Whatever you want, you have only to ask the fish bones for it." The girl followed his advice, and from then on she was able to provide herself with gold, pearls, dresses, and food whenever she wanted them.

When the time came for the cave festival, the stepmother took her own daughter with her, and left Yeh-hsien to keep watch over the fruit trees in the garden. The girl waited until they were far away, and then she followed them, wearing a cloak of material spun from **kingfisher** feathers and shoes of gold. Her stepsister saw her and said to the stepmother, "That girl looks like my sister." The stepmother suspected the same thing. The girl was aware of this and went away in such a hurry that she lost one shoe. It was picked up by one of the people of the cave. When the stepmother got home, she found the girl asleep, with her arms round one of the trees in the garden, and thought no more about it.

kingfisher: bright-colored bird that eats fish

The cave was near an island in the sea, and on this island was a kingdom called T'o-han. The man who had picked up the gold shoe sold it in T'o-han, and it was brought to the king. He ordered all the women of the court to put it on, but it was too small even for the one among them that had the smallest foot. He then ordered all the women in his kingdom to try it on, but there was not one that it fitted. It was as light as **down**, and it made no noise even when treading on stone. His search finally took him to the place where Yeh-hsien lived with her stepmother, and the shoe fitted her perfectly. She put on the other shoe, and her cape of feathers, and she was as beautiful as a heavenly being. Taking the fish bones with her, she returned with the king to T'o-han and became his chief wife. The first year, the king was very greedy and asked the fish bones for **jade** and pearls without limit. The next year, the fish bones no longer granted his requests. He buried them by the sea shore and covered them with a hundred **bushels** of pearls, and after a while they were washed away by the tide.

down: soft feathers

jade: very hard, green mineral used for jewelry

bushel: unit of measure equal to 32 quarts

The stepmother and stepsister were struck by flying rocks, and died. The cave people buried them in a stone pit, which was called the Tomb of the Two Women. Men would come there and make offerings, and the girl they prayed for would become their wife.

In the European version of the story that you probably know, Cinderella marries the prince, who is as good and deserving as she is. How would you describe the character of the king in "Yeh-hsien"? How else are the European and Chinese versions alike or different?

Source: Judy Sierra, *The Oryx Multicultural Folktale Series: Cinderella.* Phoenix: Oryx Press, 1992.

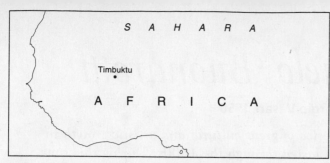

Timbuktu

by Leo Africanus, 1526

During the 1400s Songhai (SAWNG hĭ) was one of the largest kingdoms in West Africa. Timbuktu was one of the major centers of trade in Songhai and a great cultural center. Trade brought great wealth to the kingdom and to the city. It was said that in Timbuktu books were "sold for more money than any other merchandise." Why do you think books were so valued? The following description of Timbuktu is from a history of North Africa by an Arab scholar called Leo Africanus, written in the 1500s.

Timbuktu is situated within twelve miles of a certain branch of [the] **Niger**, all the houses **whereof** are now changed into cottages built of chalk, and covered with thatch. **How be it** there is a most stately temple to be seen, the walls **thereof** are made of stone and lime; and a princely palace also built by a most excellent workman of **Granada**. Here are many shops of **artificers**, and merchants, and especially of such as weave linen and cotton cloth. And **hither** do the **Barbary** merchants bring cloth of Europe....Corn, cattle, milk and butter this region **yieldeth** in great abundance; but salt is very scarce here; for it is brought hither by land from Tegaza, which is five hundred miles distant....

Niger: river in West Africa
whereof: there
How be it: Nonetheless
thereof: of which
Granada: Islamic kingdom in Spain at that time
artificers: craftspeople
hither: here
Barbary: North Africa
yieldeth: gives
scepters: staffs or rods held by a king

The rich king of Timbuktu hath many plates and **scepters** of gold, some whereof weigh 1,300 pounds: and he keeps a magnificent and well furnished court....He hath always three thousand horsemen, and a great number of footmen that shoot poisoned arrows, attending upon him. They have often skirmishes with those that refuse to pay tribute....Here are great store of doctors, judges, priests, and other learned men, that are bountifully maintained at the king's cost and charges. And hither are brought diverse manuscripts or written books out of Barbary which are sold for more money than any other merchandise. The coin of Timbuktu is of gold without any stamp or superscription; but in matters of small value they use certain shells brought hither out of the kingdom of Persia, four hundred of which shells are worth a **ducat**....The inhabitants are people of a gentle and cheerful **disposition**, and spend a great part of the night in singing and dancing through all the streets of the city: they keep great store of men and women-slaves, and their town is much in danger of fire: at my second being there half the town almost was burnt in five hours space. Without the suburbs there are no gardens or orchards at all.

ducat: type of money
disposition: way of being

Scholars from all over the world came to Timbuktu to study at its university, and the kingdom of Songhai saw many travelers and explorers from Europe seeking gold, ivory, and other riches.

Source: Adapted from Robin Hallett, *The Penetration of Africa*. New York: Frederick A. Praeger, Inc., 1965.

Michelangelo Buonarotti

by Giorgio Vasari, 1550

The Renaissance (ren uh SAHNS), a period of great cultural and artistic growth in Europe, began in Italy in the 1300s and lasted through the 1500s. During this time, people became interested in broadening their horizons and in learning about ideas that were new to them. Many artists, such as Michelangelo Buonarotti (mi kuh LAN juh loh BUO nuh ROH tee, 1474-1563) produced magnificent works of art. The following excerpt is from a book of short biographies by a friend of Michelangelo's who was also an artist. The biographer describes how Michelangelo created the paintings on the ceiling of the Sistine Chapel in Rome, which are considered to be among the finest artwork of all time. What personal qualities helped Michelangelo produce such great work?

The **master** accordingly finished the whole, completing it to perfection in twenty months, without having even the help of a man to **grind the colours**. It is true that he sometimes complained of the manner in which the **Pope** hastened forward the work, seeing that he was thereby prevented from giving it the finish which he would have desired to bestow; His Holiness constantly inquiring when it would be completed. On one occasion, therefore, Michelangelo replied, "It will be finished when I shall have done all that I believe required to satisfy Art." "And we command," rejoined the Pontiff, "that you satisfy our wish to have it done quickly"; adding finally, that if it were not at once completed, he would have him, Michelangelo, thrown headlong from the scaffolding.

…He worked with great inconvenience to himself, having to labour with the face turned upwards, and injuring his eyes so much in the progress of the work, that he could neither read letters nor examine drawings for several months afterwards….

Michelangelo found his chief pleasure in the labours of art…. For the greater **exactitude**, he made numerous **dissections** of the human frame, examining the anatomy of each part…. These labours enabled him to complete his works, whether of the pencil or chisel, with perfection, and to give them a grace, a beauty, and an animation, **wherein**…he has surpassed even **the antique**….

His powers of imagination were such that he was frequently compelled to abandon his purpose, because he could not express by the hand those grand and sublime ideas which he had conceived in his mind, nay, he has spoiled and destroyed many works for this cause; and I know too that some short time before his death he burnt a large number of his designs and sketches…that none might see the labours he had endured in his resolve not to fall short of perfection.

The master: honorary term for a great artist; here applied to Michelangelo

grind the colours: make the paints

Pope: Julius II

exactitude: accuracy

dissections: examinations

wherein: where

the antique: the artists of "antiquity," or the Greek and Roman times

New knowledge and inventions discovered during the Renaissance enabled men such as Henry the Navigator to search for a shorter, cheaper route to Asia. Later, Columbus, seeking this same route to the silk and spices of the East, reached the Americas and changed the course of history.

Source: James Hanscom, Leon Hellerman, and Ronald Posner, eds., *Voices of the Past: Readings in Medieval and Early Modern History*. New York: The Macmillan Company, 1967.

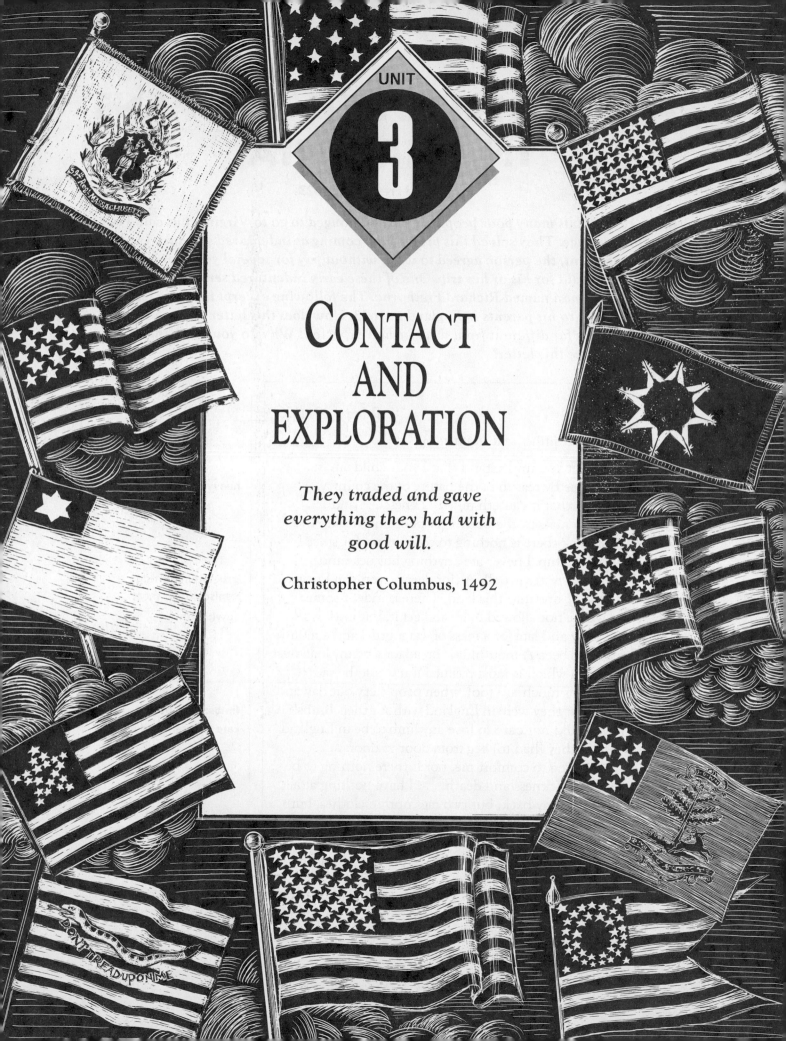

UNIT

3

CONTACT
AND
EXPLORATION

*They traded and gave
everything they had with
good will.*

Christopher Columbus, 1492

AN INDENTURED SERVANT IN VIRGINIA

by Richard Frethorne, 1623

In the early 1600s many poor people in England longed to go to Virginia but could not afford the voyage. They solved this problem by coming as indentured servants. Under this arrangement, the person agreed to work without pay for several years for a colonist who paid for his or her trip. One of these early indentured servants was a young Englishman named Richard Frethorne. The following excerpt is from a letter he wrote home to his parents in England in 1623. How does this letter show that life in Virginia was far different from what he had expected? Why do you think that Frethorne wrote this letter?

[March 20, 1623]

Loving and kind father and mother:

This is to let you understand that I your child am in a most **heavy case** by reason of the nature of the country, [which] is such that it causeth much sickness . . . and . . . diseases, which maketh the body very poor and weak. And when we are sick there is nothing to comfort us; for since I came out of the ship, I never ate anything but peas and loblollie (that is, water **gruel**). As for deer or **venison** I never saw any since I came into this land. There is indeed some **fowl**, but we are not allowed to go and get it, but must work hard both early and late for a mess of water gruel and a mouthful of bread and beef. A mouthful of bread for a penny loaf must serve for 4 men which is most pitiful. [You would be sad] if you did know as much as I [do], when people cry out day and night—Oh, that they were in England without their **limbs**! And [they] would not **care to lose** any limb to be in England again [even if] they [had to] beg from door to door. . . .

I have nothing to comfort me, nor is there nothing to be gotten here but sickness and death. . . . I have nothing at all; no, not a shirt to my back, but two rags nor no clothes, but one poor suit, nor but one pair of shoes, but one pair of stockings, but one cap, [and] but two **bands**. My cloak is stolen by one of my own **fellows**, and to his dying hour [he] would not tell me what he did with it. But some of my fellows saw him have butter and beef out of a ship, which my cloak, I doubt [not] paid for, so that I have not a penny, nor a penny

heavy case: sad condition

gruel: thin porridge
venison: deer meat
fowl: birds

limbs: arms or legs
care to lose: mind losing

bands: belts
fellows: friends

worth to help me. . . . I am not half [of] a quarter so strong as I was in England, and all is for want of **victuals**, for I do protest unto you that I have eaten more in [one] day at home than I have . . . here for a week. . . .

victuals: food

I find [myself in] . . . great grief and misery, and [I] saith, that if you love me you will **redeem me** suddenly, for which I do **entreat** and beg. And if you cannot get the merchants to redeem me for some little money, then for God's sake . . . entreat some good folks to lay out some little sum of money, in **meal** and cheese and butter and beef. Any eating meat will yield great profit. . . . Good father, do not forget me, but have mercy and pity my miserable case. I know if you did but see me you would weep to see me, for I have but one suit. . . . For God's sake, pity me. I pray you to remember my love . . . to all my friends and **kindred**. I hope all my brothers and sisters are in good health, and as for my part I have set down my **resolution** that . . . the answer of this letter will be life or death to me. Therefore, good father, send as soon as you can. . . .

redeem me: buy back my period of service

entreat: plead

meal: grains

kindred: family

resolution: belief

Richard Frethorne

What became of Richard Frethorne remains a mystery. Whether he returned to England, stayed in Virginia, or died young is unknown. Life in Virginia remained full of hunger, hardships, and disease throughout the 1600s. Still, indentured servants continued to pour into the colony in hopes of a better life. Many completed the long period of service and gained their freedom. Not only whites were indentured servants. Most of the first Africans in Virginia—although brought by force to America—were treated like indentured servants in the early and middle 1600s. Many of these Africans also gained their freedom. Altogether, more than half of the people who came to Virginia between 1607 and 1776 came, like Richard Frethorne, as indentured servants.

Source: Adapted from Susan Myra Kingsbury, ed., *The Records of the Virginia Company of London*, Vol. IV. Washington, D.C.: Government Printing Office, 1935.

The Mayflower Compact

Pilgrim Agreement, 1620

When the passengers aboard the Mayflower saw that they had reached New England instead of Virginia in 1620, they quickly realized that their new home was not subject to any European laws. How would this new colony govern itself? To answer this question, Pilgrim leaders drew up a compact, or agreement, and 41 of the ship's 101 passengers signed it before they went ashore. As you read the Mayflower Compact below and the rewritten modern version on the next page, think about what the signers are agreeing to do. Why do they believe it is important to set up a government? Note the names of the people who signed the compact. Why do you think there are no women's names?

In the Name of God, Amen. We, whose names are underwritten, the Loyal Subjects of our dread Sovereign Lord King *James*, by the Grace of God, of *Great Britain, France,* and *Ireland,* King, *Defender of the Faith,* etc. Having undertaken for the Glory of God, and Advancement of the Christian Faith, and the Honour of our King and Country, a Voyage to plant the first Colony in the northern Parts of *Virginia*; Do by these Presents, solemnly and mutually, in the Presence of God and one another, covenant and combine ourselves together into a civil Body Politick, for our better Ordering and Preservation, and Furtherance of the Ends aforesaid; And by Virtue hereof do enact, constitute, and frame, such just and equal Laws, Ordinances, Acts, Constitutions, and Officers, from time to time, as shall be thought most meet and convenient for the general Good of the Colony; unto which we promise all due Submission and Obedience. IN WITNESS whereof we have hereunto subscribed our names at *Cape-Cod* the eleventh of *November*, in the Reign of our Sovereign Lord King *James*, of *England, France,* and *Ireland,* the eighteenth, and of *Scotland,* the fifty-fourth, *Anno Domini*, 1620.

Mr. John Carver	Mr. Samuel Fuller	Edward Tilly
Mr. William Bradford	Mr. Christopher Martin	John Tilly
Mr. Edward Winslow	Mr. William Mullins	Francis Cooke
Mr. William Brewster	Mr. William White	Thomas Rogers
Isaac Allerton	Mr. Richard Warren	Thomas Tinker
Miles Standish	John Howland	John Ridgale
John Alden	Mr. Steven Hopkins	Edward Fuller
John Turner	Digery Priest	Richard Clark
Francis Eaton	Thomas Williams	Richard Gardiner
James Chilton	Gilbert Winslow	Mr. John Allerton
John Craxton	Edmund Margesson	Thomas English
John Billington	Peter Brown	Edward Doten
Joses Fletcher	Richard Bitteridge	Edward Liester
John Goodman	George Soule	

In the name of God, Amen. We, who have signed our names below, are the loyal subjects of King James of Great Britain. In honor of God, our Christian religion, our king, and our country, we took a voyage to build the first colony in northern Virginia. To keep order in this colony, we agree in this document to join together under one government. We promise to make laws and rules that are fair and will apply equally to everyone. We also promise to obey these laws and rules. We hope that the laws, rules, and leaders we choose will both improve and help preserve the colony.

Having read and agreed to this compact, we have signed our names at Cape Cod on November 11, 1620.

In addition to helping Plymouth colony grow, the Mayflower Compact helped to establish the idea of self-government among European colonists in North America. Over 150 years later this idea would be clearly expressed in another important document—the Declaration of Independence. You can read this document on pages 62–66.

Source: Ben. Perley Poore, *The Federal and State Constitutions*, Part 1. New York: Burt Franklin, 1924.

Reaching the Americas

by Christopher Columbus, 1492

On August 3, 1492, Christopher Columbus (1451–1506) and his crew of 90 sailors set sail from Spain on three ships hoping to find a new route to Asia. After stopping to get supplies in the Canary Islands, the crew sailed west across the Atlantic Ocean—a voyage no European had attempted in hundreds of years. What was this historic voyage like? Fortunately, Columbus kept a journal, or diary, of his trip. In the part of his journal you are about to read, Columbus describes the long, dangerous journey and the first sight of land, a small island in the Caribbean Sea. Notice Columbus's opinion of the Taino, the first people he meets in the Americas, and how the Taino treat the Europeans. In what ways does Columbus consider himself a trader and explorer? In what ways does he see himself as a conqueror as well?

September 9

This day we completely lost sight of land, and many men sighed and wept for fear they would not see it again for a long time. I comforted them with great promises of lands and riches. To **sustain** their hope and **dispel** their fears of a long voyage, I decided to **reckon** fewer **leagues** than we actually made. I did this that they might not think themselves so great a distance from Spain as they really were.

For myself I will keep a **confidential** accurate reckoning.

sustain: keep up
dispel: drive away
reckon: count
leagues: units of distance

confidential: secret

September 24

I am having serious trouble with the crew. . . . All day long and all night long those who are awake and able to get together never **cease** to talk to each other [as they gather] in circles, complaining that they will never be able to return home. They have said that it is insanity and **suicidal** on their part to risk their lives following the madness of a **foreigner**. . . . I am told by a few trusted men (and these are few in number!) that if I **persist** in going onward, the best course of action will be to throw me into the sea some night.

cease: stop

suicidal: very dangerous

foreigner: Columbus is called a foreigner because he was born in Italy
persist: continue

October 10

Between day and night I made 177 miles [285 km]. I told the crew 132 miles [212 km], but they could stand it no longer. They grumbled and complained of the long voyage, and I **reproached** them for their lack of spirit, telling them that, for better or worse, they had to complete the **enterprise** on which the **Catholic Sovereigns** had sent them.

October 11

About 10 o'clock at night, while standing on the **sterncastle**, I thought I saw a light to the west. It looked like a little wax candle bobbing up and down. It had the same appearance as a light or torch belonging to fishermen or travelers who **alternately** raised and lowered it, or perhaps were going from house to house. . . .

The moon, in its third quarter, rose in the east shortly before midnight. . . . Then, at two hours after midnight, the *Pinta* fired a cannon, my **prearranged** signal for the sighting of land.

I now believe that the light I saw earlier was a sign from God and that it was truly the first positive **indication** of land. When we caught up with the *Pinta*, which was always running ahead because she was a swift sailor, I learned that the first man to sight land was Rodrigo de Triana, a seaman from Lepe.

October 12

At dawn we saw . . . people, and I went ashore in the ship's boat, **armed**. . . . I **unfurled** the royal banner and the captains brought the flags which displayed a large green cross with the letters **F** and **Y** at the left and right side of the cross. . . .

No sooner had we concluded the **formalities** of taking possession of the island than people began to come to the beach. . . . All those that I saw were young people, none of whom was over 30 years old. They are very well-built people, with handsome bodies and very fine faces. . . . Their eyes are large and very pretty. . . . These are tall people and their legs, with no exceptions, are quite straight, and none of them has a **paunch**. They are, in fact, **well proportioned**. Their hair is . . . straight, and **coarse** like horsehair. They wear it short over the eyebrows, but they have a long **hank** in the back that they never cut. Many of the natives paint their faces; others paint their whole bodies; some, only the eyes or nose. Some are painted black, some white, some red; others are of different colors.

The people here called this island *Guanahaní* in their language, and their speech is very **fluent**, although I do not understand any of it. They are friendly and **well-dispositioned** people who **bear no arms** except for small spears, and they have no iron. I showed one my sword, and through **ignorance** he grabbed it by the blade and cut himself. Their spears are made of wood, to which they attach a fish tooth at one end, or some other sharp thing. . . .

fluent: smooth and rapid
well-dispositioned: easygoing
bear no arms: carry no weapons
ignorance: not knowing

They traded and gave everything they had with good will, but it seems to me that they have very little and are poor in everything. . . .

This afternoon the people . . . came swimming to our ships and in boats made from one log. They brought us parrots, balls of cotton thread, spears, and many other things. . . . For these items we **swapped** them little glass beads and **hawks' bells**. . . .

swapped: traded
hawks' bells: small bells that attach to the leg of a hawk

They ought to make good and skilled servants, for they repeat very quickly whatever we say to them. . . . I will take six of them to Your Highnesses when I depart. . . .

October 13

After sunrise people . . . again began to come to our ships in boats **fashioned** in one piece from the trunks of trees. These boats are wonderfully made . . . and every bit as fine as those I have seen in **Guinea**. They come in all sizes. Some can carry 40 or 50 men; some are so small that only one man rides in it. . . .

fashioned: built
Guinea: region of western Africa
attentive: alert

I have been very **attentive** and have tried very hard to find out if there is any gold here.

Columbus left the Caribbean on January 15, 1493, with six Taino prisoners and arrived in Spain in March. News of his voyage spread quickly through Europe and changed the world forever. Columbus's journey had joined two "worlds"—the continents of North and South America and the continents of Europe, Asia, and Africa—that had been separated for thousands of years. European explorers, conquerors, and treasure hunters soon began streaming across the Atlantic Ocean in search of gold and other riches. Columbus returned to the Americas three more times. On his later voyages he enslaved thousands of Native Americans and forced them to dig for gold. The harsh treatment and diseases brought by European explorers soon caused the death of all the Taino. To learn about the Europeans' hunger for gold, read the next document on pages 31–32.

Source: Robert H. Fuson, translator, *The Log of Christopher Columbus*. Camden, ME: International Marine Publishing Company, 1987.

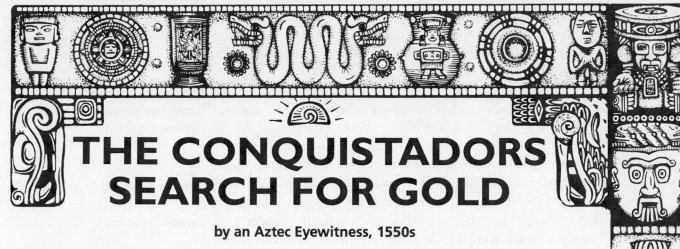

THE CONQUISTADORS SEARCH FOR GOLD

by an Aztec Eyewitness, 1550s

In the early 1500s Spanish conquerors, known as conquistadors, explored both North and South America. One of these conquistadors was 34-year-old Hernando Cortés. Like Christopher Columbus, whose journal you read on pages 28–30, Cortés hoped to find gold and other riches. In 1519 Cortés and about 500 Spanish soldiers marched through present-day Mexico and conquered one of the largest empires in the world—the Aztec empire. In the 1550s an historian interviewed an Aztec eyewitness who had seen the Spanish conquest. This witness described how Cortés and his men acted when they seized the fabulous treasures of the empire's capital city, Tenochtitlán. As you read this account, notice what the eyewitness sometimes compares the conquistadors to. Why do you suppose the eyewitness chose to make such comparisons?

When the Spaniards were **installed** in the palace, they asked **Motecuhzoma** about the city's resources and **reserves** and about the warriors' **ensigns** and shields. They questioned him closely and then demanded gold.

Motecuhzoma guided them to it. They surrounded him and crowded close with their weapons. He walked in the center, while they formed a circle around him.

When they arrived at the treasure house . . . the riches of gold and feathers were brought out to them: ornaments made of **quetzal** feathers, richly worked shields, disks of gold, the necklaces of the **idols**, . . . gold **greaves** and bracelets and crowns. . . .

The Spaniards burst into smiles; [and] their eyes shone with pleasure; they were delighted by them. They picked up the gold and fingered it like monkeys; they seemed to be **transported** by joy, as if their hearts were **illumined** and made new.

The truth is that they longed and **lusted for** gold. Their bodies swelled with greed, and their hunger was **ravenous**; they hungered like pigs for that gold. They snatched at the golden ensigns, waved them from side to side and examined every inch of them. . . .

The Spaniards immediately stripped the feathers from the gold shields and ensigns. They gathered all the gold into a great mound and set fire to everything else, regardless of its value. Then they

installed: settled

Motecuhzoma (maw tay kway SOH mah): Aztec emperor, also called Moctezuma and Montezuma

reserves: valuables

ensigns: flags

quetzal: a kind of bird

idols: statues of gods
greaves: leg armor

transported: carried away
illumined: lit up
lusted for: wanted strongly
ravenous: intense

melted down the gold into **ingots**. As for the precious green stones,   **ingots:** bars
they took only the best of them. . . .

Next they went to Motecuhzoma's storehouse . . . where his
personal treasures were kept. The Spaniards grinned like little beasts
and patted each other with delight.

When they entered the hall of treasures, it was as if they had
arrived in **Paradise**. They searched everywhere and **coveted**   **Paradise:** heaven
everything; they were slaves to their own greed. All of   **coveted:** wanted
Motecuhzoma'a possessions were brough out: fine bracelets,
necklaces with large stones, ankle rings with little gold bells,
the royal crowns and all the royal **finery**—everything that   **finery:** jewels and fancy
belonged to the king and was reserved to him only. They seized   clothing
these treasures as if they were their own, as if this **plunder** were   **plunder:** stealing
merely a stroke of good luck. And when they had taken all the
gold, they heaped up everything else in the middle of the **patio**.   **patio:** courtyard

*By 1570, 50 years after the Spanish conquest, over 1 million Aztec had been killed by
foreign diseases, warfare, and the effects of forced labor. By this time Cortés and other
Spaniards had carried much of the Aztec gold back to Europe.*

Source: Miguel Leon-Portilla, ed., *The Broken Spears: The Aztec Account of the Conquest of Mexico.*
Boston: Beacon Press, 1962.

Drawings of Roanoke
by John White, 1585

The first English colonists who built a settlement on Roanoke Island (1585–1586) faced hunger and conflicts with the Native Americans who lived there, the Roanoac. The second group of colonists (1587–?) vanished, leaving a mystery that has not yet been solved by historians. All that is known for sure is that the colony had disappeared by the time colonial governor John White returned to the island in August 1590, bringing additional supplies. The Roanoke colony, although it failed, yielded enough information about the territory and climate of the region to enable later colonists to survive. John White's hand-drawn maps and other drawings show Roanoke and the surrounding land and waterways. Why do you think this area of the coast was so dangerous to vessels attempting to land?

The Algonquin village of Pomeiooc in what is now North Carolina was painted in watercolor by John White.

White's watercolor painting of Secoton, another Algonquin village in present-day North Carolina, includes cornfields and other details of daily life.

Sources: R. Conrad Stein, *America the Beautiful: North Carolina.* Chicago: Childrens Press, 1990; William S. Powell, *The North Carolina Colony.* London: Crowell-Collier Press, 1969; *Eugenia Burney, North Carolina.* New York: Thomas Nelson Inc., 1975.

This engraving, based on a lost drawing done by John White, shows the first group of English colonists arriving at Roanoke Island in 1585.

Governor John White used his artistry to draw and paint maps and pictures of the wildlife of Virginia and North Carolina. His work helped to spark European interest in North America. In 1607 Jamestown, Virginia was to become the first permanent English colony in North America. White also sketched Native American peoples of North Carolina, leaving a body of artwork that documents a whole way of life during the late 1500s.

John White's map of the Outer Banks of Virginia depicts Cape Lookout and Chesapeake Bay.

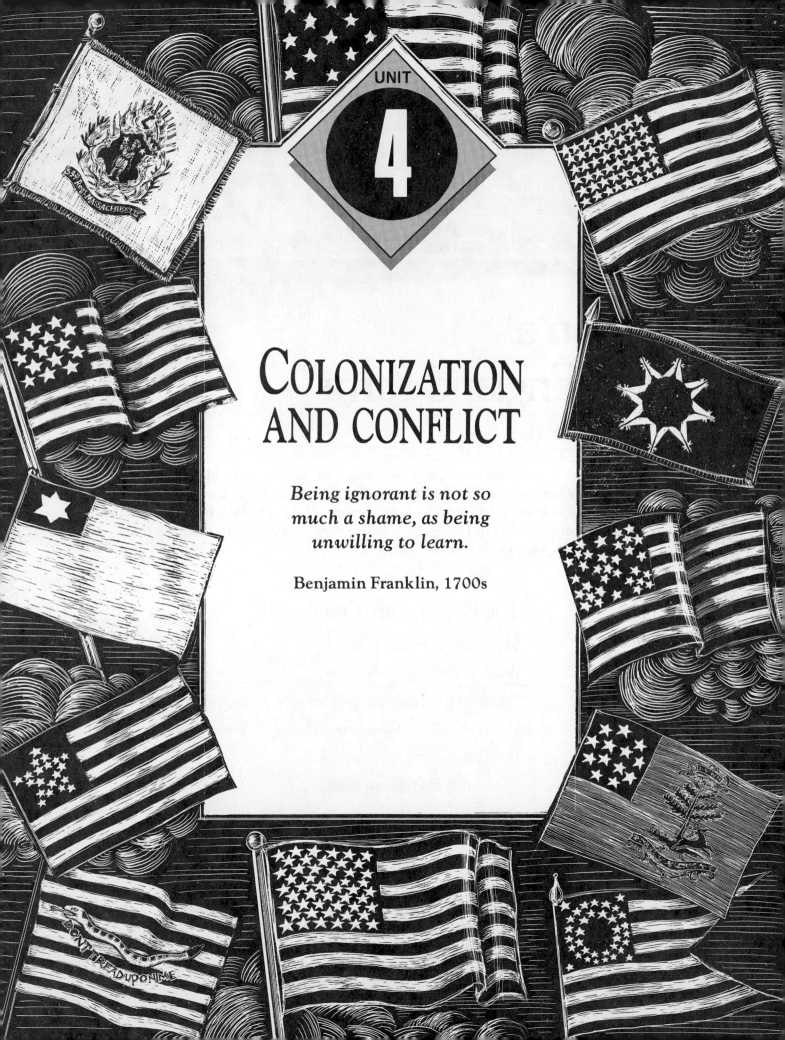

UNIT 4

COLONIZATION AND CONFLICT

Being ignorant is not so much a shame, as being unwilling to learn.

Benjamin Franklin, 1700s

Life on a New England Farm

by Ruth Belknap, 1782

What was life like on a farm in colonial New England? For most people it meant hard work, especially for women. The following poem, written in 1782, gives an idea of some of the many chores performed by farm women. The poet, Ruth Belknap, was the wife of a minister and lived in Dover, New Hampshire. Why do you think she titled her poem "The Pleasures of a Country Life"?

The Pleasures of a Country Life

Up in the morning I must rise

Before I've time to rub my eyes.

With half-**pin'd** gown, unbuckled shoe,   **pin'd:** pinned

I haste to milk my **lowing** cow.   **lowing:** mooing

But, Oh! it makes my heart to ache,

I have no bread till I can bake,

And then, alas! it makes me sputter,

For I must **churn** or have no butter.   **churn:** stir milk into butter

The hogs with **swill** too I must serve;   **swill:** garbage fed to pigs

For hogs must eat or men will starve.

Besides, my **spouse** can get no clothes   **spouse:** mate; husband or wife

Unless I much offend my nose.

36

For all that try it know it's true

There is no smell like **coloring blue**.

coloring blue: bleach

Then round the **parish** I must ride

And **make enquiry** far and wide

To find some girl that is a **spinner**,

Then hurry home to get my dinner. . . .

parish: area served by a minister

make enquiry: ask questions

spinner: person who makes yarn on a spinning wheel

All summer long I toil & sweat,

Blister my hands, and scold & **fret**.

And when the summer's work is **o'er**,

New **toils** arise from Autumn's store.

Corn must be **husk'd**, and pork be kill'd,

The house with all confusion fill'd.

O could you see the grand display

Upon our annual butchering day. . . .

fret: worry

o'er: over

toils: jobs

husk'd: stripped of its outer covering

parson: minister

Ye starch'd up folks that live in town,

That lounge upon your beds till noon,

That never tire yourselves with work,

Unless with handling knife & fork,

Come, see the sweets of country life,

Display'd in **Parson** B[elknap's] wife.

Although most women, like Ruth Belknap, worked on farms in colonial New England, many held other jobs as well. Some colonial women worked as printers, doctors, and merchants. Others ran inns and restaurants and owned their own businesses. For both women and men, there was never a lack of work in colonial New England.

Source: Laurel Thatcher Ulrich, *Good Wives: Image and Reality in the Lives of Women in Northern New England, 1650–1750.* New York: Oxford University Press, 1982.

A PILGRIM'S JOURNAL OF PLYMOUTH PLANTATION

by William Bradford, 1620

Europeans came to North America in the 1600s for many different reasons. The Pilgrims came in search of religious freedom and a life they thought would be better than the one they left behind in England. William Bradford (1590-1657) was one of the Pilgrims who came to what is now Massachusetts aboard the Mayflower. He later became governor of Plymouth, the new colony founded by the Pilgrims. Below is an entry from Bradford's journal. It was written shortly after the Pilgrims first reached North America. What did the Pilgrims find when they landed? Why were these discoveries so important to them?

December 18th. Monday, we went **a-land, manned with** the master of the ship and three or four of the sailors and marched along the coast in the woods some seven or eight miles. We found where **formerly** had been some inhabitants and where they had planted their corn, but saw not an Indian nor an Indian house. We found no **navigable** river but saw four or five small running brooks of very sweet fresh water that all run into the sea. **The crust of the earth is excellent black mold for a spit's depth**, and more in some places. There are two or three great oaks but not very thick, **pines, walnuts, beech, ash, birch, hazel, holly, asp, sassafras** in abundance, vines everywhere, cherry trees, plum trees, and many others which we know not.

Many kinds of herbs we found here in winter: strawberry leaves **innumerable**, sorrel, yarrow, chervil, brook-lime, liverwort, watercress, great store of leeks and onions, and an excellent strong kind of flax, and hemp. Here is sand, gravel, and excellent clay, no better in the world, excellent for pots and will wash like soap, and great store of stone, though somewhat soft. The best water that ever we drunk is here, and the streams now begin to be full of fish. That night, many of us being weary with marching, we went aboard again.

a-land: ashore

manned with: along with

formerly: previously

navigable: sailable by boats

The crust . . . a spit's depth: A spit holds meat while it's being roasted; Bradford is saying that the soil is rich and good for farming to a depth of perhaps two or three feet.

pines . . . sassafras: types of trees

innumerable: without number; that is, so many it's impossible to count them

The Pilgrims paved the way for other Europeans who came to North America during the 1600s and 1700s. These new groups built cities, towns, and farms. They established what is now the United States as a place where people from all over the world can seek a new and better life.

Source: William Bradford, et. al., "A Pilgrim's Journal of Plymouth Plantation in 1620" in *Homes in the Wilderness,* Margaret Wise Brown, ed. Hamden, CT: Linnet Books, 1988.

Penn's Woods

by Navidad O'Neill, 1996

In 1681, a Quaker named William Penn received a land grant from King Charles I to establish a colony in North America where Quakers could practice their religion freely. This play tells about the founding of this colony, which became the modern-day state of Pennsylvania. Besides religious freedom, what other ideals were important to Penn and his followers?

CAST OF CHARACTERS

William Penn, Quaker and founder of Pennsylvania
Charles, the king of England
Samantha, a colonist
Margaret, a colonist
Samuel, a colonist
Ben, a colonist
Sarah, a colonist

The playing area is divided into three sections: 1. The banks of a river in England; 2. The ship Welcome; 3. Philadelphia, Pennsylvania. The time is the late 1680s.

There is one important prop, the rolled-up document which King Charles II gives to William Penn, and which is later used as a banner reading "Welcome." A second rolled-up piece of paper is also needed for the Charter of Liberty.

King Charles and William Penn stand in a circle made by the colonists squatting down. Charles is writing on a document with a quill pen.

King: (*looking up at Penn*) What shall we call this land? We can't simply say, here, William Penn, take this 45,000 square miles in a rectangle shape, somewhere in America. Here, William Penn, govern this land about the size of England. Here, William Penn, for the debt I owe your father, instead of money take this piece of land. It needs a name, this broad rectangular land.

Penn: New Wales would be a good name for the new land, since it is mountainous like Wales in England.

King: No. No. Something else.

Penn: How about Sylvania, which means woods? I am told that the forests are magnificent in this new land across the sea.

King: I like that, but let's call it "Penn's woods." That is, "Pennsylvania."

Penn: You cannot name a land after me!

King: After your father then. The Admiral in whose debt I shall forever be.

Penn: As you wish: Pennsylvania.

King: Now according to this document you must send to me two beaver skins to be delivered at our home, Windsor Castle, on the first day of January every year, and of course, one-fifth of all the gold and silver you may find.

Penn: Happily.

(*They both sign the document, and Penn takes it under his arm.*)

Penn: My colony will be a place where Quakers like me can live in peace, but people of all religions will be welcome.

(*He unrolls the document and reads in a loud voice.*)

Penn: Wanted: brave adventurers who wish to form a free colony for all people! Must be willing to travel 3,000 miles across the ocean. Must be willing to work hard and treat everyone as an equal! 5,000 acres for sale!

(*One of the colonists, Margaret, stands up.*)

Margaret: Count me in! I would like to live in a land where I can practice my religion freely, where I don't need to hide when I pray because I am a Quaker.

(*Two other colonists, Samuel and Samantha, stand up.*)

Samantha: We'll go! We've been wanting to start a family in a country where everyone is equal, no matter what their family background is.

Samuel: Where do we sign?

Penn: Right here.

(Two other colonists, Ben and Sarah, stand up.)

Ben: We'd like to go but we can't afford a high price.

Sarah: We don't have a lot of money.

Penn: Rent up to 200 acres at a penny an acre!

Ben and Sarah: Can we borrow that quill?

(They sign up.)

(Everyone gives coins to Penn as they move from this area to the ship area, lining up to board the boat.)

Penn: Be prepared for hardships!

Margaret and Samantha: *(together)* We have hardships here. We can't speak out without fear of being jailed for our beliefs.

Penn: Our boat, the Welcome is ready!

(He unrolls the Welcome banner and hangs it aboard the ship. Everyone stands on board swaying slightly through this scene to show that they are at sea.)

Ben: Cows and chickens are safely in their cages!

Sarah: The furniture is roped in tight!

Samuel: The *Welcome* is a strong ship.

Margaret: William Penn's three horses are safe!

Samantha: The *Welcome* is 108 feet long with three strong sails—a very seaworthy vessel.

Ben: A hundred colonists are safely aboard!

Penn: And I have the most precious cargo of all: THE CHARTER OF LIBERTY.

(Penn reads from a new parchment.)

Penn: What I have in my hand is a plan for good government. Our plans call for power to be placed in the hands of the people. To protect people from misuses of power, there are laws that must be followed for the good of all. I have written, "Liberty without obedience is confusion, and obedience without liberty is slavery."

(All repeat this line.)

Penn: "Let men be good, and the government cannot be bad..."

Samantha: There will be free elections in this new land. We will have a council and assembly that are chosen by the colonists.

Margaret: Our new set of forty laws includes freedom of worship, which is very important to so many of us Quakers who are aboard.

Ben: It also includes the right to a trial by jury.

Samuel: Nobody can be put to death in this new land except for murder or plotting to overthrow the government.

Margaret: With laws aboard we set sail happily.

Ben: *(talks to the audience)* Unfortunately, midway across the Atlantic Ocean, tragedy struck. A passenger came down with smallpox. In one week, 31 passengers died. Penn, who had already had the disease, went about the ship helping the sick.

Sarah: *(talks to the audience)* Seven weeks after we set sail we arrived in the new land, on October 24, 1682.

Margaret: We are in Pennsylvania!

Penn: Let us go up the river to the city I named Philadelphia, which means "Brotherly Love" in Greek.

Samuel: What shall we find in Philadelphia?

Penn: I have sent planners ahead of us and told them to begin building a city where houses have "ground on each side for gardens and orchards and fields."

Margaret: I have always wanted to live in a city which has parks and greenery.

Sarah: I would think that the greenery would help protect us from chimney fires and wind.

Penn: Yes, it is both beautiful to the eye and safer for the people who live there. Shall we leave the ship?

Ben: Lower the gang plank if you please!

(All depart from the ship area. They are now in Philadelphia.)

Penn: One of the first items of business for our new city will be to visit the Native Americans. Other colonists have not always treated them well. As a Quaker, I regard all people as equals and aim to live together with them in peace.

Samuel: May I go with you when you visit?

Penn: Yes, but you must leave all weapons at home.

Samuel: I carry only a hunting gun, William.

Penn: Still, there must be no weapons, whatsoever. It is a matter of respect.

Samuel: All right. I agree.

Samantha: Can you teach us how to speak to the Native Americans?

Penn: First you should know that our Pennsylvania is home to three peoples: the Lenni Lenape, the Susquehannock and the Shawnee. It will take time to learn their language but today I shall teach you one important word, *netap*.

All: *Netap.*

Ben: What does *netap* mean?

Penn: It is a word that will be important to all of us: "friend."

All: *Netap.*

Margaret: I have learned two new words on my first day in this new world of America. *Netap* or "friend," and *adelphos*, meaning "brother" in Greek.

Penn: I think we are off to a good start in Pennsylvania.

Samantha: Don't forget another important word, the word under which we sailed to this new land: WELCOME.

Penn: Yes, let us welcome all of those who wish to come to Pennsylvania and live in peace and harmony.

All: Welcome.

THE END

William Penn, and other Quaker colonists in Pennsylvania, believed in treating Native Americans with respect. Penn paid the Native Americans for their land, and relations with them remained peaceful for many years.

Poor Richard's Almanac

by Benjamin Franklin, 1732–1757

In the 13 English colonies, there were no television or radio news shows to tell people what the weather would be like each day or when community events such as fairs would take place. Instead, people depended on little booklets called almanacs for such information. Because almanacs were so popular among the colonists, many printers wrote their own versions and competed with one another for buyers. When Benjamin Franklin (1706–1790) first printed his Poor Richard's Almanac in 1732, there were at least six other almanacs on sale in Philadelphia alone. Yet Franklin's almanac quickly became the most popular in the English colonies because he included many clever and funny sayings. How do the sayings below help us to understand some of the ideas and values that English colonists considered important?

When the well's dry, we know the worth of water.

Keep conscience clear, Then never fear.

Three may keep a secret, if two of them are dead.

He that is of opinion money will do every thing may
    well be suspected of doing every thing for money.

Wish not so much to live long,
  as to live well.

If your head is wax, don't walk
  in the sun.

Plough deep while sluggards sleep; and
  you shall have corn to sell and to keep.

Genius without education
is like silver in the mine.

Well done, is twice done.

The family of fools is ancient.

Men and melons are hard to know.

Lost time is never found again.

An empty bag cannot stand upright.

Glass, china, and reputation, are easily
crack'd, and never well mended.

Little strokes, Fell great oaks.

Dost thou love life? Then do not squander
time; for that's the stuff life is made of.

There are three things extremely hard, steel,
a diamond and to know one's self.

Being ignorant is not so much a shame,
as being unwilling to learn.

Don't throw stones at your neighbors', if
your own windows are glass.

The honey is sweet, but the bee has a sting.

Where there is hunger, law is not regarded; and where
law is not regarded, there will be hunger.

A slip of the foot you may soon recover, but a slip
of the tongue you may never get over.

Paintings and fightings are best seen at a distance.

Ben Franklin continued to publish Poor Richard's Almanac *until 1757. From then until he died in 1790, Franklin was an important leader in the colonies and in the struggle for independence from England.*

Source: Benjamin Franklin, *Poor Richard's Almanack*. Mount Vernon, NY: The Peter Pauper Press, n.d.

SHIP OF HORRORS

by Olaudah Equiano, 1789

By the late 1600s, slavery existed throughout the English colonies. For the slave traders, buying and selling human beings was a money-making business. But for the Africans kidnapped from their homeland, the forced ocean voyage to the Americas involved some of the greatest horrors that human beings have ever endured. In the excerpt below, adapted from his autobiography written in 1789, Olaudah Equiano (1745-1797) describes some of these horrors. Olaudah was an 11-year-old boy living in West Africa in 1756 when slave traders kidnapped him in order to take him to North America. The excerpt begins just as Olaudah arrives at the coast of Africa, about to begin the overseas voyage. What are some of the reactions of Olaudah and the other prisoners to the way in which they are treated? What are some of the things Olaudah wishes for?

The first thing I saw when I arrived at the coast was the sea and a slave ship waiting to pick up its cargo. The sight of the slave ship amazed me. This amazement turned into terror when I was carried on board. The crew immediately grabbed me and tossed me in the air to see if I was healthy. I was now convinced that I had gotten into a world of bad spirits and that they were going to kill me. The fact that their skin color differed so much from ours, that their hair was so long, and that the language they spoke was unlike any I had ever heard, strengthened my belief that they planned to kill me. I was so filled with horror and fear at that moment that if I had possessed 10,000 worlds, I would have given them all away to trade places with the poorest slave in my own country.

THE
INTERESTING NARRATIVE
OF
THE LIFE
OF
OLAUDAH EQUIANO,
OR
GUSTAVUS VASSA,
THE AFRICAN.
WRITTEN BY HIMSELF.

VOL. I.

Behold, God is my salvation · I will trust and not
be afraid, for the Lord Jehovah is my strength
and my song: he also is become my salvation.
And in that day shall ye say, 'Praise the Lord, call
upon his name, declare his doings among the people.
Isaiah xii. 2, 4.

FIRST AMERICAN EDITION.

NEW-YORK:
Printed and Sold by W. DURELL, at his
Book-Store and Printing-Office, No. 19, Q. Street.
M,DCC,XCI.

When I looked around the ship and saw large numbers of black people chained together—every one of them looking sad and unhappy—I no longer doubted my fate. Overpowered by horror and fright, I fell on the deck and fainted. When I woke up I was surrounded by black people. I asked them if these white men with their long hair and horrible looks were going to eat us up. They told me no. They tried to cheer me up, but I still felt miserable.

I now realized I would never again return to my native country. Never again would I see the shores of Africa. As I was realizing all of this, the crew sent me to the lower decks of the ship. Everybody down there was crying and the smell was worse than anything I had ever smelled in my life. It was so bad I became sick and could not eat. I did not feel like tasting a thing. I now wished only for death. At that moment two white men offered me food. When I refused they grabbed my hands, stretched me across a barrel, tied my feet, and whipped me.

Never in my life had I been treated in this way. As much as I feared drowning, I thought of jumping overboard. But the ship had nets all around it to prevent people from jumping into the ocean. Also, those prisoners who were not chained down were watched very closely by the crew to keep them from jumping overboard. Some prisoners who tried were beaten, and those who refused to eat were whipped every hour. This was often the case with myself.

A little later I came across some people from my own nation. Although we were all in chains, seeing them made me feel better. I asked them what was going to happen to us. They told me we were being carried to the white people's country to work for them. This cheered me up a little. After all, if all I had to do was work then things could not be so bad. But I still feared I would be put to death. The white people, I thought, looked and acted like savages. I had never seen such brutal cruelty in my life. They acted this way not only toward us blacks but toward each other. I saw them whip one white man so cruelly with a large rope that he died as a result. Then they tossed him over the side of the boat like an animal. This made me fear these people all the more, for I expected to be treated in the same manner.

After all the cargo was loaded, the smell in the lower decks became even worse. Everybody dripped with sweat and the air became unfit for breathing. We were packed together in chains so tightly we could hardly move or turn over. The cramped surroundings and the deadly heat almost suffocated us. Many slaves fell sick and died—a result of being packed so closely. The only reason they were packed so closely was to increase the profits of the slave dealers. This wretched situation was made even worse by the scraping of the chains. Children often fell into the tubs used for bathrooms and almost choked to death. The shrieks of the women and the groans of the dying made this scene a horror beyond belief.

One day the crew caught a large number of fish and feasted upon them. We begged and prayed for some of the fish that were left over. But to our amazement, they refused to give us any. Instead, they threw the fish overboard! Before they did this, however, some of my countrymen who were starving tried to grab some of the fish when they thought no one was looking. But they were discovered and whipped horribly.

One day, when the sea was smooth and the wind mild, two prisoners decided they would rather die than endure such a life of misery. Although they were chained together, they somehow managed to jump beyond the nets and into the sea. Immediately, another prisoner also jumped overboard. I believe many more would have done the same thing if the crew had not prevented them. The boat stopped at once to pick up the three prisioners who had jumped into the sea. The first two had drowned but they rescued the last one. They later whipped him extra cruelly for preferring death to slavery. In this manner we continued to undergo more hardships than I can now describe. These hardships were all caused by the wretched and terrible slave trade.

Olaudah Equiano was one of hundreds of thousands of Africans kidnapped and brought by force to North America at the hands of slave traders in the 1600s and 1700s. Roughly 200,000 more died on the ocean voyage. Equiano survived the voyage and worked as a slave in both Barbados, an island in the Caribbean, and the colony of Virginia. A British sea captain soon bought him and made him a sailor. Although enslaved, Equiano managed to earn money and bought his freedom in 1766. As a free man, he traveled the world and explored the northern Arctic. Years later he settled in England and wrote his autobiography. The book was widely read in the 1790s and contributed to the growth of the anti-slavery movement.

Source: Adapted from Olaudah Equiano, *The Interesting Narrative of the Life of Olaudah Equiano, or Gustavus Vassa, the African. Written by Himself.* New York: W. Durell, 1791.

SLAVE SALES

Advertisements, 1700s

During the 1700s European and American merchants forcibly transported more Africans to American shores than in any other century. Once these Africans arrived they were sold as slaves—and they could be resold at any time. As a result, slave sales were common events in the New England, Middle, and Southern colonies. Below is a selection of advertisements from newspapers and posters that appeared in colonial America. (Note that the letter s sometimes appeared as ſ.) How do these advertisements attempt to deprive Africans and African Americans of their humanity? How did one of these African Americans try to escape slavery?

TO BE SOLD on board the Ship *Bance-Iſland*, on tueſday the 6th of *May* next, at *Aſhley-Ferry*; a choice cargo of about 250 fine healthy

NEGROES,

juſt arrived from the Windward & Rice Coaſt. —The utmoſt care has already been taken, and ſhall be continued, to keep them free from the leaſt danger of being infected with the SMALL-POX, no boat having been on board, and all other communication with people from *Charles-Town* prevented.

Auſtin, Laurens, & Appleby.

N. B. Full one Half of the above Negroes have had the SMALL-POX in their own Country.

RUN away, on the 3d Day of *May* laſt, a young Negro Boy, named *Joe*, this Country born, formerly belonged to Capt. *Hugh Heſt*. Whoever brings the ſaid Boy the Subſcriber at *Ediſto*, or to the Work Houſe in *Charles Town*, ſhall have 3 l reward. On the contrary whoever harbours the ſaid Boy, may depend upon being ſeverely proſecuted, by

Thomas Chiſbam.

TO BE SOLD by William Yeomans, (in Charles Town Merchant,) a parcel of good Plantation Slaves. Encouragement will be given by taking Rice in Payment, or any leg ſaddles and Furniture, choice Barbados and Boſton Rum, alſo Cordial Waters and Limejuice, as well as a parcel of extraordinary Indian trading Goods, and many of other ſorts ſuitable for the Seaſon. Time Credit, Security to be given if required There's likewiſe to be ſold, very good Troop-

TO BE SOLD,

A Likely negro Man, his Wife and Child; the negro Man capable of doing all ſorts of Plantation Work, and a good Miller: The Woman exceeding fit for a Farmer, being capable of doing any Work, belonging to a Houſe in the Country, at reaſonable Rates, inquire of the Printer hereof.

In the late 1700s slavery slowly began to die out in the North. Sales of enslaved people, however, continued to be daily events in the South until after the Civil War.

Father Junípero Serra

by Ivy Bolton, 1952

In 1769 a Spanish priest named Father Junípero Serra (hoo NEE pair roh SEH rah) came on foot from Mexico to build a series of missions throughout California. In this excerpt from a biography of Father Serra, the priest is on his way to found his first mission in California, San Diego. According to this biographer, what kind of man was Father Serra?

"This is sheer folly. You can go no farther, Father Serra. How could you ever have hoped to do missionary work in the wilds of Upper California with a leg like that? Look at it! I shall make a **litter** and send four men with you to carry you home." Comandante Portolá spoke with his usual decision.

litter: kind of stretcher, or cot, to carry the sick

Father Serra stretched out the leg obediently and looked at it with a rueful smile. His face was white with fatigue and pain, but there was laughter still in his dark eyes and the little quirk at the side of his mouth told his **exasperated** commander that, as usual, Father Serra was finding something amusing in a situation which was not funny at all. He did not realize that his own excitement was the cause of the laughter now.

exasperated: frustrated

The leg was a sorry sight, swollen and inflamed from knee to toe, with an open sore from the ankle halfway up the leg.

"It is one of the only two that I possess," Father Serra answered thoughtfully. "There is no need for all this worry, Comandante. The leg has been in this state, more or less, all the years I have been in the New World. I admit that at present it is a little more. God has called me to preach and found missions and I can trust Him to help me to do the task. He knows all about this handicap and has enabled me to come twelve hundred **leagues**. Surely, I can trust Him to get me the rest of the way."

leagues: units of measure; one league equals about 3 miles

"And you will not go home? You should have had a doctor long ago."

"I have had doctors and none of them have been able to help me," Father Serra answered quietly. "This is the first present that the New World gave to me. Father Pedro and I were walking from **Vera Cruz** to Mexico City when the snake crossed our path. It struck at me and then went about its business in the undergrowth. The walk that afternoon was somewhat of an **ordeal** and the place has never healed. Wise doctors have told me that most people die of a similar snake bite. God had something for me to do and I lived. The 'something' is here in California and I have not the slightest **intention** of going home. If I delay you too much, leave me here with a little food and I will follow you with what speed I can."

Vera Cruz: city on the Gulf coast of Mexico

ordeal: difficult trial

intention: idea of

"And run into Indians and wild beasts, not to mention more snakes," the comandante grumbled.

"I came here to find Indians and I am not afraid of snakes or wild beasts," Father Serra informed him. "Thus far we have seen nothing but desert, and the Indians, who are really important, must be looked for in good **earnest**. Leave off worrying. I shall be all right."

earnest: sincerity

Portolá pondered. "I am not going to leave you behind," he said obstinately and turned to summon two of his soldiers, who came running at his call.

"Cut wood and make a litter on which we can carry Father Serra," he commanded them. "Until you can walk again, that is what I intend to do and it is of no use for you to say any more, Father."

"Then I will not." Father Serra leaned back against a rock and surveyed the scene around him.

It was a glorious sight. In the west the sun was setting in a blaze of crimson and gold, the flaming cacti and desert plants greeted his beauty-loving eyes. The camp was being made ready and the men were gathering around the fires drawn by the scent of a cooking meal. Father Serra felt far too sick and weary to eat. He was grave enough now. Something had to be done, that was certain. He could not be a burden on the expedition. Men and animals had quite enough to do without adding the task of carrying a sick man.

One of the animals was in trouble. It was the mule that had gone lame yesterday. The beast was making no secret of its discomfort and was making life as hard as possible for the **muleteer** by kicks and squeals and struggles—together with futile efforts to bite his doctor. The muleteer was trying to **poultice** the open sore. Even at this distance, the smell of the ingredients of the steaming mass was overpowering.

muleteer: person who handles mules

poultice: apply medicine to

Father Serra watched, idly at first, then with real interest. He could sympathize with the mule. If the sore was anything like his own, no wonder the animal wanted to bite and kick.

The muleteer was skillful. His voice was going on in a murmur to reassure his patient. Very gradually the mule grew quieter. At last a bandage was fixed in place, and water and a nose bag were carried over to comfort the invalid.

The muleteer rose to his feet. "You will be able to go on tomorrow," he assured the mule and then turned to answer the call of Father Serra.

His dark eyes were full of concern as he saw the father's leg.

"My son, you know how to care for your animals," Father Serra said. "What can you do for my leg?"

"I know nothing about medicine, Father. I can cure a wound on a mule's back or a sore on its leg. You need a good doctor."

Father Serra laughed. "The doctors are twelve hundred leagues away and so I must have you. Make a remedy and apply it as you do to an animal. Pretend that I am a mule."

A snort behind him made Father Serra look around. His eyes met the sulky ones of Portolá.

"A good description?" Father Serra questioned, and the grim face of the comandante lightened a little.

"An excellent one," he agreed, and turned away.

The muleteer was still uneasy and unwilling to take the risk, but like everyone else in the expedition, he would do anything for Father Serra. All through the long trek over the scorching desert, when spirits were low, Father Serra could always inspire people with courage and his hand and strength were always at the service of a tired man.

"Go on, Juan," he urged the muleteer. "I need your help."

The muleteer went to work. He melted yellow **tallow** over the smoky fire and stirred in oil and herbs, a remedy no other man would have dared to try.

tallow: animal fat used to make candles

Even Father Serra clenched his hands and bit his lip to keep back a groan as the hot mass was laid on his open sore. His face grew whiter still and tears, forced out by sheer pain, made the eyes behind the glasses misty.

He managed a grateful "Thank you," when the leg was bandaged. He found himself lifted in strong arms and laid upon a couch of straw and leaves, which eager hands had made ready. The muleteer's cloak was rolled up for a pillow and a mule's blanket was used for a covering.

Juan brought broth and fed it to Father Serra by spoonfuls and then rose to his feet.

"The pain will be easier soon," he promised. "You will sleep. God grant that you are better in the morning."

"God grant it indeed," Father Serra murmured.

He lay quiet as the waves of pain engulfed him. Pain was no new experience to Father Serra. While he lay he prayed earnestly that God—who had brought him all this way to the land of his heart's desire—would make it possible for him to walk on. A missionary who had to be carried would delay the expedition badly. If the eyes of unseen Indians were watching—and almost certainly they were—would they ever listen to a man who was so helpless?

Oh, these were stupid thoughts, Father Serra decided. There were so many things that he had wanted to do which were out of his reach, things which had seemed utterly impossible at the time. Suddenly, in his own way, God had opened a path here, a friend there, and a great desire had been won.

By 1823 Father Serra had founded 21 missions in California, each only a day's journey apart, stretching all the way north to San Francisco.

Source: Ivy Bolton, *Father Junipero Serra*. New York: Julian Messner, Inc., 1952.

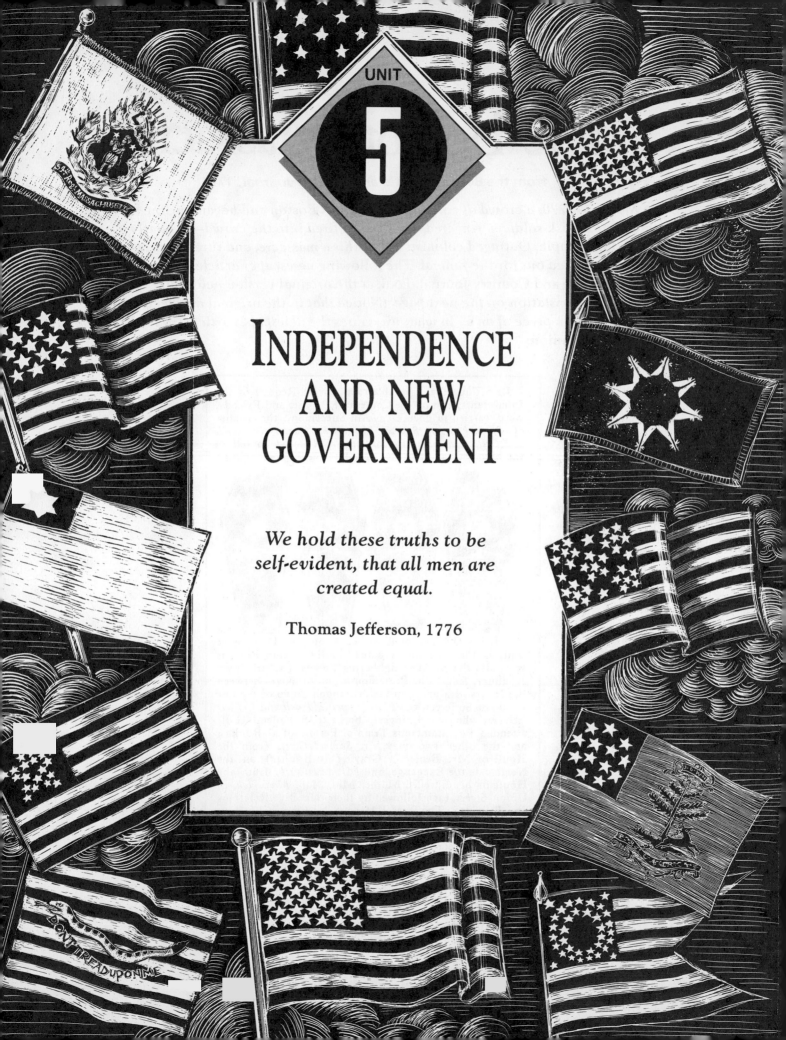

INDEPENDENCE AND NEW GOVERNMENT

We hold these truths to be self-evident, that all men are created equal.

Thomas Jefferson, 1776

The Boston Massacre

from the Boston *Gazette and Country Journal*, 1770

On March 5, 1770, a crowd of colonists gathered in Boston and began hurling rocks at a group of British soldiers. Angered, the soldiers fired into the crowd—instantly killing four people. Outraged colonists called this a massacre, and three days later thousands turned out for the funeral. The following newspaper article appeared in the Boston Gazette and Country Journal. Look at the original version below and then read the modern translation on the next page. (Notice that in the original article, the letter ſ is often used in place of an s.) In what ways does the newspaper article try to shape the reader's opinions?

Laſt Thurſday, agreeable to a general Requeſt of the Inhabitants, and by the Conſent of Parents and Friends, were carried to their *Grave* in Succeſſion, the Bodies of *Samuel Gray, Samuel Maverick, James Caldwell,* and *Criſpus Attucks,* the unhappy Victims who fell in the bloody Maſſacre of the Monday Evening preceeding !

On this Occaſion moſt of the Shops in Town were ſhut, all the Bells were ordered to toll a ſolemn Peal, as were alſo thoſe in the neighboring Towns of Charleſtown Roxbury, &c. The Proceſſion began to move between the Hours of 4 and 5 in the Afternoon ; two of the unfortunate Sufferers, viz. Meſſ. *James Caldwell* and *Criſpus Attucks,* who were Strangers, borne from Faneuil-Hall, attended by a numerous Train of Perſons of all Ranks ; and the other two, viz. Mr. *Samuel Gray,* from the Houſe of Mr. Benjamin Gray, (his Brother) on the North-ſide the Exchange, and Mr. *Maverick,* from the Houſe of his diſtreſſed Mother Mrs. *Mary Maverick,* in Union-Street, each followed by their reſpective Relations and Friends : The ſeveral Hearſes forming a Junction in King-Street, the Theatre of that inhuman Tragedy ! proceeded from thence thro' the Main-Street, lengthened by an immenſe Concourſe of People, ſo numerous as to be obliged to follow in Ranks of ſix, and brought up by a long Train of Carriages belonging to the principal Gentry of the Town. The Bodies were depoſited in one Vault in the middle Burying-ground : The aggravated Circumſtances of their Death, the Diſtreſs and Sorrow viſible in every Countenance, together with the peculiar Solemnity with which the whole Funeral was conducted, ſurpaſs Deſcription.

Last Thursday, the bodies of Samuel Gray, Samuel Maverick, James Caldwell, and Crispus Attucks were carried to their graves. All four had died the unhappy victims of the bloody massacre three days earlier! Local citizens had requested a public funeral, and the victims' parents and friends agreed to it.

The funeral procession began between 4:00 and 5:00 in the afternoon. Most of the stores in town were closed, and all the bells in Boston, Charlestown, Roxbury, and elsewhere rang solemnly in honor of the dead. Two of the unfortunate sufferers, James Caldwell and Crispus Attucks, were both unknown in Boston. Beginning at Faneuil (fan' yəl) Hall, a group made up of all kinds of people marched behind their coffins. A second group of people marched from the house of Samuel Gray's brother, and a third from the house of Samuel Maverick's very sad mother. The three groups came together at King Street, where the terrible tragedy had taken place! The procession then continued down Main Street. Huge crowds of people joined the march—so many, in fact, that they had to walk in rows of six people across. The procession was completed by a long train of carriages owned by the town's wealthier people. The bodies were at last buried in the ground. The alarming way in which the victims died, the sadness visible on everyone's faces, and the seriousness of the entire funeral are beyond description.

About 10,000 of Boston's 16,000 people turned out for the funeral. This heavy turnout was very surprising because two of those killed—a pair of sailors named James Caldwell and Crispus Attucks, a former slave—knew very few people in Boston. Newspapers all over the colonies reported the funeral, and the event that became known as the Boston Massacre increased colonists' anger against the British. As tensions between Britain and the American colonies grew during the next few years, many newspapers printed articles in favor of independence.

Source: Boston *Gazette and Country Journal,* March 12, 1770.

Paul Revere's Ride

by Henry Wadsworth Longfellow, 1863

Every country has its heroes and a body of literature that celebrates their heroic deeds. In 1861, the poet Henry Wadsworth Longfellow remembered Paul Revere and his midnight ride. Revere, a silversmith and soldier, was a leading member of the Sons of Liberty. Less than twenty-four hours before the shots that marked the beginning of the Revolutionary War, Revere and two other Patriots galloped across the countryside. They warned the sleeping citizens of Middlesex and Concord of the upcoming British attack. What do you think would have happened had the midnight riders failed to deliver their message to their countrymen?

Listen, my children, and you shall hear
Of the midnight ride of Paul Revere,
On the eighteenth of April, in Seventy-five;
Hardly a man is now alive
Who remembers that famous day and year.

He said to his friend, "If the British march
By land or sea from **the town** tonight,
Hang a lantern aloft in the **belfry** arch
Of the North Church tower as a signal light,—
One, if by land, and two, if by sea;
And I on the opposite shore will be,
Ready to ride and spread the alarm
Through every **Middlesex** village and farm,
For the country folk to be up and to arm."

Then he said, "Good-night!" and with **muffled** oar
Silently rowed to the Charlestown shore.
Just as the moon rose over the bay,
Where swinging wide at her **moorings** lay
The *Somerset*, British **man-of-war**;
A phantom ship, with each mast and **spar**
Across the moon like a prison bar,
And a huge black hulk, that was magnified
By its own reflection in the tide.

Meanwhile, his friend, through alley and street,
Wanders and watches with eager ears.
Till in the silence around him he hears
The **muster** of men at the **barrack** door,
The sound of arms, and the tramp of feet,
And the measured tread of the **grenadiers**,
Marching down to their boats on the shore.

He: Paul Revere
the town: Boston
belfry: bell tower

Middlesex: county north of Boston, including Lexington and Concord

muffled: quiet, perhaps wrapped in cloth to reduce the sound

moorings: ropes and anchors keeping a ship in place

man-of-war: warship

spar: pole that holds a ship's sails

muster: gathering

barrack: housing for soldiers

grenadiers: soldiers

Then he climbed the tower of the Old North Church,
By the wooden stairs, with stealthy tread,
To the belfry-chamber overhead,
And startled the pigeons from their perch
On the **sombre** rafters, that round him made
Masses and moving shapes of shade,—
By the trembling ladder, steep and tall,
To the highest window in the wall,
Where he paused to listen and look down
A moment on the roofs of the town,
And the moonlight flowing over all.

sombre: (English spelling of *somber*) gloomy

Beneath, in the churchyard, lay the dead,
In their **night-encampment** on the hill,
Wrapped in silence so deep and still
That he could hear, like a **sentinel's** tread,
The watchful night-wind, as it went
Creeping along from tent to tent.
And seeming to whisper, "All is well!"
A moment only he feels the spell
Of the place and the hour, and the secret dread
Of the lonely belfry and the dead;
For suddenly all his thoughts are bent
On a shadowy something far away,
Where the river widens to meet the bay,—
A line of black that bends and floats
On the rising tide, like a bridge of boats.

night-encampment: cemetery

sentinel's: guard's or watchman's

Meanwhile, impatient to mount and ride,
Booted and spurred, with a heavy stride
On the opposite shore walked Paul Revere.
Now he patted his horse's side,
Now gazed at the landscape far and near,
Then, impetuous, stamped the earth,
And turned and tightened his **saddle-girth**;
But mostly he watched with eager search
The belfry-tower of the Old North Church,
As it rose above the graves on the hill,
Lonely and **spectral** and sombre and still.
And **lo**! as he looks, on the belfry's height
A glimmer, and then a gleam of light!
He springs to the saddle, the bridle he turns,
But lingers and gazes, till full on his sight
A second lamp in the belfry burns!

Booted and spurred: wearing boots and spurs

saddle-girth: belt that holds a saddle on the horse

spectral: ghostly
lo: look

A hurry of hoofs in a village street,
A shape in the moonlight, a bulk in the dark,
And beneath, from the pebbles, in passing a spark
Struck out by a steed flying fearless and fleet:
That was all! And yet, through the gloom and the light,
The fate of a nation was riding that night;
And the spark struck out by that steed in his flight,
Kindled the land into flame with its heat.

He has left the village and **mounted the steep**,
And beneath him, tranquil and broad and deep,
Is the **Mystic**, meeting the ocean tides;
And under the **alders** that skirt its edge,
Now soft on the sand, now loud on the ledge,
Is heard the tramp of his steed as he rides.

mounted the steep:
climbed the hill

Mystic: river running
through Medford,
Massachusetts

alders: type of trees

It was twelve by the village clock,
When he crossed the bridge into Medford town.
He heard the crowing of the cock,
And the barking of the farmer's dog,
And felt the damp of the river fog
That rises after the sun goes down.

It was one by the village clock,
When he galloped into Lexington.
He saw the **gilded weathercock**
Swim in the moonlight as he passed,
And the meeting-house windows, blank and bare,
Gaze at him with a spectral glare,
As if they already stood aghast
At the bloody work they would look upon.

gilded weathercock: gold-
coated weather vane
shaped like a rooster

It was two by the village clock,
When he came to the bridge in Concord town.
He heard the **bleating of the flock**,
And the twitter of birds among the trees,
And felt the breath of the morning breeze
Blowing over the meadows brown.
And one was safe and asleep in his bed
Who at the bridge would be first to fall,
Who that day would be lying dead,
Pierced by a British musket-ball.

bleating of the flock: crying
of sheep

You know the rest. In the books you have read,
How the British Regulars fired and fled,—
How the farmers gave them ball for ball,
From behind each fence and farm-yard wall,
Chasing the red-coats down the lane,
Then crossing the fields to emerge again
Under the trees at the turn of the road,
And only pausing to fire and load.

So through the night rode Paul Revere;
And so through the night went his cry of alarm
To every Middlesex village and farm,—
A cry of defiance and not of fear,
A voice in the darkness, a knock at the door,
And a word that shall echo forevermore!
For, **borne** on the night-wind of the Past,   **borne:** carried
Through all our history, to the last,
In the hour of darkness and peril and need,
The people will waken and listen to hear
The hurrying hoof-beats of that steed,
And the midnight message of Paul Revere.

*Longfellow (1807–1882) was a professor of modern languages
at Bowdoin and Harvard colleges. His work includes a number
of long poems about historic events. He wrote "Paul Revere's
Ride" in 1861, during the Civil War between the North and
the South. Why do you think he might have written this poem
at that time?*

Source: George Gesner, ed., *Anthology of American Poetry*. New York: Avenel
Books, 1983.

Concord Hymm

by Ralph Waldo Emerson, 1837

The battles of Lexington and Concord marked the beginning of the Revolutionary War. The writer and philosopher Ralph Waldo Emerson (1803–1882) wrote the poem "Concord Hymn" for the unveiling of a monument to the patriots of Concord. It was first sung as a hymn at the 1837 ceremony and was later distributed as a printed leaflet. In 1876 it was published in Emerson's book of Selected Poems. Emerson's poem has since been read by millions of schoolchildren. What did Emerson mean by the phrase "the shot heard round the world"?

July 4, 1837

By the **rude** bridge that arched the flood,
    Their flag to April's breeze unfurled,
Here once the embattled farmers stood
    And fired the shot heard round the world.

> **rude:** simple, rustic

The foe long since in silence slept;
    Alike the conqueror silent sleeps;
And Time the ruined bridge has swept
    Down the dark stream which seaward creeps.

On this green bank, by this soft stream,
    We set to-day a **votive** stone;
That memory may their deed **redeem**,
    When, like our **sires**, our sons are gone.

> **votive:** in fulfillment of a promise or vow
> **redeem:** reclaim
> **sires:** fathers, parents

Spirit, that made those heroes dare
    To die, and leave their children free,
Bid Time and Nature gently spare
    The shaft we raise to them and thee.

The poem is dated July 4, 1837, in honor of Independence Day. The colonies could not have achieved their independence from Britain without the blood that was shed at Lexington and Concord. Emerson's poem expresses the bittersweet feelings of pride in the Patriots and sorrow for the heroes who gave their lives for freedom.

Source: Sculley Bradley, Richmond Croom Beatty, E. Hudson Long, and George Perkins, eds., *The American Tradition in Literature*, Fifth Edition. New York: Random House, 1981.

Declaration of Independence

by Thomas Jefferson, 1776

By the spring of 1776, American colonists had been at war with Britian for about a year. During that time colonists debated whether they were fighting for more rights from Britain or for total independence. As the fighting went on, more and more colonists argued that peace with Britain was no longer possible. In June 1776 members of the Second Continental Congress asked 33-year-old Thomas Jefferson (1743–1826) of Virginia to write a statement explaining why the colonies ought to be independent. Read the Declaration of Independence that Jefferson wrote and the notes of explanation beside it. Notice Jefferson's ideas about government, rebellion, and people's rights. Notice also what injustices he accuses King George III of Great Britain of having committed against the colonists. How do King George's actions take away the rights that Jefferson believes people and governments should have?

When in the Course of human events,

it becomes necessary for one people to dissolve the political bands which have connected them with another, and to assume, among the Powers of the earth, the separate and equal station to which the Laws of Nature and of Nature's God entitle them, a decent respect to the opinions of mankind requires that they should declare the causes which impel them to the separation.

At certain times in history, it is necessary for a group of people to break away from the government that has ruled them and to form a new, independent nation. At such a time, their reasons for separation and independence should be clearly stated.

We hold these truths to be self-evident, that all men are created equal, that they are endowed by their Creator with certain unalienable Rights, that among these are Life, Liberty, and the pursuit of Happiness.

We believe that everyone agrees on certain basic ideas: All people are created equal and they have basic rights that can never be taken away. People have the right to live, the right to be free, and the right to seek happiness.

That, to secure these rights, Governments are instituted among Men, deriving their just Powers from the consent of the governed.

That, whenever any Form of Government becomes destructive of these ends, it is the Right of the People to alter or to abolish it, and to institute new Government, laying its foundation on such Principles, and organizing its powers in such form, as to them shall seem most likely to effect their Safety and Happiness.

Prudence, indeed, will dictate that Governments long established should not be changed for light and transient causes; and, accordingly all experience hath shown, that mankind are more disposed to suffer, while evils are sufferable, than to right themselves by abolishing the forms to which they are accustomed. But, when a long train of abuses and usurpations, pursuing invariably the same Object, evinces a design to reduce them under absolute Despotism, it is their right, it is their duty, to throw off such Government, and to provide new Guards for their future security.

Such has been the patient sufferance of these Colonies; and such is now the necessity which constrains them to alter their former Systems of Government. The history of the present King of Great Britain is a history of repeated injuries and usurpations, all having in direct object the establishment of an absolute Tyranny over these States.

To prove this, let Facts be submitted to a candid world.

He has refused his Assent to Laws the most wholesome and necessary for the public good.

He has forbidden his Governors to pass Laws of immediate and pressing importance, unless suspended in their operation till his Assent should be obtained; and when so suspended, he has utterly neglected to attend to them.

He has refused to pass other Laws for the accommodation of large districts of People, unless those People would relinquish the right of Representation in the Legislature, a right inestimable to them and formidable to tyrants only.

He has called together legislative bodies at places unusual, uncomfortable, and distant from the depository of their Public Records, for the sole purpose of fatiguing them into compliance with his measures.

To preserve these rights, people create governments. Every government must have the support of the people it governs.

If a government loses this support or tries to take away basic freedoms, people have the right to change their government or to get rid of it and form a new government that will protect their rights.

However, people should not change governments that have long been in power for minor or temporary problems. We have learned from history that people are usually more willing to put up with a bad government than to get rid of it. But when people see their government misusing its power and mistreating its people time after time, it is the right and duty of the people to get rid of their government and to form a new one.

The colonies have suffered patiently long enough, and it is now time to change our government. King George III of Great Britain has ruled badly for many years. His main goal has been to establish total control over the colonies.

These statements are proven by the following facts:

King George III has rejected much-needed laws passed by the colonists.

He has not permitted important laws to be passed by his governors in the 13 English colonies.

He has refused to redraw the borders of large voting districts unless the people living there agreed to give up their right to be represented in the legislature.

He has ordered lawmakers in the colonies to meet far from their homes and offices in places that are unusual and difficult to get to. His only reason for doing this has been to tire out the lawmakers so that they will accept his rule.

He has dissolved Representative Houses repeatedly, for opposing, with manly firmness, his invasions on the rights of the people.

When lawmakers have criticized the king for attacking their rights, he has broken up the legislature's meetings.

He has refused for a long time, after such dissolutions, to cause others to be elected; whereby the Legislative Powers, incapable of Annihilation, have returned to the People at large for their exercise; the State remaining in the mean time exposed to all the dangers of invasion from without, and convulsions within.

After breaking up their meetings, the king has refused to allow new elections. As a result, colonists have been living in danger, unable to protect themselves or pass new laws.

He has endeavoured to prevent the Population of these States; for that purpose obstructing the Laws of Naturalization of Foreigners; refusing to pass others to encourage their migration hither, and raising the conditions of new Appropriations of Lands.

He has tried to stop colonists from moving west and settling in new lands. He has also tried to prevent people from foreign countries from settling in America by making it hard for newcomers to become citizens.

He has obstructed the Administration of Justice, by refusing his Assent to Laws for establishing Judiciary Powers.

In some places, he has not let colonists set up a system of courts.

He has made Judges dependent on his Will alone, for the tenure of their offices, and the amount and payment of their salaries.

He has forced colonial judges to obey him by deciding how long they can serve and how much they are paid.

He has erected a multitude of New Offices, and sent hither swarms of Officers to harass our People, and eat out their substance.

He has sent officials from Britain to fill new government offices in the colonies. These officials have mistreated people and demanded unfair taxes.

He has kept among us, in times of Peace, Standing Armies, without the Consent of our legislature.

In times of peace he has kept soldiers in the colonies even though the colonists did not want them.

He has affected to render the Military independent of and superior to the Civil Power.

He has tried to give soldiers power over colonial legislatures.

He has combined with others to subject us to a jurisdiction foreign to our constitution, and unacknowledged by our laws; giving his Assent to their Acts of pretended Legislation:

He and other leaders in Great Britain have passed laws for the colonies that the colonists did not want. In these laws the British government has:

For quartering large bodies of armed troops among us:

forced colonists to house and feed British soldiers;

For protecting them, by a mock Trial, from Punishment for any Murders which they should commit on the Inhabitants of these States:

protected these soldiers by giving them phony trials and not punishing them for murdering colonists;

For cutting off our Trade with all parts of the world:

cut off trade between colonists and people in other parts of the world;

For imposing Taxes on us without our Consent:

demanded taxes that colonists never agreed to;

For depriving us, in many cases, of the benefits of Trial by Jury:

prevented colonists accused of crimes from having their trials decided fairly by a jury;

For transporting us beyond Seas to be tried for pretended offences:

brought colonists falsely accused of crimes to Great Britain to be put on trial;

For abolishing the free System of English Laws in a neighbouring Province, establishing therein an Arbitrary government, and enlarging its Boundaries, so as to render it at once an example and fit instrument for introducing the same absolute rule into these Colonies:

extended the borders of the neighboring province of Quebec to include lands stretching to the Ohio River, thus forcing colonists in this region to obey harsh French laws rather than English laws. The goal of the British government is to force all colonists to obey these harsh laws;

For taking away our Charters, abolishing our most valuable Laws, and altering fundamentally the Forms of our Governments:

taken away our charters, or documents that make governments legal, canceled important laws, and completely changed our forms of government;

For suspending our own Legislatures, and declaring themselves invested with Power to legislate for us in all cases whatsoever.

broken up our legislatures and claimed that Great Britain has the right to pass all laws for the colonies.

He has abdicated Government here, by declaring us out of his Protection and waging War against us.

King George III has ended government in the colonies by waging war against us and not protecting us.

He has plundered our seas, ravaged our Coasts, burnt our towns, and destroyed the Lives of our People.

He has robbed colonists' ships at sea, burned down our towns, and ruined people's lives.

He is at this time transporting large Armies of foreign Mercenaries to compleat the works of death, desolation and tyranny, already begun with circumstances of Cruelty & perfidy scarcely paralleled in the most barbarous ages, and totally unworthy the Head of a civilized nation.

He is right now bringing foreign soldiers to the colonies to commit horrible and brutal deeds. These actions by the king are some of the cruelest ever committed in the history of the world.

He has constrained our fellow Citizens taken Captive on the high Seas to bear Arms against their Country, to become the executioners of their friends and Brethren, or to fall themselves by their Hands.

He has forced colonists captured at sea to join the British Navy and to fight and kill other colonists.

He has excited domestic insurrections amongst us, and has endeavoured to bring on the inhabitants of our frontiers, the merciless Indian Savages, whose known rule of warfare, is an undistinguished destruction of all ages, sexes and conditions.

He has urged enslaved people in the colonies to rebel, and he has tried to get Native Americans to fight against colonists.

In every stage of these Oppressions We have Petitioned for Redress in the most humble terms: Our repeated Petitions have been answered only by repeated injury. A Prince, whose character is thus marked by every act which may define a Tyrant, is unfit to be the ruler of a free People.

For years we have asked King George III to correct these problems and safeguard our rights. Unfortunately, the king has refused to listen to our complaints and he continues to treat us badly. The king is such an unfair ruler that he is not fit to rule the free people of the 13 colonies.

Nor have We been wanting in attention to our British brethren. We have warned them from time to time of attempts by their legislature to extend an unwarrantable jurisdiction over us. We have reminded them of the circumstances of our emigration and settlement here. We have appealed to their native justice and magnanimity, and we have conjured them by the ties of our common kindred to disavow these usurpations, which, would inevitably interrupt our connections and correspondence. They too have been deaf to the voice of justice and of consanguinity. We must, therefore, acquiesce in the necessity, which denounces our Separation, and hold them, as we hold the rest of mankind, Enemies in War, in Peace Friends.

We have also asked the British people for help. We have told them many times of our problems and pointed out the unfair laws passed by their government. We hoped they would listen to us because they believed in reason and justice. We hoped they would listen to us because we are related to each other and have much in common. But we were wrong: The British people have not listened to us at all. They have ignored our pleas for justice. We must, therefore, break away from Great Britain and become a separate nation.

We, therefore, the Representatives of the United States of America, in General Congress Assembled, appealing to the Supreme Judge of the world for the rectitude of our intentions, do, in the Name, and by Authority of the good People of these Colonies, solemnly publish and declare, That these United Colonies are, and of Right ought to be Free and Independent States; that they are Absolved from all Allegiance to the British Crown, and that all political connection between them and the State of Great Britain, is and ought to be totally dissolved; and that as Free and Independent States, they have full Power to levy War, conclude Peace, contract Alliances, establish Commerce, and to do all other Acts and Things which Independent States may of right do. And for the support of this Declaration, with a firm reliance on the protection of divine Providence, we mutually pledge to each other our Lives, our Fortunes and our sacred Honour.

In the name of the American people, we members of the Continental Congress declare that the United States of America is no longer a colony of Great Britain but is, instead, a free and independent nation. The United States now cuts off all its relations with Great Britain. As a free nation the United States has the right and power to make war and peace, make agreements with other nations, conduct trade, and do all the things that independent nations have the right to do. To support this Declaration of Independence, we promise to each other our lives, our fortunes, and our personal honor.

On July 4, 1776, the members of the Second Continental Congress approved the Declaration of Independence. This action made it clear that Americans were no longer colonists, but rather citizens of a new country called the United States of America. For more than 200 years, Jefferson's words have inspired people all over the world in their struggle for liberty and independence. To learn how African Americans applied some of the ideas in the Declaration of Independence, read their petition for freedom on pages 71–72.

Common Sense

by Thomas Paine, 1776

Thomas Paine was an American patriot (1737-1809) whose ability to express his ideas through the use of bold and graphic language made his political theories easily understandable to the public. In January 1776 Paine published a pamphlet called Common Sense. In this pamphlet, Paine argued for independence from Great Britain. He said that Great Britain's rule was not kindly. Further, he wrote that the colonies had nothing to lose by leaving the British empire since Britain was too far away to rule effectively. In just three months the colonists bought nearly 12,000 copies of Common Sense. Why were the colonists ready to listen to Thomas Paine?

In the following pages I offer nothing more than simple facts, plain arguments, and common sense....

The sun never shined on a **cause** of greater worth.'Tis not the affair of a city, a county, a province, or a kingdom, but of a continent—of at least one eighth part of the **habitable** globe.'Tis not the concern of a day, a year, or an age; **posterity** are virtually involved in the contest, and will be more or less affected, even to the end of time, by the **proceedings** now. Now is the **seed-time** of continental union, faith and honor....

I have heard it asserted by some, that as America hath flourished under her former **connexion** with Great-Britain, that the same connexion is necessary towards her future happiness, and will always have the same effect. Nothing can be more **fallacious** than this kind of argument. We may as well assert that because a child has thrived upon milk, that it is never to have meat, or that the first twenty years of our lives is to become a **precedent** for the next twenty. But even this is admitting more than is true, for I answer **roundly**, that America would have flourished as much, and probably much more, had no European power had anything to do with her. The commerce, by which she hath enriched herself, are the **necessaries** of life, and will always have a market while eating is the custom of Europe.

But she has protected us, say some. That she has **engrossed** us is true, and defended the continent at our **expence** as well as her own is admitted, and she would have defended Turkey from the same motive, **viz.** the sake of trade and dominion....

cause: here refers to independence from Britain

habitable: livable

posterity: future generations

proceedings: events

seed-time: time when seed is planted for later harvest; that is, the beginning

connexion: connection, tie to

fallacious: false

precedent: model

roundly: confidently

necessaries: vital things

engrossed: enlarged

expence: expense

viz: that is

Europe is too thickly planted with kingdoms to be long at peace, and whenever a war breaks out between England and any foreign power, the trade of America goes to ruin, *because of her connection with Britain.* ... Every thing that is right or natural pleads for separation. The blood of the slain, the weeping voice of nature cries, **'TIS** TIME TO PART. Even the distance at which the **Almighty** hath placed England and America, is a strong and natural proof, that the authority of the one, over the other, was never the design of Heaven. ...

'TIS: it is
Almighty: God

As to government matters, it is not in the power of Britain to do this continent justice: The business of it will soon be too weighty, and intricate, to be managed with any tolerable degree of convenience, by a power so distant from us, and so very ignorant of us; for if they cannot conquer us, they cannot govern us. To be always running three or four thousand miles with a tale or a petition, waiting four or five months for an answer, which when obtained requires five or six more to explain it in, will in a few years be looked upon as **folly** and childishness—There was a time when it was proper, and there is a proper time for it to cease.

folly: foolishness

Small islands not capable of protecting themselves, are the proper objects for kingdoms to take under their care; but there is something very absurd, in supposing a continent to be perpetually governed by an island. In no instance hath nature made the **satellite larger than its primary planet**, and as England and America, with respect to each other, reverses the common order of nature, it is evident they belong to **different systems**; England to Europe, America to itself. ...

satellite ... planet: object in outer space that moves in a circle around larger objects; for example, the moon around Earth
different systems: any group of planets revolving around a star
shew: show

TO CONCLUDE, however strange it may appear to some, or however unwilling they may be to think so, matters not, but many strong and striking reasons may be given, to **shew**, that nothing can settle our affairs so expeditiously as an open and determined declaration for independance. ...

These proceedings may at first appear strange and difficult; but, like all other steps which we have already passed over, will in a little time become familiar and **agreeable**; and, until an independance is declared, the **Continent** will feel itself like a man who continues putting off some unpleasant business from day to day, yet knows it must be done, hates to set about it, wishes it over, and is continually haunted with the thoughts of its necessity.

agreeable: nice
Continent: America

In Common Sense, *Thomas Paine presented his arguments clearly and appealed to reason and common sense. Many say that his writings inspired two of the greatest revolutions in history—the American Revolution in 1776 and the French Revolution in 1789.*

Source: Thomas Paine, *Common Sense, The Rights of Man, and other Essential Writings of Thomas Paine*. New York: Meridian, 1984.

Johnny Tremain

by Esther Forbes, 1943

The English had a long history of fighting for liberty in their own country. In 1215 the Magna Carta, an early English charter of rights, limited the powers of the monarchy. In 1649 King Charles I was beheaded for abusing his power. In 1689 Parliament passed a Bill of Rights that increased the power of citizens. Thus, it was probably natural that the 13 English colonies in North America would eventually fight for the same kind of liberty. In the novel Johnny Tremain, the author depicts some of the major events that led up to the American Revolution as seen by a teenager growing up in Boston. This excerpt from the novel takes place in April 1775, immediately before the battles of Lexington and Concord. How does Johnny feel about the British?

Suddenly there was silence along the whole great length of the **brigade**. Slim Earl Percy on a white horse, escorted by a group of officers, was cantering slowly across the **Common**.

Five mounted men. The sun was bright that day with only breeze enough to **ruffle** the horses' manes, **flaunt** scarlet riding capes, float the flag of England. Johnny was an Englishman. The sullen, rebellious people standing about watching Percy and his staff approaching, waiting for the brigade to march, all were Englishmen. The flag—it stood for Magna Carta, the Bill of Rights, Charles the First's head upon a block, centuries of struggle for 'English liberty.' But over here there had grown up a broader interpretation of the

brigade: military unit
Common: village green

ruffle: disturb the calmness
flaunt: show off

69

word 'liberty': no man to be ruled or taxed except by men of his own choice. But we are still fighting for 'English liberty', and don't you forget it. French slaves to the north of us, Spanish slaves to the south of us. Only English colonies are allowed to taste the forbidden fruit of liberty—we who grew up under England. Johnny thought of **James Otis**'s words. Upholding the torch of liberty—which had been lighted on the fires of England.

James Otis: American patriot who opposed the Stamp Act

Not since the soldiers had come to Boston had Johnny removed his hat when the British flag went by except once when it had been knocked off his head by a soldier. He started to remove it now—for the first time and doubtless the last. Thought better of it—It was too late. He knew the shooting had begun.

The sword in Earl Percy's hand flashed. There was a command which was instantly picked up and repeated and echoed and repeated again. The **regimental** drummers struck up. The artillery horses threw their weight against their collars. Wagoners cracked their whips and the **scarlet dragon** swung forward, sluggishly at first, heading for the town gates. Thousands of separate feet merged into only one gigantic pair. Left, right, left, right. The earth shook to their rhythm. Johnny watched them pass. Every button was sewed on. Every buckle in place. Every cartridge box held exactly thirty-six cartridges. Every musket had a bayonet, and there was not one old **fowling piece** among them. Every horse had four new shoes. It was a magnificent sight, but Johnny felt a little sick.

regimental: belonging to a regiment, a military unit similar in size to a brigade

scarlet dragon: British brigade

fowling piece: gun for shooting fowl or birds

What chance—what shadow of a chance—had those poor, untrained, half-armed farmers at Concord? O God, be with us now. But even as he prayed, he kept an eye out for the regimental markings on the men's uniforms. It was the Fourth, the Twenty-Third, and the Forty-Seventh who were being sent out, plus five hundred marines, plus a small artillery train, and a few baggage wagons. Twelve hundred for a guess.

The drums throbbed. The heavy dragon marched on its thousands of feet, and now above the drums came the **shrilling** of **fifes**. They played a tune they always played when they wished to insult Yankees. For once more Yankee Doodle was going to town on a **spanking** stallion, with that forlorn feather in his cap, asking those **unmilitary questions**.

shrilling: unpleasantly high-pitched sound

fifes: flutes

spanking: very nice, fancy

unmilitary questions: questions regarding independence from Britain

Poor Yankee Doodle. Whatever could he do against this great scarlet dragon?

In this excerpt the author paints a vivid picture of the military might of the British redcoats that the colonists faced. Yet the colonists' desire for liberty was so strong that they eventually defeated the British and won their independence.

Source: Esther Forbes, *Johnny Tremain*. Santa Barbara, CA: Cornerstone Books, 1943.

A Petition for Freedom

by African Americans of Massachusetts, 1777

When the American Revolution began, slavery was legal in all 13 colonies. However, the aims and ideals of the Revolution—independence and freedom—were important to all Americans. During the 1770s African Americans in Massachusetts wrote many petitions to colonial leaders, seeking an end to slavery. The following 1777 petition to the new Massachusetts state government was signed by Prince Hall, a leading Boston minister, and seven other African Americans. As you read this excerpt, notice how the writers compare their struggle for freedom to the American struggle for independence from Great Britain. Which words and ideas in the petition can also be found in the Declaration of Independence, which you read on pages 62–66?

To the Honorable Counsel and House of Representatives for the
State of Massachusetts Bay in General Court assembled,
January 13, 1777

The petition of a great number of Blacks detained in a state
of slavery in the **bowels** of a free and Christian country humbly
show that your petitioners **apprehend** that they have in common
with all other men a natural and **unalienable** right to that
freedom which the Great Parent of the Universe hath **bestowed**
equally on all mankind and which they have never **forfeited**
by any compact or agreement whatever. But they were unjustly
dragged by the hand of cruel power from their dearest friends
and some of them even torn from the embraces of their tender
parents—from a **populous**, pleasant, and plentiful country and
in violation of laws of nature and of nations and in **defiance of**
all the tender feelings of humanity brought here [to America]
. . . to be sold like beasts of burden and like them condemned to
slavery for life. . . . A life of slavery like that of your petitioners
deprived of every social privilege of everything **requisite** to
render life tolerable is far worse than **nonexistence**. . . .

Your petitioners have long and patiently waited the event of
petition after petition by them presented to the legislative body

bowels: deepest parts
apprehend: understand
unalienable: incapable of
being taken away
bestowed: given
forfeited: given up

populous: filled with
people
defiance of: opposition to

requisite: necessary
render: make
nonexistence: death

of this state and [they] . . . **cannot but** express their astonishment
that it has never been considered that every principle from
which America has acted in the course of their unhappy
difficulties with Great Britain pleads stronger than a thousand
arguments in favor of your petitioners. They therefore humbly
beseech your honors to give this petition its due weight and
consideration and cause an act of the Legislature to be passed
whereby they may be restored to the enjoyments of that which is
the natural right of all men—and [that] their children who were
born in this land of liberty may not to be held as slaves. . . .
And your petitioners, as in duty bound shall ever pray.

cannot but: can only

beseech: beg

Lancaster Hill	Jack Purpont
Peter Bess	Nero Suneto
Brister Slenten	Newport Symner
Prince Hall	Job Lock

*Lawmakers in Massachusetts ignored this petition for freedom just as they had ignored
earlier petitions. Continued pressure by African Americans during the Revolutionary
War, however, along with the ideals of the Revolution itself, led people in Massachusetts
to end slavery in the 1780s. By 1800 most states in the North had outlawed slavery.*

Source: *Collections of the Massachusetts Historical Society,* Vol. III, Fifth Series. Boston, 1877.

Song of Marion's Men

by William Cullen Bryant, 1831

The Revolutionary War was fought by resourceful men and women who drew upon their familiarity with the terrain to drive off the larger and professionally trained British army. One of these legendary Patriots was Captain Frances Marion (1732–1795), a brave South Carolinian who earned the nickname of "Swamp Fox." Marion's strategy was to make sneak, lightning-quick attacks on the British and then take cover in the swamps of Carolina. In 1831 the poet William Cullen Bryant wrote a poem in admiration of Marion's men. Marion's outfit was small, yet he and his men were highly successful. How do you think Marion's style of fighting differed from that of the British?

Our band is few but true and tried,
    Our leader frank and bold;
The British soldier trembles
    When Marion's name is told.
Our fortress is the good **greenwood**,   **greenwood:** forest
    Our tent the cypress-tree;
We know the forest round us,
    As seamen know the sea.
We know its walls of thorny vines,
    Its glades of reedy grass,
Its safe and silent islands
    Within the dark **morass**.   **morass:** swamp

Woe to the English soldiery
    That little dread us near!
On them shall light at midnight
    A strange and sudden fear:
When, waking to their tents on fire,
    They grasp their arms in vain,
And they who stand to face us
    Are beat to earth again;
And they who fly in terror deem
    A mighty host behind,
And hear the tramp of thousands

73

Upon the hollow wind.
Then sweet the hour that brings release
    From danger and from toil:
We talk the battle over,
    And share the battle's spoil.
The woodland rings with laugh and shout,
    As if a hunt were up,
And woodland flowers are gathered
    To crown the soldier's cup.
With merry songs we mock the wind
    That in the pine-top grieves,
And slumber long and sweetly
    On beds of oaken leaves.

Well knows the fair and friendly moon
    The band that Marion leads—
The glitter of their rifles,
    The scampering of their steeds.
'Tis life to guide the fiery **barb**
    Across the moonlight plain;
'Tis life to feel the night-wind
    That lifts the tossing mane.
A moment in the British camp—
    A moment—and away
Back to the pathless forest,
    Before the peep of day.

barb: horse

Grave men there are by broad **Santee**,
    Grave men with **hoary** hairs;
Their hearts are all with Marion,
    For Marion are their prayers.
And lovely ladies greet our band
    With kindliest welcoming,
With smiles like those of summer,
    And tears like those of spring.
For them we wear these trusty arms,
    And lay them down no more
Till we have driven the Briton,
    Forever, from our shore.

Santee: a river in South
Carolina

hoary: ancient, old

William Cullen Bryant (1794–1878) was born in Cummington, Massachusetts. The poet and editor was part-owner of the newspaper The Evening Post. *Through his paper, Bryant voiced his support for an end to slavery and other reforms. He also translated the* Iliad *and the* Odyssey, *two great epic poems of the ancient Greeks. An epic poem is a narrative that tells of the deeds of a hero or of a nation. Although "Song of Marion's Men" is not as lengthy or ambitious as an epic, it has some of the same qualities. What deeds or characteristics of Marion and his band does the poem celebrate?*

Source: George Gesner, ed., *Anthology of American Poetry*. New York: Avenel Books, 1983.

Washington's Farewell to His Officers

from an eyewitness account by Benjamin Tallmadge, 1783

George Washington, Commander-in-Chief of the Continental Army, took an army of raw recruits and shaped them into a disciplined team. He fought with Congress for better pay to induce men to extend their term of service. Ultimately, he created an army that was able to defeat the British. By the time Washington bid farewell to his officers on December 4, 1783, he had become a military leader who was much loved by his troops. Why do you think this was so? The following excerpt is from an eyewitness account of this event, written by one of Washington's aides.

The time now drew near when the Commander-in-Chief intended to leave this part of the country for his beloved retreat at Mount Vernon.

On Thursday, the 4th of December, it was made known to the officers then in New York that General Washington intended to commence his journey on that day. At 12 o'clock the Officers **repaired** to Fraunces Tavern, in Pearl Street, where General Washington had **appointed** to meet them, and to take his final

repaired: went

appointed: decided, named as the place

leave of them. We had assembled but a few moments, when his excellency entered the room. His emotion, too strong to be concealed, seemed to be **reciprocated** by every Officer present.

After **partaking** of a slight refreshment, in almost breathless silence, the General filled his glass with wine, and, turning to the Officers, he said: "With a heart full of love and gratitude, I now take leave of you. I most devoutly wish that your latter days may be as prosperous and happy as your former ones have been glorious and honorable."

After the Officers had taken a glass of wine, General Washington said: "I cannot come to each of you, but shall feel obliged if each of you will come and take me by the hand."

General Knox, being nearest to him, turned to the Commander-in-Chief, who, **suffused** in tears, was incapable of **utterance** but grasped his hand when they embraced each other in silence.

In the same affectionate manner, every Officer in the room marched up to, kissed, and parted with his General-in-Chief.

Such a scene of sorrow and weeping I had never before witnessed, and I hope may never be called upon to witness again. It was indeed too **affecting** to be of long **continuance**—for tears of deep **sensibility** filled every eye—and the heart seemed so full that it was ready to burst from its **wonted abode**. Not a word was uttered to break the solemn silence that **prevailed**, or to interrupt the tenderness of the interesting scene. The simple thought that we were then about to part from the man who had conducted us through a long and bloody war, and under whose conduct the glory and independence of our country had been achieved, and that we should see his face no more in this world, seemed to me utterly **insupportable**.

But the time of separation had come, and waving his hand to his grieving **children** around him, he left the room and, passing through a **corps** of **light infantry** who were paraded to receive him, he walked silently on the **whitehall**, where a barge was in waiting.

We all followed in mournful silence to the wharf, where a **prodigious** crowd had assembled to witness the departure of the man, who, under God, had been the great agent in establishing the glory and independence of these United States.

As soon as he was seated, the barge put off into the river, and, when out in the stream, our great and beloved General waved with hat, and **bid** us a silent **adieu**.

After the war Washington returned to Mount Vernon where he believed he would lead a peaceful life on his farm. This was not to be. The newly created United States was to call upon him again to lead their efforts to form a national government and to serve as our first President.

Source: Col. Benjamin Tallmadge, *Memoir of Colonel Benjamin Tallmadge*. New York: The New York Times & Arno Press, 1963.

reciprocated: returned equally

partaking: taking part

suffused: overflowing

utterance: talking

affecting: touching the emotions

continuance: duration

sensibility: feeling

wonted abode: usual home

prevailed: lasted

insupportable: unbearable

children: the officers, who look on Washington as a "father"

corps: military unit

light infantry: foot soldiers carrying small weapons

whitehall: boat dock

prodigious: large, huge

bid: offered

adieu: French for good-bye

Shh! We're Writing the Constitution

by Jean Fritz, 1987

In May 1787, 55 delegates from the 13 states met in Philadelphia at a Constitutional Convention. There they discussed problems that the states were having under the existing plan of government, the Articles of Confederation. In her book Shh! We're Writing the Constitution Jean Fritz makes this historical period come alive by painting vivid pictures with words of the drama and the personalities involved in writing the Constitution. In this excerpt from the book, the delegates debate fiercely over what kind of government the young country needs. They argue over whether to revise the Articles or to come up with a new plan entirely. Why do you think the debate was so fierce?

If the people of the country were afraid of what might happen in the convention, so were the delegates themselves. They didn't call the document they were working on a "constitution"; they referred to it as "the plan." Because they knew that the country was sensitive to the word "national," they tried to stick to "federal," a word they were used to and one which didn't reduce the power of the states. But after Edmund Randolph, Governor of Virginia, had presented what came to be called the Virginia Plan, he spoke right out.

In the Virginia Plan, Randolph explained, there would be three branches of government. The executive branch would have a head who would be responsible for running the government. The legislative branch would be made up of two houses which would make laws. The House of Representatives would be elected directly by the people; the Senate, the smaller and supposedly more coolheaded body, would be elected by the House. Together they would be called the Congress. The third branch would be the judiciary headed by a Supreme Court, which would make sure that laws were constitutional and were properly obeyed.

Edmund Randolph was a tall, handsome, likable man and nothing he said at first seemed alarming. Some of the states had constitutions that were similar to the one he described. Besides, the members knew that after Randolph's plan had been discussed, other members would have a chance to present their plans. But at the end of his speech Randolph did **arouse** his audience. It should be clear, he said, that his resolutions were not merely for a federal government but for a national government that would be supreme over the states.

arouse: to cause an action or strong feeling

There was dead silence.

Pierce Butler of South Carolina was one of the first to recover. He jumped down hard on the word "national" but John Dickinson of Delaware said there was nothing wrong with the word. "We *are* a nation!" he declared.

No! For Elbridge Gerry of Massachusetts this kind of talk was scary. He was a thin, worrying sort of man who was sometimes called "Grumbletonian" behind his back. National? he sputtered. How could they think national? They had been sent here to revise the Articles of Confederation, not to destroy them.

As the meetings went on, all kinds of fear surfaced. The smaller states with fewer people were afraid of the larger states which had more people. In the past the votes of all states, no mater what their population, had counted the same. But a national government would be more concerned with individual people than with the states themselves. So what would happen to the small states now? And what kind of government were they forming? Some people were afraid of a "**high-toned**" or **aristocratic** government run by a small, privileged, wealthy group, the way a monarchy was usually run. Others were just as afraid of the common people having too much power. They weren't capable of governing, it was said.

high-toned: having to do with wealth and social position

aristocratic: born to a high social position

Eventually the convention did agree on a national legislature to consist of two houses but before final acceptance, the word "national" was crossed out.

Still, there were so many questions to decide. What about the person who was to be the executive or head of the government?

Should there be just one person? If so, would he seem like a king? Why not three people, each representing a different part of the country? But what if they fought among themselves? What if they couldn't reach an agreement? Should the executive be paid a salary? (Yes, said Madison. Don't count on patriotism.) But who should pay the salary—the states or the government of the United States? How should the executive be chosen? By the people? By the states? By a branch of the United States legislature? By **electors**? By **lot**? (They had to vote sixty times before they could settle this question.) And how long should the executive serve? If he were thought to be guilty of misconduct, could they **impeach** him? Could they remove him from office?

Alexander Hamilton was one of the few who wanted the president to serve a long term, perhaps even for life. He thought it would be embarrassing to watch a lot of ex-presidents wandering around like ghosts. But suppose you had a long-term president, Franklin pointed out. And suppose he turned out to be a bad president? What then? Out of simple kindness they ought to provide some way to get rid of him. Otherwise, Franklin chuckled, the only thing they could do would be to shoot him.

In the end it was decided that there should be a single executive who would be paid out of the Treasury of the new government. He

electors: people selected by a political party to vote in an election

lot: a piece of paper or other material used to decide something by chance

impeach: bring formal charges against a public official for crime or misconduct in office

J. MADISON   W. PATERSON

would be chosen by electors from each state, and he would serve four years. And yes, if it was necessary, he could be impeached.

But what if he should die while in office? Or be impeached? Who would take his place? So there had to be a vice president, the one who came in second in the presidential election. And since the vice president should do more than just wait around to see if the president would make it through his term, he was given the job of presiding over the Senate.

Mr. Randolph finished presenting his plan on May 29 and for the next two weeks—until June 13—the convention went over it. Some **measures** were voted on, some would be revised, and all would be discussed again and again. But there was also the chance that the whole plan would be scrapped for something else. After a day's recess, on June 15, William Paterson of New Jersey stood up. Only five feet two, he wasn't as impressive a figure as Mr. Randolph, but he was a cheerful, modest, likable man. Still, he didn't approve of a single idea of Mr. Randolph's.

The government should be a federation of states as it was now, with each state having an equal vote, he said. It should consist of one legislative body with several executives at its head.

measures: legislative acts or bills

According to Mr. Paterson, the Virginia Plan was impractical, illegal, and expensive. How could so many members of Congress, he asked, find the money to travel from all over the country to attend meetings?

When James Madison answered Mr. Paterson, it was as if he were fencing. Madison danced all around Mr. Paterson's arguments, **thrusting** at first one point, then another until it seemed as if there were nothing left of William Paterson's plan. And there wasn't. When the delegates were asked to vote in favor of one of the two plans, Mr. Randolph's won. Seven states against three. (Maryland's delegation was divided.) Randolph's plan still had to be thrashed out, but the idea of a federation was dead. With this vote the delegates committed themselves to write a constitution for a new nation, whether all of them were willing to call it that or not.

thrusting: forceful, sudden pushing

When the convention ended in September 1787, the Articles of Confederation were no more, and the new Constitution of the United States had been signed. The delegates had adopted in large part a new plan for government written by James Madison and presented at the convention by Edmund Randolph of Virginia. This plan would establish a republic with a national government consisting of three branches. Throughout the convention, the delegates made many compromises until they created a written plan of government that all could support. The Constitution and its amendments still serve as the basis of the government of the United States.

Source: Jean Fritz, *Shh! We're Writing the Constitution.* New York: G. P. Putnam's Sons, 1987.

Two Views on Women's Rights

by Abigail Adams and John Adams, 1776

In the spring of 1776, many Americans were expecting the 13 colonies to declare their independence from Britain. Once independence was achieved, some people hoped that the new government would treat women and men as equals under the law. One of these people was Abigail Adams (1744-1818), the 31-year-old wife of colonial leader John Adams (1735-1826). At the time, American women had few legal rights or powers. The Adamses were a close couple, and Abigail called John her "dearest friend" and "beloved partner." On the issue of women's rights, however, the Adamses had very different opinions. The excerpts below are from three letters that were written in 1776 while Abigail was in Massachusetts running the family farm and John was in Philadelphia serving in the Continental Congress. How do their views differ on women's rights and equality?

Abigail to John, March 31, 1776

I long to hear that you have declared **an independency**—and by the way in the new code of laws which I suppose it will be necessary for you to make I desire you would remember the ladies, and be more generous and favorable to them than your ancestors. Do not put such unlimited power into the hands of the husbands. Remember all men would be **tyrants** if they could. If particular care and attention is not paid to the ladies we are determined to **foment** a rebellion, and will not hold ourselves bound by any laws in which we have no voice, or representation.

That your sex are naturally tyrannical is a truth so thoroughly established as to **admit** of no **dispute**, but such of you as wish to be happy willingly give up the harsh title of master for the more tender and endearing one of friend. Why then, not put it out of the power of the vicious and the lawless to use us with cruelty and indignity. . . . Men of sense in all ages **abhor** those customs which treat us only as the **vassals** of your sex. Regard us then as beings placed by **providence** under your protection and in imitation of the Supreme Being make use of that power only for our happiness.

an independency: independence

tyrants: oppressive rulers

foment: stir up

admit: be
dispute: disagreement

abhor: hate
vassals: servants
providence: God

John to Abigail, April 14, 1776

As to Declarations of Independency, be patient. . . .

As to your extraordinary code of laws, I cannot but laugh. We have been told that our struggle has loosened the **bands** of government every where. That children and **apprentices** were disobedient—that schools and colleges were grown **turbulent**—that Indians **slighted** their guardians and Negroes grew **insolent** to their masters. But your letter was the first **intimation** that another tribe more numerous and powerful than all the rest were grown discontented. . . .

Depend upon it, we know better than to **repeal** our masculine systems. Although they are in full force, you know that they are little more than **theory**. We dare not exert our power in its full **latitude**. We are obliged to go fair, and softly, and in practice you know we are the **subjects**. We have only the name of masters, and rather than give up this, which would completely subject us to the **despotism** of the **petticoat**, I hope General Washington, and all our brave heroes would fight.

bands: ties

apprentices: workers learning a trade

turbulent: stormy
slighted: showed disrespect to
insolent: disrespectful
intimation: clue
repeal: undo

theory: unsure belief
latitude: strength
subjects: ones who obey

despotism: oppressive rule
petticoat: woman's skirt; old symbol for a woman

Abigail to John, May 7, 1776

I can not say that I think you very generous to the ladies, for whilst you are **proclaiming** peace and good will to men, **emancipating** all nations, you insist upon retaining an absolute power over wives. But you must remember that **arbitrary** power is like most other things which are very hard, very **liable** to be broken—and notwithstanding all your wise laws and **maxims** we have it in our power not only to free ourselves but to **subdue** our masters, and without violence throw both your natural and legal authority at our feet. . . .

proclaiming: announcing
emancipating: freeing

arbitrary: unlimited
liable: likely
maxims: truths
subdue: conquer

John Adams later served as second President of the United States from 1797 to 1801. His views of women's rights and equality were similar to those of most American men of his day. As First Lady, Abigail Adams assisted her husband in the White House. It would be many years, however, before women received the same rights as men.

Source: L. H. Butterfield, ed., *Adams Family Correspondence*, Vol. I. Cambridge, MA: The Belknap Press of Harvard University Press, 1963.

The Federalist, Number 10

by James Madison, 1787

By September 1787 the new Constitution of the United States was finished. It was now up to the states to ratify it. Opinion was divided between those who favored a strong central government, called Federalists, and those who favored more control by the states. One of the leading Federalists was James Madison. Madison and others wrote a series of unsigned letters to the newspapers in New York City arguing in favor of the Constitution. Below is an excerpt from one of these letters. Why do you think Madison did not sign the letters?

*T*he question resulting is whether small or extensive republics are most favorable to the election of proper guardians of the public **weal**; and it is clearly decided in favor of the latter by two obvious considerations.

weal: well-being

In the first place it is to be remarked that however small the republic may be the representatives must be raised to a certain number in order to guard against the **cabals** of a few; and that however large it may be they must be limited to a certain number in order to guard against the confusion of a **multitude**....

cabals: secret plots

multitude: crowd

In the next place, as each representative will be chosen by a greater number of citizens in the large than in the small republic, it will be more difficult for unworthy candidates to practise with success the vicious arts by which elections are too often carried; and the **suffrages** of the people being more free, will be more likely to center on men who possess the most attractive merit and the most **diffusive** and established characters....

suffrages: votes

diffusive: well-rounded

Extend the **sphere** and you take in a greater variety of parties and interests; you make it less probable that a majority of the whole will have a common motive to invade the rights of other citizens; or if such a common motive exists, it will be more difficult for all who feel it to discover their own strength and to act in unison with each other....

sphere: a round object like a ball; here meaning the group of voters

The influence of **factious leaders** may **kindle** a flame within their particular States but will be unable to spread a general **conflagration** through the other States.

factious leaders: leaders who try to divide people from each other

kindle: start, as in a fire

conflagration: large, uncontrollable fire

The letters, numbering 85, sent between 1787 and 1788, have been called "the best commentary on the principles of government ever written." This statement was made by Thomas Jefferson, who did not support the Federalist position.

Source: Alexander Hamilton, James Madison, and John Jay, *The Federalist Papers.* New York: New American Library, 1961.

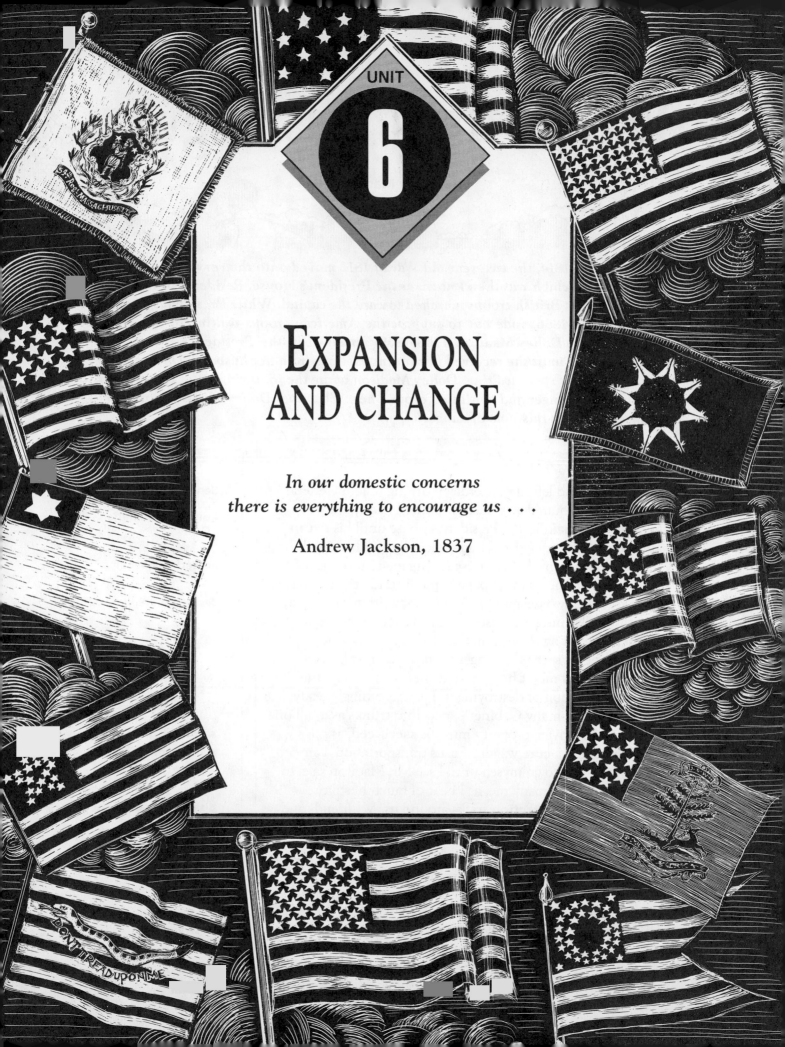

EXPANSION AND CHANGE

*In our domestic concerns
there is everything to encourage us . . .*

Andrew Jackson, 1837

Escape from Washington

by Dolley Madison, 1814

On August 23, 1814, the two-year-old War of 1812 moved onto the very doorstep of the White House, which was then known as the President's House. Residents of the city began fleeing as British troops marched toward the capital. While President James Madison (1751-1836) rode out to support the American troops waiting to fight the British, his wife Dolley Madison (1768-1849) remained in the President's House. She refused to leave until she received further instructions from her husband. During these long, tense hours spent waiting, Dolley Madison wrote the following letter to her sister, describing the danger and confusion around her. What does Dolley Madison consider her main duties in this time of danger?

Dear Sister,   Tuesday, August 23, 1814

My husband left me yesterday morning to join **General Winder.** He inquired anxiously whether I had courage or firmness to remain in the President's house until his return . . . and on my assurance that I had no fear but for him, and the success of our army, he left, **beseeching** me to take care of myself, and of the Cabinet papers, public and private. I have since received two **despatches** from him, written with a pencil. The last is alarming, because he desires I should be ready at a moment's warning to enter my carriage, and leave the city; that the enemy seemed stronger than had at first been reported, and it might happen that they would reach the city with the intention of destroying it. I am accordingly ready; I have pressed as many Cabinet papers into trunks as to fill one carriage; our private property must be **sacrificed,** as it is impossible to **procure** wagons for its transportation. I am determined not to go myself until I see Mr. Madison safe, so that he can accompany me, as I hear of much hostility towards him. **Disaffection** stalks around us. My friends and acquaintances are all gone. . . .

Wednesday Morning, August 24, 1814, twelve o'clock
Since sunrise I have been turning my spy-glass in every direction, and watching with unwearied anxiety, hoping to discover the approach of my dear husband and his friends; but, alas! I can **descry** only groups of military, wandering in all

General Winder: commander of troops outside Washington, D.C.

beseeching: begging

despatches: reports

sacrificed: given up
procure: get

disaffection: disloyalty

descry: spot

directions, as if there was a lack of **arms**, or of spirit to fight for their own fireside.

Three o'clock

Will you believe it, my sister? we have had a battle, or skirmish, near **Bladensburg**, and here I am still, within sound of the cannon! Mr. Madison comes not. May God protect us! Two messengers, covered with dust, come to bid me fly; but here I mean to wait for him. . . . At this late hour a wagon has been procured, and I have had it filled with **plate** and the most valuable **portable** articles, belonging to the house. Whether it will reach its destination . . . or fall into the hands of British soldiery, events must determine. Our kind friend, Mr. Carroll, has come to hasten my departure, and [is] in a very bad **humor** with me, because I insist on waiting until the large picture of General Washington is **secured**, and it requires to be unscrewed from the wall. This process was found too **tedious** for these **perilous** moments; I have ordered the frame to be broken, and the canvas taken out. It is done! and the precious portrait [is now] placed . . . for safe keeping. And now, dear sister, I must leave this house, or the retreating army will make me a prisoner in it by filling up the road I am directed to take. When I shall again write to you, or where I shall be tomorrow, I cannot tell!

arms: weapons

Bladensburg: Maryland town bordering Washington, D.C.

plate: costly dishes and silverware
portable: movable

humor: mood
secured: safe

tedious: long and difficult
perilous: dangerous

A few hours after Dolley Madison left Washington, D.C., on August 24, 1814, British soldiers marched in and set fire to the President's House and the rest of the city. Light from the enormous blaze could be seen 40 miles (64 km) away. Dolley Madison, dressed in the disguise of a poor country woman, escaped safely through the burning city to nearby Virginia. Several days later she returned to Washington and found much of the capital in ruins. Because the President's House had burned down, Dolley Madison and her husband had to live in a different house for the next two and a half years. When the President's House was rebuilt several years later, its outside walls were painted white. This is probably why it became known as the White House.

Source: *Memoirs and Letters of Dolley Madison, Wife of James Madison, President of the United States.* Boston: Houghton, Mifflin and Company, 1887.

The Journals of Lewis and Clark

Journal Entry by Meriwether Lewis, 1805

In 1803 at the request of President Thomas Jefferson, Meriwether Lewis and William Clark led an expedition to explore the land that the United States had just purchased from France, known as the Louisiana Territory. Their job included exploring the Missouri River and finding a safe passage west to the Pacific Ocean. President Jefferson asked them to write a description of everything they saw on their expedition. Why do you suppose President Jefferson wanted this? Below is a journal entry from their expedition.

August 12, 1805

We fell in with a large and plain Indian road, which came into the cove from the northeast and led along the foot of the mountains to the southwest, **obliquely** approaching the main stream, which we had left yesterday. This road we now pursued to the southwest. At 5 miles it passed a stout stream which is a principal fork of the main stream and falls into it just above the narrow pass between the two cliffs before mentioned, which we now saw below us. Here we halted and breakfasted on the last of our **venison**, having yet a small piece of pork in reserve. After eating, we continued our route through the low bottom of the main stream along the foot of the mountains on our right. The valley for 5 miles farther in a southwest direction was from 2 to 3 miles wide.

obliquely: indirectly

venison: deer meat

At the distance of 4 miles further, the road took us to the most distant fountain of the waters of the mighty Missouri in search of which we have spent so many **toilsome** days and restless nights. Thus far I had accomplished one of those great objects on which my mind has been unalterably fixed for many years. Judge, then, of the pleasure I felt in **allaying** my thirst with this pure and ice-cold water which issues from the base of a low mountain or hill of a gentle ascent for 1/2 a mile.... Two miles below, McNeal had exultingly stood with a foot on each side of this little rivulet and thanked his God that he had lived to bestride the mighty, and heretofore deemed endless, Missouri.

toilsome: full of toil or work

allaying: relieving

After refreshing ourselves, we proceeded on to the top of the dividing ridge, from which I discovered immense ranges of high mountains still to the west of us, with their tops partially covered with snow. I now descended the mountain about 3/4 of a mile, which I found much steeper than on the opposite side, to a handsome bold running creek of cold, clear water. Here I first tasted the water of the great Columbia River.

The Lewis and Clark expedition left St. Louis, Missouri, in May 1803, and reached the Pacific Ocean in November 1805. Lewis and Clark mapped and explored over 3,000 miles of land, making it easier for new settlers to find their way west.

Source: John Bakeless, ed., *The Journals of Lewis and Clark.* New York: New American Library, 1964.

The Removal of the Cherokee

by John G. Burnett, 1890

During the 1830s many Cherokee and other Native Americans fought the Indian Removal Act, which ordered them to leave their homes in the southeastern United States. The Cherokee, who had their own constitution and government, took their case to the Supreme Court. The Court supported their right to the land, but President Andrew Jackson and his successor, Martin Van Buren, refused to follow the Court's decision. In 1838 the United States Army began to remove more than 15,000 Cherokee from their homeland by force. One of the soldiers in the army was John G. Burnett, a 27-year-old native of Tennessee who had grown up among the Cherokee. Over 50 years later, in 1890, Burnett wrote down his memories of this forced 800-mile (1,287-km) march of the Cherokee, which came to be known as the "Trail of Tears." As you read this excerpt, think about why Burnett might have written down what happened.

In the year of 1828, a little Indian boy living on Ward creek had sold a Gold nugget to a white trader, and that nugget sealed the doom of the Cherokees. In a short time the country was over run with armed **brigands** claiming to be Government Agents, who paid no attention to the rights of the Indians who were the legal possessors of the country. Crimes were committed that were a disgrace to civilization. Men were shot in cold blood, lands were **confiscated**. Homes were burned and the inhabitants driven out by these Gold hungry brigands. . . .

brigands: bandits

confiscated: taken away

Chief John Ross sent . . . an **envoy** to plead with President Jackson for protection for his people, but Jackson's manner was cold and indifferent. . . . "Sir [Jackson said] your audience is ended, there is nothing I can do for you." The doom of the Cherokee was sealed, Washington, D.C. had decreed that they must be driven West, and their lands given to the white man, and in May 1838 an Army of four thousand regulars, and three thousand volunteer soldiers . . . marched into the Indian country and wrote the blackest chapter on the pages of American History. . . .

Chief John Ross: leader of the Cherokee
envoy: representative

The removal of the Cherokee Indians from their life long homes in the year of 1838 found me . . . a Private soldier in the American Army. Being acquainted with many of the Indians and able to **fluently** speak their language, I was sent as interpreter into the **Smoky Mountain Country** in May, 1838, and witnessed the execution of the most brutal order in the History of American Warfare. I saw the helpless Cherokees arrested and dragged from their homes, and

fluently: easily
Smoky Mountain Country: mountain region of Georgia, North Carolina, and Tennessee

driven at the **bayonet** point into the **stockades**. And in the chill of a drizzling rain on an October morning I saw them loaded like cattle or sheep into six hundred and forty-five wagons and started toward the west.

bayonet: steel blade on the tip of a rifle

stockades: military prisons

One can never forget the sadness and **solemnity** of that [October] morning [in 1838]. Chief John Ross led in prayer and when the bugle sounded and the wagons started rolling many of the children rose to their feet and waved their little hands good-by to their mountain homes, knowing they were leaving them forever. Many of these helpless people did not have blankets and many of them had been driven from home barefooted.

solemnity: seriousness

On the morning of November the 17th we encountered a terrific sleet and snow storm with freezing temperatures and from that day until we reached the end of the fateful journey on March the 26th 1839, the sufferings of the Cherokees were awful. The trail of the **exiles** was a trail of death. They had to sleep in the wagons and on the ground without fire. And I have known as many as twenty-two of them to die in one night of pneumonia due to ill treatment, cold, and exposure. Among this number was the . . . wife of Chief John Ross. This noble hearted woman died a **martyr** to childhood, giving her only blanket for the protection of a sick child. She rode thinly clad through a blinding sleet and snow storm, developed pneumonia and died in the still hours of a bleak winter night, with her head resting on Lieutenant Gregg's saddle blanket. . . .

exiles: people forced from their country

martyr: person who suffers death for a cause

I was on guard duty the night Mrs. Ross died. When **relieved** at midnight I did not **retire**, but remained around the wagon out of sympathy for Chief Ross, and at daylight was **detailed** by Captain McClellan to assist in the burial. . . . Her uncoffined body was buried in a shallow grave by the roadside far from her native mountain home, and the sorrowing **Cavalcade** moved on. . . .

relieved: freed from duty

retire: go to bed

detailed: ordered

The long painful journey to the west ended March 26th, 1839, with four-thousand silent graves reaching from the foothills of the Smoky Mountains to what is known as Indian territory in the West. And **covetousness** on the part of the white race was the cause of all that the Cherokees had to suffer. . . .

cavalcade: group of wagons

School children of today do not know that we are living on lands that were taken . . . at the bayonet point to satisfy the white man's greed for gold. . . . Let the Historian of a future day tell the sad story with its sighs, its tears and dying groans.

covetousness: greed, wanting another's possessions

Not all the Cherokee made this tragic trip. A few hundred managed to hide in the mountains of North Carolina and escape removal from their land. Today their descendants are known as the Eastern Cherokee. Those who survived the Trail of Tears settled in present-day Oklahoma. There the Cherokee and other Native Americans set up new homes and governments based on written constitutions. White settlers, however, soon began taking these lands just as they had in the Southeast. In the late 1800s many of the same Cherokee and other Native Americans would be forced out of Oklahoma.

Source: *Journal of Cherokee Studies,* Vol. 3, Summer 1978.

Farewell Address

by Andrew Jackson, 1837

President Andrew Jackson believed that one way to end the tensions between Native Americans and white settlers in the Southeast was to relocate the Native Americans to lands west of the Mississippi River. Read the following excerpt from Jackson's farewell address to the American people. Why do you think President Jackson thought relocation was an acceptable idea?

We have now lived almost fifty years under the Constitution framed by the sages and patriots of the Revolution. The conflicts in which the nations of Europe were engaged during a great part of this period, the spirit in which they waged war against each other, and our **intimate commercial** connections with every part of the civilized world rendered it a time of much difficulty for the Government of the United States. We have had our seasons of peace and of war, with all the evils which precede or follow a state of hostility with powerful nations. We encountered these trials with our constitution yet in its infancy, and under the disadvantages which a new and untried government must always feel when it is called upon to put forth its whole strength without the lights of experience to guide it or the weight of **precedents** to justify its measures. But we have passed triumphantly through all these difficulties. Our Constitution is no longer a doubtful experiment, and at the end of nearly half a century we find that it has preserved **unimpaired** the liberties of the people, secured the rights of property, and that our country has improved and is flourishing beyond any former example in the history of nations.

> **intimate commercial:** close business

> **precedents:** prior examples

> **unimpaired:** not lessened, whole, complete

In our domestic concerns there is everything to encourage us, and if you are true to yourselves nothing can **impede** your march to the highest point of national prosperity. The states which had so long been **retarded** in their improvement by the Indian tribes residing in the midst of them are at length relieved from the evil, and this unhappy race—the original dwellers in our land—are now placed in a situation where we may well hope that they will share in the blessings of civilization and be saved from that **degradation** and destruction to which they were rapidly hastening while they remained in the States; and while the safety and comfort of our own citizens have been greatly promoted by their removal, the **philanthropist** will rejoice that the remnant of that ill-fated race has been at length placed beyond the reach of injury or oppression, and that the **paternal** care of the General Government will hereafter watch over them and protect them.

> **impede:** interrupt, delay, block

> **retarded:** delayed, held back

> **degradation:** lowering in quality

> **philanthropist:** one who helps others

> **paternal:** fatherly, parental

As you have read, in 1837 the United States government forced the Cherokee to relocate to the Indian Territory, which is now the state of Oklahoma.

Source: Francis Newton Thorpe, ed., *The Principles of American Statesmanship.* New York: Tandy-Thomas Company, 1909.

The Factory Bell

by an Unknown Factory Girl, 1844

The first large group of factory workers in the United States was made up of New England girls and women ranging in age from about 11 to 25. In the early and middle 1800s many left their small farms in the country for jobs in the mill towns. On the farm, the rising and setting of the sun and the changing of the seasons had determined which tasks people did each day. In the factory, however, all this changed. In mill towns across New England, daily life was suddenly shaped by clocks and bells that told workers when to wake, when to eat, when to work, and when to sleep. Look at the timetable of the Lowell Mills in Massachusetts printed on the next page. How might it have felt to live by such a strict schedule? To get an idea, read the poem below by an unknown factory girl. This poem first appeared on May 25, 1844, in the Factory Girl's Garland, a mill workers' newspaper in Exeter, New Hampshire. Why do you think the poet wrote a poem about bells?

Loud the morning bell is ringing,
  Up, up sleepers, haste away;
Yonder sits the redbreast singing,
  But to **list** we must not stay.

Not for us is morning breaking,
  Though we with **Aurora** rise;
Nor for us is Nature waking,
  All her smiles through earth and skies.

Sisters, haste, the bell is **tolling**,
  Soon will close the dreadful gate;
Then, alas! we must go strolling,
  Through the **counting-room**, too late.

Now the sun is upward climbing,
  And the breakfast hour has come;
Ding, dong, ding, the bell is chiming,
  Hasten, sisters, hasten home.

Quickly now we take our **ration**,
  For the bell will babble soon;
Each must hurry to her station,
  There to toil till weary noon.

Mid-day sun in heaven is shining,
  Merrily now the clear bell rings,
And the grateful hour of dining,
  To us weary sisters brings.

Now we give a welcome greeting,
  To these **viands** cooked so well;
Horrors! oh! not half done eating—
  Rattle, rattle goes the bell!

Sol behind the hills descended,
  Upward throws his ruby light;
Ding dong ding,—our toil is ended,
  Joyous bell, good night, good night.

list: listen
Aurora: dawn
tolling: ringing
counting-room: business
  room in the factory
ration: food
viands: meals
Sol: sun

TIME TABLE OF THE LOWELL MILLS,

Arranged to make the working time throughout the year average 11 hours per day.

TO TAKE EFFECT SEPTEMBER 21st., 1853.

The Standard time being that of the meridian of Lowell, as shown by the Regulator Clock of AMOS SANBORN, Post Office Corner, Central Street.

From March 20th to September 19th, inclusive.

COMMENCE WORK, at 6.30 A. M.   LEAVE OFF WORK, at 6.30 P. M., except on Saturday Evenings.
BREAKFAST at 6 A. M.   DINNER, at 12 M.   Commence Work, after dinner, 12.45 P. M.

From September 20th to March 19th, inclusive.

COMMENCE WORK at 7.00 A. M.   LEAVE OFF WORK, at 7.00 P. M., except on Saturday Evenings.
BREAKFAST at 6.30 A. M.   DINNER, at 12.30 P.M.   Commence Work, after dinner, 1.15 P. M.

BELLS.

From March 20th to September 19th, inclusive.

Morning Bells.	Dinner Bells.	Evening Bells.
First bell,..........4.30 A. M.	Ring out,.............12.00 M.	Ring out,............6.30 P. M.
Second, 5.30 A. M.; Third, 6.20.	Ring in,...........12.35 P. M.	Except on Saturday Evenings.

From September 20th to March 19th, inclusive.

Morning Bells.	Dinner Bells.	Evening Bells.
First bell,..........5.00 A. M.	Ring out,..........12.30 P. M.	Ring out at..........7.00 P. M.
Second, 6.00 A. M.; Third, 6.50.	Ring in,............1.05 P. M.	Except on Saturday Evenings.

SATURDAY EVENING BELLS.

During APRIL, MAY, JUNE, JULY, and AUGUST, Ring Out, at 6.00 P. M.
The remaining Saturday Evenings in the year, ring out as follows :

SEPTEMBER.	NOVEMBER.	JANUARY.
First Saturday, ring out 6.00 P.M.	Third Saturday ring out 4.00 P.M.	Third Saturday, ring out 4.25 P.M.
Second " " 5.45 "	Fourth " " 3.55 "	Fourth " " 4.35 "
Third " " 5.30 "		
Fourth " " 5.20 "	**DECEMBER.**	**FEBRUARY.**
	First Saturday, ring out 3.50 P.M.	First Saturday, ring out 4.45 P. M.
OCTOBER.	Second " " 3.55 "	Second " " 4.55 "
First Saturday, ring out 5.05 P.M.	Third " " 3.55 "	Third " " 5.00 "
Second " " 4.55 "	Fourth " " 4.00 "	Fourth " " 5.10 "
Third " " 4.45 "	Fifth " " 4.00 "	
Fourth " " 4.35 "		**MARCH.**
Fifth " " 4.25 "		First Saturday, ring out 5.25 P.M.
	JANUARY.	Second " " 5.30 "
NOVEMBER.	First Saturday, ring out 4.10 P.M.	Third " " 5.35 "
First Saturday, ring out 4.15 P.M.	Second " " 4.15 "	Fourth " " 5.45 "
Second " " 4.05 "		

YARD GATES will be opened at the first stroke of the bells for entering or leaving the Mills.

SPEED GATES commence hoisting three minutes before commencing work.

During the 1800s factory towns like Lowell, Massachusetts, and Exeter, New Hampshire, began growing throughout the United States. More and more Americans began to live according to clocks, rather than the sun, as they took jobs in new factories and cities. Today it is hard for most Americans to think of living without clocks. How much does your own life revolve around clocks and bells? Imagine living without them. How would your life be different?

Source: *Factory Girl's Garland*, May 25, 1844, reprinted in Philip S. Foner, ed., *The Factory Girls*. Urbana, IL: University of Illinois Press, 1977.

Last Appeal for Aid

by William Travis, 1836

By the middle 1800s large numbers of Americans had settled in Texas, which was then part of Mexico. As their numbers grew, talk of independence became widespread. Such talk alarmed President Santa Anna of Mexico, and soon he and his army were on the march into Texas. In December 1835 pro-independence forces, under the leadership of William Travis, took control of the Alamo. The Alamo was an old Spanish mission in San Antonio that had been turned into a fort. Below is an excerpt from Travis's last appeal to the United States government for more help for his small army of 200 at the Alamo. Why were the Texans at the Alamo prepared to defend it to the death?

March 3, 1836

*S*ir,— . . . I beg leave to communicate to you the situation of this **garrison**. You have doubtless already seen my official report of the action . . . to Gen. Sam. Houston, together with the various communications **heretofore** sent by express. I shall therefore **confine** myself to what has **transpired** since that date. . . . The spirits of my men are still high, although they have had much to depress them. We have **contended** for ten days against an enemy whose numbers are variously estimated at from fifteen hundred to six thousand men. I hope your honourable body will hasten on reinforcements, ammunition, and **provisions** to our aid, as soon as possible. We have provisions for twenty days for the men we have—our supply of ammunition is limited. . . .

garrison: military post

heretofore: before this time

confine: limit

transpired: happened

contended: fought

provisions: supplies

If these things are promptly sent and large reinforcements are hastened to this frontier, this neighborhood will be the great and decisive battle ground. The power of Santa Anna is to be met here, or in the colonies; we had better meet them here, than to suffer a war of desolation to rage in our settlements. . . . They have declared us [rebels] and demanded that we should surrender **at discretion**, or that this garrison should **be put to the sword**. Their threats have had no influence on me, or my men, but to make all fight with desperation, and that high souled courage which characterizes the patriot, who is willing to die in defence of his country's liberty and his own honor. . . .

at discretion: on their (in this case, the Mexican army's) terms

be put to the sword: executed

The bearer of this will give your honorable body a statement more in detail, should he escape through the enemy's lines—God and Texas—*Victory or Death!*

P.S. The enemy's troops are still arriving, and the reinforcement will probably amount to two or three thousand.

On March 6, 1836, the Alamo fell to the Mexican army. All of the Texans lost their lives in this battle. "Remember the Alamo!" became the rallying cry in the Texas fight for independence.

Source: Ernest Wallace, David M. Vigness, and George B. Ward, eds., *Documents of Texas History.* Austin: State House Press, 1994.

ERIE CANAL

Traditional Song, 1800s

When the Erie Canal opened in 1825, it became one of the busiest transportation routes in the United States. The canal carried travelers and goods between Albany and Buffalo in New York State. As they labored, canal workers made up songs describing their lives, their jobs, and even the mules that towed the boats under very low bridges by walking on paths alongside the canal. What does the following song tell you about working on the Erie Canal?

I got a mule, her name is Sal, Fif-teen miles on the E-rie Ca-nal!__ She's a good old work-er and a good old pal, Fif-teen miles on the E-rie Ca-nal!__ We've hauled some barg-es in our day, Filled with lum-ber, coal and hay, And we know ev-'ry inch of the way From Al-ba-ny__ to__ Buf-fa-lo.__ Low bridge, ev-'ry-bod-y down, Low bridge, 'cause we're com-ing to a town; And you'll al-ways know your neigh-bor, You'll al-ways know your pal, If you ev-er nav-i-gat-ed on the E-rie Ca-nal.__

Source: *Music and You*. New York: Macmillan Publishing Company, 1988.

SWEET BETSY FROM PIKE

Traditional Song, 1800s

In 1849, soon after the discovery of gold in California, thousands of people rushed to the Sierra Nevada mountains, hoping to strike it rich. As many of these "Forty-Niners" bumped along in their covered wagons, they sang songs to help them pass the time. The song below was one of their favorites. What parts of the song do you think held a special meaning for those traveling west?

Adapted by Merrill Staton

1. Oh, do you re-mem-ber sweet Bet-sy from Pike, Who crossed the wide prai-ries with her broth-er Ike? With two yoke of ox-en, a big yal-ler dog, A tall Shang-hai roos-ter, and one spot-ted hog.

Refrain

Hoo-dle dang, fol-de-dye-do, hoo-dle dang, fol-de-day. Hoo-dle dang, fol-de dye-do, hoo-dle dang, fol-de-day.

2. They soon reached the desert where Betsy gave out,
And down in the sand she lay rollin' about.
When Ike saw sweet Betsy he said with surprise,
"You'd better get up, you'll get sand in your eyes." *Refrain*

3. Said Ike, "Ole Pike County, I'll go back to you,"
Said Betsy, "You'll go by yourself if you do,
There's no time for pleasure and no time for rest,
In spite of our troubles we'll keep headin' west." *Refrain*

4. They camped on the prairie for weeks upon weeks.
They swam the wide rivers and crossed the tall peaks.
And soon they were rollin' in nuggets of gold.
You may not believe it but that's what we're told. *Refrain*

Source: *Music and You*. New York: Macmillan Publishing Company, 1988.

Diary of an Overland Journey to California

by Sallie Hester, 1849

During the middle 1800s up to half a million people made the rugged overland journey to California and Oregon. Among them were 12-year-old Sallie Hester and her family from Indiana. Like many pioneers, Sallie kept a diary of her seven-month, westward journey across the continent in 1849. As you read excerpts of Sallie's diary, think of the adventures she experienced and the hardships she faced. What type of skills and personal qualities would it have taken to survive this journey?

Bloomington, Indiana, March 20, 1849. Our family, consisting of father, mother, two brothers and one sister, left this morning for that far and much talked of country, California. Our **train** numbered fifty wagons. The last hours were spent in bidding goodby to old friends. My mother is heartbroken over this separation of relatives and friends. . . . The last goodby has been said, the last glimpse of our old home on the hill, and wave of hand at the old **Academy** with a goodby to kind teachers and schoolmates, and we are off.

train: traveling group

academy: school

New Albany, March 24. This is my first experience of a big city. We have been several days reaching it on account of the terrible conditions of the roads. Our carriage **upset** at one place. All were thrown out but no one was hurt. My mother thought it a bad **omen** and wanted to give up the trip.

upset: overturned
omen: sign

March 26. Took the steamboat *Meteor* this evening for **St. Joe.** Now sailing on the broad Ohio [River], toward the far west.

St. Joe: St. Joseph, Missouri

St. Joe, April 27. Here we are at last, safe and sound, laying in supplies and waiting our turn to be ferried across the river. As far as the eye can reach, so great is the **emigration**, you see nothing but wagons. This town presents a striking appearance — a vast army on wheels — crowds of men, women, and lots of children, and last but not least the cattle and horses upon which our lives will depend.

emigration: number of people moving

May 21. Camped on the beautiful [**Big**] **Blue River**, 215 miles [346 km] from St. Joe, with plenty of wood and water and good grazing for cattle. . . . We had two deaths in our train within the past week of **cholera** — young men going west to seek their fortunes. We buried them on the banks of the Blue River, far from home and friends.

Big Blue River: river in southeastern Nebraska

cholera: a deadly disease

We are now in the Pawnee Nation. . . . When we camp at night we form a **corral** with our wagons and pitch our tents on the outside, and inside of this corral we drive our cattle, with guards stationed on the outside of the tents.

corral: circle

We have a cooking stove made of sheet iron, a **portable** table, tin plates and cups, cheap knives and forks (best ones packed away) and camp stools. We sleep in our wagons on feather beds. The men who drive for us sleep in the tent. We live on bacon, ham, rice, dried fruits, molasses, packed butter, bread, coffee, tea and milk as we have our own cows. Occasionally the men kill an antelope and then we have a feast; and sometimes we have fish on Sunday.

portable: movable

June 3. Our tent is now pitched on the beautiful **Platte River**, 315 miles [507 km] from St. Joe. The cholera is raging. A great many deaths. Graves everywhere. We [my family] are all in good health. **Game** is scarce; a few antelope in sight. Roads bad.

Platte River: river in central Nebraska

game: animals hunted for food

adobe: bricks made of dried earth

lighten up: relax

struck: arrived at

Fort Laramie, Wyoming, June 19. This fort is of **adobe**, enclosed with a high wall. The entrance is a hole in the wall just large enough for a person to crawl through. The impression you have on entering is that you are in a small town. Men are engaged in all kinds of business from blacksmith up. We camped a mile from the fort, where we remained a few days to wash and **lighten up**.

June 21. Started over sixty miles [97 km] of the worst road in the world. Have again **struck** the Platte [River] and followed it until we came to the ferry. We had a great deal of trouble swimming our cattle across [and] taking our wagons to pieces. . . . A number of accidents happened here. A lady and four children were drowned through the carelessness of those in charge of the ferry.

July 2. Passed **Independence Rock**. This rock is covered with names. With great difficulty I found a place to cut mine. . . .

During the week we went over the South Pass and the **summit** of the Rocky Mountains.

Independence Rock: stone landmark in central Wyoming on which pioneers carved their names when they passed by

summit: peak

July 4. Had the pleasure of eating ice. . . . Had neither wood nor water for fifty-two miles [84 km]. Traveled in the night. At the

SALLIE HESTER'S ROUTE WEST, 1849

········ Sallie Hester's route

● City or town

🏰 Fort

)(Mountain pass

■ Landmark

N

Green River we lay by two days to rest man and beast after our long and weary journey.

August 18. This week some of our company left us, all young men. They were jolly, merry fellows and gave life to our lonely evenings. We all miss them very much. Some had violins, others guitars, and some had fine voices. They were anxious to hurry on without the Sunday stops. Roads are rocky and trying to our wagons, and the dust is horrible. The men wear veils tied over their hats as a protection. When we reach camp at night they are covered with dust from head to heels.

Humboldt River, August 20. We are now 348 miles [560 km] from the [gold] mines. We expect to travel that distance in three weeks and a half. Water and grass scarce. Though the water is not fit to drink— **slough** water—we are obliged to use it for it's all we have.

September 7. Stopped and cut grass for the cattle and supplied ourselves with water for the desert. Had a **trying** time crossing it. Several of our cattle gave out and we left one. Our journey through the desert was from Monday, three o'clock in the afternoon, until Thursday morning at sunrise. The weary journey that last night, the mooing of the cattle for water, the cry, "Another ox down," the

Green River: river in southwestern Wyoming

Humboldt River: river in northern Nevada

slough: swamp

trying: hard

stopping of the train to **unyoke** the poor dying **brute**, to let him follow at will or stop by the wayside and die, and the weary, weary tramp of men and beasts, worn out with heat and **famished** for water, will never be erased from my memory. Just at dawn in the distance we had a glimpse of the **Truckee River**, and with it the feeling: Saved at last! Poor cattle; they kept on mooing even when they stood knee deep in water. The long, dreaded desert has been crossed and we are all safe and well. Grass green and beautiful, and the cattle are up to their eyes in it.

unyoke: free
brute: animal
famished: dying of thirst

Truckee River: river in northwestern Nevada

September 11. Made eighteen miles [29 km]. Crossed Truckee River ten times. Came near being drowned at one of the crossings. Got frightened and jumped out of the carriage into the water. The current was very swift and carried me some distance down the stream. In jumping I expected to reach the shore; instead I landed in the water, but was rescued in time all right.

September 14. It was night when we crossed the summit of the **Sierra Nevada**, and I shall never forget our descent to the place where we are now encamped— our **tedious** march with pine **knots** blazing in the darkness and the tall, majestic pines towering above our heads. The scene was grand and gloomy beyond description. We could not ride—roads too narrow and rocky. It was a footsore and weary crowd that reached this camp.

Sierra Nevada: mountain range in California and Nevada
tedious: tiring
knots: branches

September 21. Reached Bear Valley by descending a tremendous hill. We let the wagons down with ropes. Left one of our wagons and the springs of our carriage. Cut down trees for our cattle to **browse** on.

browse: graze

Vernon, California, October 6. Well, after a five-months trip from St. Joe, Missouri, our party of fifty wagons, now only thirteen, has at last reached this **haven** of rest. Strangers in a strange land, what will our future be?

Vernon: town near San Francisco
haven: peaceful place

Fremont, October 10. This is a small town on the opposite side of the river from Vernon. My father has decided to remain here for the winter. We have had a small house put up of two rooms made of boards with **puncheon** floor.

puncheon: split log

April 27 [1850]. Have met a number of nice young men here. I am too young for **beaux**, but the young men don't seem to think so.

beaux (bōz): boyfriends

Despite the attention that she received from young men upon her arrival in California in 1849, Sallie chose not to get married until 1871, when she was 34 years old. By that time, just 22 years after Sallie's seven-month journey from Indiana, people could travel across the entire country to California by train—a trip that took only six days!

Source: Josef and Dorothy Berger, *Small Voices.* New York: Paul S. Eriksson, Inc., 1966.

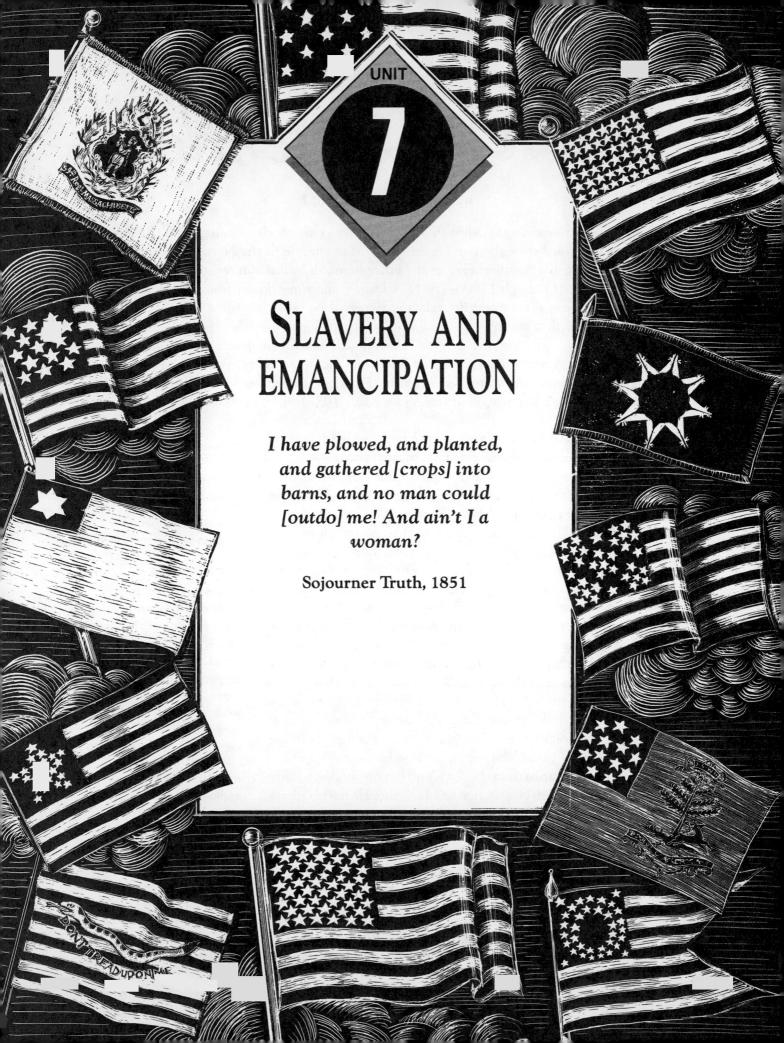

SLAVERY AND EMANCIPATION

I have plowed, and planted, and gathered [crops] into barns, and no man could [outdo] me! And ain't I a woman?

Sojourner Truth, 1851

Slavery Defended

by George Fitzhugh, 1857

Was slavery right or wrong? Although today the answer seems clear to us, in the 1800s Americans disagreed strongly with one another. Many people in the North felt slavery was evil. Many white Southerners, on the other hand, defended slavery and believed it was right. George Fitzhugh (1806–1881), a lawyer and slave owner from Port Royal, Virginia, was one of the fiercest defenders of slavery. In a book published in 1857, Fitzhugh claimed that slavery was good for black people, good for white people, and good for the country. As you read the excerpt below, notice how he compares the life of enslaved African Americans to the life of free white factory workers. What differences does he see between them? After reading what Fitzhugh wrote, compare his account with Frederick Douglass's description of slavery on pages 103–104.

The negro slaves of the South are the happiest, and, in some sense, the freest people in the world. The children and the aged and **infirm** work not at all, and yet have all the comforts and **necessaries** of life provided for them. They enjoy liberty, because they are **oppressed** neither by care nor labor. The women do little hard work, and are protected from the **despotism** of their husbands by their **masters**. The negro men and stout boys work, on the average, in good weather, not more than nine hours a day. The balance of their time is spent in perfect **abandon**. Besides, they have their **Sabbaths** and holidays. White men, with so much of **license** and liberty, would die of **ennui**; but negroes **luxuriate in corporeal** and mental **repose**. With their faces upturned to the sun, they can sleep at any hour. . . . [This sleep] results from contentment with the present, and confident **assurance** of the future. We do not know whether free laborers [in the North] ever sleep. They are fools to do so; for, whilst they sleep, the **wily** and watchful **capitalist** is devising means to **ensnare** and **exploitate** them. The free laborer must work or starve. He is more of a slave than the negro, because he works longer and harder for less **allowance** than the slave, and has no holiday, because the cares of life with him begin when its labors end. He has no liberty, and not a single right. . . .

Free laborers have not a thousandth part of the rights and liberties of negro slaves. Indeed, they have not a single right or a single liberty, unless it be the right or liberty to die.

infirm: sick

necessaries: needed items

oppressed: burdened

despotism: cruel misuse of power

masters: owners

abandon: relaxation

Sabbaths: Sundays

license: freedom

ennui: boredom

luxuriate in: enjoy totally

corporeal: physical

repose: rest

assurance: certainty

wily: clever

capitalist: business or factory owner

ensnare: trap

exploitate: misuse

allowance: reward

Many Southerners agreed with Fitzhugh. They believed that slavery was fair and that enslaved African Americans lived comfortable lives.

Source: George Fitzhugh, *Cannibals All! or, Slaves Without Masters*. Richmond, VA: Adolphus Morris, 1857.

Slavery Denounced

by Frederick Douglass, 1852

No person in the United States spoke out more forcefully against slavery than Frederick Douglass (1817–1895). Born into slavery in Maryland, Douglass escaped to New England in 1838. He became an abolitionist in the 1840s and began touring the North to denounce, or condemn, slavery. He settled in Rochester, New York, and started the North Star, an antislavery newspaper. In 1852 the people of Rochester asked Douglass to give a speech in honor of the Fourth of July. They expected him to speak about Independence Day and the greatness of the United States. But Douglass had a different message—one that shocked his listeners. As you read this excerpt from Douglass's Fourth of July speech, keep in mind the account of George Fitzhugh that you read on page 102. How does Douglass's argument concerning slavery and the equality of African Americans compare with Fitzhugh's? How does he argue for the rights and accomplishments of African Americans?

Fellow Citizens—Pardon me, and allow me to ask, why am I called upon to speak here today? What have I, or those I represent, to do with your national independence? Are the great **principles** of political freedom and of natural justice, **embodied** in that Declaration of Independence, extended to us? . . .

principles: ideas
embodied: contained

Such is not the state of the case. I say it with a sad sense of the **disparity** between us. I am not included within the **pale** of this glorious anniversary! Your high independence only reveals the immeasurable distance between us. The blessings in which you this day rejoice, are not enjoyed **in common**. The rich inheritance of justice, liberty, prosperity, and independence, **bequeathed** by your fathers, is shared by you, not by me. The sunlight that brought life and healing to you, has brought **stripes** and death to me. This Fourth of July is *yours*, not *mine*. *You* may rejoice, *I* must mourn. . . .

disparity: difference
pale: boundary

in common: by all
bequeathed: handed down

stripes: whippings

Fellow-citizens, above your national, **tumultuous** joy, I hear the mournful wail of millions, whose chains, heavy and **grievous** yesterday, are to-day **rendered** more **intolerable** by the **jubilant** shouts that reach them. If I do forget, if I do not faithfully remember those bleeding children of sorrow this day, "may . . . my tongue **cleave** to the roof of my mouth!" . . . My subject, then, fellow-citizens, is AMERICAN SLAVERY. I shall see this day and its popular **characteristics** from the slave's point of view. Standing there, identified with the American **bondman**, making his wrongs mine, I do not hesitate to declare, with all my soul, that the character and conduct of this nation never looked blacker to me than on this Fourth of July. Whether we turn to the declarations of the past, or to the **professions** of the present, the conduct of the nation seems

tumultuous: excited
grievous: painful
rendered: made
intolerable: unbearable
jubilant: joyful
cleave: stick

characteristics: features
bondman: slave

professions: beliefs

equally hideous and revolting. America is false to the past, false to the present, and solemnly **binds** herself to be false to the future. Standing with God and the crushed and bleeding slave on this occasion, I will . . . **denounce**, with all the emphasis I can command, everything that serves to **perpetuate** slavery—the great sin and shame of America! . . .

binds: forces

denounce: attack

perpetuate: continue

For the present, it is enough to **affirm** the equal manhood of the Negro race. Is it not astonishing that, while we are plowing, planting, and reaping, using all kinds of mechanical tools, erecting houses, constructing bridges, building ships, working in metals of brass, iron, copper, silver, and gold; that, while we are reading, writing, and **cyphering**, acting as clerks, merchants, and secretaries, having among us lawyers, doctors, ministers, poets, authors, editors, **orators**, and teachers; that, while we are engaged in all manner of **enterprises** common to other men—digging gold in California, capturing the whale in the Pacific, feeding sheep and cattle on the hillside, living, moving, acting, thinking, planning, living in families as husbands, wives, and children, and, above all, **confessing** and worshiping the Christian's God, and looking hopefully for life and **immortality** beyond the grave,—we are called upon to prove that we are men! . . .

affirm: declare

cyphering: doing mathematics

orators: speakers

enterprises: businesses

confessing: believing in

immortality: life after death

What! am I to argue that it is wrong to make men **brutes**, to rob them of their liberty, to work them without wages, to keep them **ignorant** of their relations to their fellow-men, to beat them with sticks, to **flay** their flesh with the **lash**, to load their limbs with irons, to hunt them with dogs, to sell them at auction, to **sunder** their families, to knock out their teeth, to burn their flesh, to starve them into obedience and submission to their masters? Must I argue that a system, thus marked with blood and stained with pollution, is wrong? No; I will not. I have better **employment** for my time. . . .

brutes: animals

ignorant: unaware

flay: strip away

lash: whip

sunder: break apart

employment: use

What to the American slave is your Fourth of July? I answer, a day that reveals to him, more than all other days in the year, the **gross** injustice and cruelty to which he is the constant victim. To him, your celebration is a **sham**; . . . your sounds of rejoicing are empty and heartless; . . . your shouts of liberty and equality [are] hollow mockery; your prayers and hymns . . . are to him mere . . . **fraud** . . . and hypocrisy—a thin veil to cover up crimes which would disgrace a nation of savages. There is not a nation on the earth guilty of practices more shocking and bloody, than are the people of these United States, at this very hour.

gross: outright

sham: fake

fraud: dishonesty

Frederick Douglass's speech in 1852 made clear that Americans had a long way to go to live up to the ideals of liberty and equality expressed in the Declaration of Independence. The powerful words of Douglass and other abolitionists helped convince many people of the evils of slavery.

Source: Frederick Douglass, *My Bondage and My Freedom*. New York and Auburn: Miller, Orton & Mulligan, 1855.

Follow the Drinking Gourd

Spiritual, 1800s

Enslaved people often expressed their pain and sorrow, hopes and dreams, in song. They also used music as a kind of code for communicating with one another. Perhaps no other song has served this urgent purpose so well as "Follow the Drinking Gourd." In the years leading up to and through the Civil War, slaves passed this song along from plantation to plantation. No ordinary set of lyrics, the words to the song told slaves how to travel through the countryside to reach the free North. The Big Dipper, or Drinking Gourd, pointed the way north. The three rivers mentioned in the song were the Tombigbee, the Tennessee, and the Ohio. The old man in the song was Peg Leg Joe, a white sailor who ferried escaping people across the river. Can you guess to what season the phrase "When the sun comes back and the first quail calls" refers?

Adapted by Paul Campbell

Verse
mp

1. When the sun comes back and the first quail calls,_____
2. Now the riv-er bank-'ll make____ a might-y good road;____ The
3. Now the riv - er ends____ be - tween two hills;____

Fol - low_____ the Drink - in' Gourd.____ Then the
dead trees - 'll show you the way. And the
Fol - low_____ the Drink - in' Gourd.____ And____

Old Man is a - wait - in' for to car - ry you to
left___ foot,___ peg - foot,___ trav - el - in'___
there's an - oth - er riv - er on the oth - er___

free - dom,___ Fol - low the Drink - in' Gourd.
on; just you fol - low the Drink - in' Gourd.
side, Just you fol - low the Drink - in' Gourd.

Refrain

Fol - low___ the Drink - in' Gourd,___

Fol - low___ the Drink - in' Gourd,___

For the Old Man is a - wait - in' for to

car - ry you to free - dom, Fol - low the Drink - in' Gourd.

The Abolitionist cause, furthered by brave people like Harriet Tubman, Levi and Catherine Coffin, Frederick Douglass, and Sojourner Truth, came to a head during the middle 1800s. Still, for many years to come, the movement for equal rights for African Americans faced serious opposition. This struggle has given birth to many songs and other works of art. Can you think of any poems, paintings, books, movies, or other songs that deal with this subject?

Source: Adapted from *Share the Music, Book 6*. New York: Macmillan/McGraw-Hill, 1995.

Declaration of Sentiments and Resolutions

Declaration of the Seneca Falls Convention, 1848

Women's rights, like those of African Americans, were won slowly and painfully. In 1848 Lucretia Mott and Elizabeth Cady Stanton organized the first women's rights convention, which was held in Seneca Falls, New York. At this convention, the participants drafted a declaration that echoed the Declaration of Independence. Below is an excerpt from their Declaration of Sentiments and Resolutions, which is also known as the Declaration of Rights and Sentiments. What basic rights did these women seek?

When, in the course of human events, it becomes necessary for one portion of the family of man to assume among the people of the earth a position different from that which they have hitherto occupied, but one to which the laws of nature and of nature's God entitle them, a decent respect to the opinions of mankind requires that they should declare the causes that impel them to such a course.

We hold these truths to be self-evident: that all men and women are created equal; that they are endowed by their Creator with certain **inalienable** rights; that among these are life, liberty, and the pursuit of happiness; that to secure these rights governments are instituted, **deriving** their just powers from the consent of the governed. Whenever any form of government becomes destructive of these ends, it is the right of those who suffer from it to refuse allegiance to it. . . .

inalienable: can't be taken away

deriving: getting

The history of mankind is a history of repeated injuries and **usurpations** on the part of man toward woman, having in direct object the establishment of an absolute tyranny over her. To prove this, let facts be submitted to a candid world.

usurpations: taking over by force

He has never permitted her to exercise her inalienable right to the **elective franchise**.

He has compelled her to submit to laws, in the formation of which she had no voice.

He has withheld from her rights which are given to the most ignorant and degraded men—both natives and foreigners.

Having deprived her of this first right of a citizen, the elective franchise, thereby leaving her without representation in the halls of legislation, he has oppressed her on all sides.

He has made her, if married, in the eye of the law, **civilly dead**.

He has taken from her all right in property, even to the wages she earns.

He has made her, morally, an irresponsible being, as she can commit many crimes with **impunity**, provided they be done in the presence of her husband. In the **covenant** of marriage, she is

elective franchise: right to vote

civilly dead: without rights

impunity: without punishment

covenant: agreement, contract

compelled to promise obedience to her husband, he becoming, to all intents and purposes, her master—the law giving him power to deprive her of her liberty, and to **administer chastisement**.

He has so framed the laws of divorce, as to what shall be the proper causes, and in case of separation, to whom the guardianship of the children shall be given, as to be wholly regardless of the happiness of women—the law, in all cases, going upon the false **supposition** of the supremacy of man, and giving all power into his hands.

After depriving her of all rights as a married woman, if single, and the owner of property, he has taxed her to support a government which recognizes her only when her property can be made profitable to it.

He has monopolized nearly all the profitable employments, and from those she is permitted to follow, she receives but a **scanty remuneration**. He closes against her all the avenues to wealth and distinction which he considers most honorable to himself. As a teacher of **theology**, medicine, or law, she is not known.

He has denied her the facilities for obtaining a thorough education, all colleges being closed against her.

He allows her in Church, as well as State, but a subordinate position, claiming **Apostolic** authority for her exclusion from the ministry, and, with some exceptions, from any public participation in the affairs of the Church.

He has created a false public sentiment by giving to the world a different code of morals for men and women, by which moral **delinquencies** which exclude women from society, are not only tolerated, but deemed of little account in man.

He has **usurped** the **prerogative** of **Jehovah** himself, claiming it as his right to assign for her a sphere of action, when that belongs to her conscience and to her God.

He has **endeavored**, in every way that he could, to destroy her confidence in her own powers, to lessen her self-respect, and to make her willing to lead a dependent and abject life.

Now, in view of this entire **disfranchisement** of one-half the people of this country, their social and religious degradation—in view of the unjust laws above mentioned, and because women do feel themselves aggrieved, oppressed, and **fraudulently** deprived of their most sacred rights, we insist that they have immediate admission to all the rights and privileges which belong to them as citizens of the United States.

adminster chastisement: punish

supposition: belief

scanty remuneration: small payment

theology: religion

Apostolic: from the Apostles, or immediate followers, of Jesus

delinquencies: failings

usurped: taken over
prerogative: sole right
Jehovah: Hebrew word for God
endeavored: tried

disfranchisement: taking away of rights

fraudulently: falsely

Other leaders such as Susan B. Anthony, Carrie Chapman Catt, and Lucy Stone also fought for equal rights for women. Although Wyoming women were granted the right to vote in 1869, it wasn't until 1920 that American women gained the freedom to vote in elections at all levels of government.

Source: Diane Ravitch, ed., *The American Reader: Words That Moved a Nation.* New York: HarperCollins Publishers, 1990.

"Ain't I a Woman?"

by Sojourner Truth, 1851

Like Frederick Douglass, whose speech you read on pages 103–104, Sojourner Truth (1797?–1883) was one of the country's leading abolitionists. She also fought strongly for the rights of women. Enslaved in New York State for the first 30 years of her life, Sojourner Truth was freed in 1827. She became a preacher and a speaker and published her autobiography (which is shown on page 110) in 1850. One year later she attended a women's rights meeting in Akron, Ohio. As some men in the audience jeered one of the speakers, Truth suddenly stood up and began talking. The meeting's leader, Frances D. Gage, later wrote down Truth's unplanned speech. In her speech how does Sojourner Truth connect the rights of African Americans to the rights of women?

*W*ell, children, where there is so much racket there must be something out of **kilter**. I think that **'twixt** the Negroes of the South and the women of the North, all talking about rights, the white men will be in a fix pretty soon. But what's all this here talking about?

> **kilter:** place
>
> **'twixt:** between

That man over there says that women need to be helped into carriages, and lifted over ditches, and to have the best place everywhere. Nobody ever helps me into carriages, or over mud-puddles, or gives me any best place! And ain't I a woman? Look at me! Look at my arm! I have plowed, and planted, and gathered [crops] into barns, and no man could **head** me! And ain't I a woman? I could work as much and eat as much as a man—when I could get it—and bear the **lash** as well! And ain't I a woman? I have **borne** thirteen children, and seen them most all sold off to slavery, and when I cried out with my mother's grief, none but Jesus heard me! And ain't I a woman?

> **head:** outdo
>
> **lash:** whip
>
> **borne:** given birth to

Then they talk about this thing in the head; what's this they call it? (**"Intellect,"** whispered someone near.) That's it, honey. What's that got to do with women's rights or Negroes' rights? If my cup won't hold but a **pint**, and yours holds a quart, wouldn't you be mean not to let me have my little half-measure full?

> **intellect:** ability to think
>
> **pint:** half-quart

Then that little man in black there, he says women can't have as much rights as men, because Christ wasn't a woman! Where did your Christ come from? Where did your Christ come from? From God and a woman! Man had nothing to do with Him.

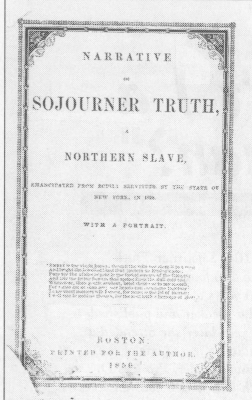

If the first woman God ever made was strong enough to turn the world upside down all alone, these women together ought to be be able to turn it back, and get it right side up again! And now that they are asking to do it, the men had better let them.

Obliged to you for hearing me, and now old Sojourner hasn't got anything more to say.

obliged: many thanks

When Sojourner Truth finished speaking, the audience roared its approval. Truth went on to speak at many other meetings around the country. She was not always welcomed. In Kansas she was clubbed, and in Missouri she was attacked by a mob, yet Truth continued to speak out bravely for the rights of both African Americans and women. During the 1840s and 1850s women abolitionists such as Sojourner Truth helped to make freedom and equal rights for all people a major issue in the United States. To learn how some others reacted to the issue of women's rights, read the next document on page 111.

Source: Adapted from Elizabeth Cady Stanton, Susan B. Anthony, and Matilda Joslyn Gage, eds., *History of Woman Suffrage*, Volume 1. New York: Fowler & Wells, 1881.

Opposition to Women's Rights

from the *New York Herald*, 1850

After women delegates were not allowed full participation at the World Antislavery Convention in London in 1840, some of them began to meet to discuss the rights of women. After the Seneca Falls Convention in 1848, a number of women's rights conventions were held every year. The press reported on these meetings from a variety of differing viewpoints. What is the viewpoint expressed in the excerpt from the New York Herald, below, which appeared after the national convention in 1850? In this editorial, the Herald singles out Lucy Stone, Antoinette Brown, and Harriot K. Hunt, who were key women's rights leaders of the time.

What do the leaders of the women's rights convention want? They want to vote and **hustle** with the rowdies at the polls. They want to be members of Congress, and in the heat of debate **subject** themselves to **coarse jests** and indecent language. They want to fill all other posts which men are ambitious to occupy, to be lawyers, doctors, captains of vessels and generals in the field. How funny it would sound in the newspapers that Lucy Stone, pleading a cause, took suddenly ill in the pains of **parturition** and perhaps gave birth to a fine bouncing boy in court? Or that Rev. Antoinette Brown was arrested in the pulpit in the middle of her sermon from the same causes and presented a **"pledge"** to her husband and the congregation; or that Dr. Harriot K. Hunt while **attending** a gentleman for a fit of **gout** . . . found it necessary to send for a doctor, there and then, and to be delivered of a man or woman child, perhaps twins. A similar event might happen on the floor of Congress, in a storm at sea or in the raging tempest of battle, and then what is to become of the woman legislator?

hustle: mix
subject: expose
coarse jests: rude jokes

parturition: childbirth

"pledge": here used to mean the newborn child
attending: taking care of
gout: disease that causes painful swelling, often in the arms or legs

After 1860 the women's rights movement took a backseat as the country became involved in the Civil War. In the late 1800s women became active once again in fighting for their rights. Opposition to full equality for women continues today.

Source: Eleanor Flexner, *A Century of Struggle.* New York: Atheneum, 1973.

UNCLE TOM'S CABIN

by Harriet Beecher Stowe, 1852

Uncle Tom's Cabin by Harriet Beecher Stowe first appeared in a weekly newspaper in 1851. In 1852 it was published as a book and quickly became a bestseller. Why do you think so many people were anxious to read it? In this excerpt from the novel, a slave named Eliza has just learned that her master has decided to sell her baby to a slave trader named Haley. In response, Eliza escapes with her baby from the plantation in the middle of the night. Mr. Haley has pursued her, along with two slaves named Sam and Andy, who have done their best to mislead him as to where Eliza might have gone.

In consequence of all the various delays, it was about three quarters of an hour after Eliza had laid her child to sleep in the village tavern that the party came riding into the same place. Eliza was standing by the window, looking out in another direction, when Sam's quick eye caught a glimpse of her. Haley and Andy were two yards behind. At this crisis, Sam **contrived** to have his hat blown off, and uttered a loud and characteristic **ejaculation**, which startled her at once; she drew suddenly back; the whole **train** swept by the window, round to the front door.

contrived: managed, usually according to some plan

ejaculation: shout

train: group

A thousand lives seemed to be concentrated in that one moment to Eliza. Her room opened by a side door to the river. She caught her child, and sprang down the steps towards it. The trader caught a full glimpse of her, just as she was disappearing down the bank, and throwing himself from his horse, and calling loudly on Sam and Andy, he was after her like a hound after a deer. In that dizzy moment her feet to her **scarce** seemed to touch the ground, and a moment brought her to the water's edge. Right on behind her they came; and, **nerved** with strength such as God gives only to the desperate, with one wild cry and flying leap, she **vaulted sheer** over the **turbid current** by the shore, on to the raft of ice beyond. It was a desperate leap,—impossible to anything but madness and despair; and Haley, Sam, and Andy instinctively cried out, and lifted up their hands, as she did it.

scarce: hardly

nerved: given courage

vaulted sheer: jumped completely

turbid current: muddy water

The huge green fragment of ice on which she alighted pitched and creaked as her weight came on it, but she stayed there not a moment. With wild cries and desperate energy she leaped to another and still another cake;—stumbling,—leaping,—slipping,—springing upwards again! Her shoes are gone,—her stockings cut from her feet,—while blood marked every step; but she saw nothing, felt nothing, till dimly, as in a dream, she saw **the Ohio side**, and a man helping her up the bank.

the Ohio side: of the Ohio River

When Eliza crossed the Ohio, she reached freedom in the North. The man who helped her up the bank was one of many white people who helped enslaved people escape. Stowe wrote this novel as a protest against the Fugitive Slave Law, which required Northerners to return escaped slaves to their masters.

Source: Harriet Beecher Stowe, *Uncle Tom's Cabin.* New York: New American Library, 1981.

CIVIL WAR PHOTOGRAPHS

by Mathew Brady, 1860–1865

The Civil War was the first war to be documented by photographers. Mathew Brady (1823–1896) was a pioneer of American photography. In 1844 he opened his own studio in New York City. When the Civil War broke out, Brady was on the scene to capture unforgettable images of the politicians and soldiers in the throes of the great conflict. His still photographs of President Lincoln, Jefferson Davis, and Generals Grant, Lee, and McClellan are priceless portraits that show the characters of the men who conducted the Civil War. If this war were being fought today, what kinds of media would be used to document events?

Ulysses S. Grant

Robert E. Lee

Battle of Fredericksburg, 1863. First actual photo of the United States Army in combat.

Jefferson Davis

Abraham Lincoln at Sharpsburg, 1862

Mathew Brady

Historians and filmmakers continue to use Mathew Brady's photographs from the Civil War era. Brady's original work is housed in the Library of Congress in Washington, D.C.

Source: Roy Meredith, *Mr. Lincoln's Camera Man: Mathew B. Brady,* 2nd rev. ed. New York: Dover Publications, 1974.

The Emancipation Proclamation

by Abraham Lincoln, 1863

The War Between the States began as a fight to save the Union. Issued by President Lincoln on January 1, 1863, the Emancipation Proclamation refueled the war spirit of both North and South. The year before, Congress had passed a law that freed Confederate slaves who entered Union territory. Now, the Emancipation Proclamation freed those slaves under Confederate rule as well. After the war the 13th Amendment to the Constitution (December 18, 1865) ended slavery throughout the nation. The Proclamation gave strength to the North, which gained over 500,000 former slaves for the war effort and helped secure the support of England and France. What other changes did this decree announce?

Whereas, on the twenty-second day of September, in the year of our Lord one thousand eight hundred and sixty-two, a proclamation was issued by the President of the United States, containing, among other things, the following, **to wit**:

Whereas: since, because

to wit: namely

That on the first day of January, in the year of our Lord one thousand eight hundred and sixty-three, all persons held as slaves within any State, or designated part of a State, **the people whereof** shall then be in rebellion against the United States, shall be **then, thenceforward**, and forever free; and the Executive Government of the United States, including the military and naval authority thereof, will recognize and maintain the freedom of such persons, and will do no act or acts to **repress** such persons, or any of them, in any efforts they may make for their actual freedom.

the people whereof: where the people

then, thenceforward: at that time and in the future

repress: stop

That the **Executive** will, on the first day of January **aforesaid**, by proclamation, **designate** the States and parts of States, if any, in which the people thereof respectively shall then be in rebellion against the United States; and the fact that any State, or the people thereof, shall on that day be in good faith represented in the Congress of the United States by members chosen thereto at elections wherein a majority of the qualified voters of such State shall have participated, shall in the absence of strong **countervailing** testimony be deemed **conclusive** evidence that such State and the people thereof are not then in rebellion against the United States.

Executive: the President

aforesaid: already mentioned; meaning here, the year 1863

designate: name

countervailing: opposing

conclusive: final, not to be disputed

Now, therefore, I, Abraham Lincoln, President of the United States, by virtue of the power in me **vested** as Commander-in-Chief of the Army and Navy of the United States, in time of actual armed rebellion against the authority and government of the United States, and as a fit and necessary war measure for suppressing said rebellion, do on this first day of January, in the year of our Lord one thousand eight hundred and sixty-three, and in accordance with my purpose so to do, publicly proclaimed for the full period of 100 days

vested: placed, given

from the day first above mentioned, order and designate as the States and parts of States wherein the people thereof, respectively, are this day in rebellion against the United States, the following, to wit:

Arkansas, Texas, Louisiana (except the parishes of St. Bernard, Plaquemines, Jefferson, St. John, St. Charles, St. James, Ascension, Assumption, Terre Bonne, Lafourche, St. Mary, St. Martin, and Orleans, including the city of New Orleans), Mississippi, Alabama, Florida, Georgia, South Carolina, North Carolina, and Virginia (except the forty-eight counties designated as West Virginia, and also the counties of Berkeley, Accomac, Northampton, Elizabeth City, York, Princess Anne, and Norfolk, including the cities of Norfolk and Portsmouth), and **which excepted parts** are for the present left precisely as if this proclamation were not issued.

which excepted parts: those areas not listed

the power: i.e., as President

And by virtue of **the power** and for the purpose aforesaid, I do order and declare that all persons held as slaves within said designated States and parts of States are, and henceforward shall be, free; and that the Executive Government of the United States, including the military and naval authorities thereof, shall recognize and maintain the freedom of said persons.

And I hereby **enjoin** upon the people so declared to be free to **abstain from** all violence, unless in necessary self-defense; and I recommend to them that, in all cases where allowed, they labor faithfully for reasonable wages.

enjoin: order, request
abstain from: not take part in

And I further declare and make known that such persons of suitable condition will be received into the armed service of the United States to **garrison** forts, positions, stations, and other places, and to man vessels of all sorts in said service.

garrison: guard

And upon this act, sincerely believed to be an act of justice, **warranted** by the Constitution upon military necessity, I invoke the considerate judgment of mankind and the gracious favor of Almighty God.

warranted: justified, allowed

In witness whereof, I have hereunto set my hand and caused the seal of the United States to be affixed.

In witness whereof, I have hereunto set my hand: To show what I intend to do, I have written this

Done at the city of Washington, the first day of January, in the year of our Lord one thousand eight hundred and sixty-three, and of the independence of the United States of America the eighty-seventh.

By the President: Abraham Lincoln
William H. Seward, Secretary of State.

By drawing former slaves North, the Emancipation Proclamation directly bolstered the Union armed forces. Thousands of African Americans joined or worked for the Union army or navy, and helped bring about its victory in 1865.

Source: Abraham Lincoln, *The Emancipation Proclamation.* Reprinted in *The World Book Encyclopedia, Vol. 6.* Chicago: World Book, Inc., 1993.

Destruction of the South

by Eliza Frances Andrews, 1864

Fierce fighting during the Civil War left much of the South in ruins. In November 1864 General William Tecumseh Sherman and 60,000 Union soldiers began a march from Atlanta, Georgia, to Savannah, Georgia, aiming to destroy everything in their path. In the following journal excerpt from December 1864, a Georgia woman named Eliza Frances Andrews (1840-1931) describes some of the destruction they caused. How does Andrews feel about the damage done to the South?

About three miles from **Sparta** we struck the "Burnt Country," . . . and then I could better understand the **wrath** and desperation of these poor people. I almost felt as if I should like to hang a **Yankee** myself. There was hardly a fence left standing all the way from Sparta to **Gordon**. The fields were trampled down and the road was lined with **carcasses** of horses, hogs, and cattle that the invaders, unable either to consume or to carry away with them, had **wantonly** shot down to starve out the people and prevent them from making their crops. The **stench** in some places was unbearable; every few hundreds yards we had to hold our noses or stop them with the cologne Mrs. Elzey had given us, and it proved a great **boon**.

The dwellings that were standing all showed signs of **pillage**, and on every plantation we saw the **charred** remains, . . . while here and there, lone chimney-stacks, **"Sherman's Sentinels,"** told of homes laid in ashes. The **infamous** wretches! I couldn't wonder now that these poor people should want to put a rope round the neck of every [one of them that] they could lay their hands on.

Hay ricks and **fodder stacks** were demolished, **corn cribs** were empty, and every bale of cotton that could be found was burnt by the savages. I saw no grain of any sort, except little patches they had spilled when feeding their horses and which there was not even a chicken left in the country to eat. A bag of oats might have lain anywhere along the road without danger from the beasts of the field, though I cannot say it would have been safe from the assaults of hungry man. . . .

I saw [soldiers] seated on the roadside greedily eating raw turnips, meat skins, **parched** corn—anything they could find, even picking up the loose grains that Sherman's horses had left.

Sparta: town in central Georgia

wrath: deep anger

Yankee: Southern term for a Northerner

Gordon: town about 30 miles (48 km) from Sparta

carcasses: dead bodies

wantonly: without caring

stench: bad smell

boon: help

pillage: destruction, robbery

charred: burned

"Sherman's Sentinels": name for chimneys left standing after Sherman's troops had destroyed the rest of the house

infamous: wicked

hay ricks: haystacks

fodder stacks: stacks of food for livestock

corn cribs: containers for storing corn

parched: dried

General William Tecumseh Sherman's march through Georgia in 1864 weakened the will of many Southerners to keep fighting. On April 9, 1865, the South surrendered, ending the bloodiest war in the country's history. Southerners spent many years rebuilding their war-torn region.

Source: Eliza Frances Andrews, *The War-Time Journal of a Georgia Girl*. Boston: D. Appleton and Co., 1908.

Teaching Freed People

by Charlotte Forten, 1864

Before the 1860s it was against the law to teach enslaved African Americans how to read and write. Some slaves went to school secretly—and illegally— but most were prevented from getting an education. As the world of slavery crumbled during the Civil War, however, one of the first things African Americans did was set up schools and begin holding classes throughout the South. They hired teachers, both black and white, to teach them. One of the first to head south to educate these newly freed people was a 25-year-old African American abolitionist from Philadelphia named Charlotte Forten (1837-1914). Forten arrived at St. Helena, an island along the coast of the area. Forten began teaching at once—to classes sometimes as large as 140 students! Two years later she wrote two magazine articles about her experiences as a teacher. An excerpt from these articles is printed below. According to Forten, how important was education to the freed people of the South?

The first day at school was rather trying. Most of my children were very small, and **consequently** restless. Some were too young to learn the alphabet. These little ones were brought to school because the older children—in whose care their parents leave them while at work—could not come without them. We were therefore willing to have them come, although they seemed to have discovered the secret of **perpetual** motion, and **tried** one's patience sadly. But after some days of positive, though not **severe** treatment, order was brought out of **chaos**, and I found but little difficulty in managing and quieting the tiniest and most restless spirits. I never before saw children so eager to learn, although I had several years' experience in New-England schools. Coming to school is a constant delight and recreation to them. They come here as other children go to play. The older ones, during the summer, work in the fields from early morning until eleven or twelve o'clock, and then come into school, after their hard toil in the hot sun, as bright and as anxious to learn as ever. . . .

consequently: as a result

perpetual: constant
tried: tested
severe: harsh
chaos: confusion

The majority learn with wonderful **rapidity**. Many of the grown people **are desirous of** learning to read. It is wonderful how a people who have been so long crushed to the earth . . . can have so great a desire for knowledge, and such a **capability** for **attaining** it. . . .

The tiniest children are delighted to get a book in their hands. Many of them already know their letters. The parents are eager to have them learn. . . .

They are willing to **make many sacrifices** [so] that their children may attend school. One old woman, who had a large family of children and grandchildren, came regularly to school in the winter, and took her seat among the little ones. She was at least sixty years old. Another woman—who had one of the best faces I ever saw— came daily, and brought her baby in her arms.

rapidity: speed
are desirous of: want to

capability: ability
attaining: reaching

make many sacrifices:
  give up many things

Charlotte Forten returned home to Philadelphia in 1864. She later became a writer and translator, and also worked for the United States Treasury Department. With the help of teachers like Charlotte Forten, African Americans built hundreds of schools that were open to both black and white students during the period of Reconstruction that followed the Civil War. African Americans also donated more than $1 million to education in the South. The Freedmen's Bureau, an agency of the federal government, also built schools to teach freed people. This vast system of education became one of the major achievements of Reconstruction.

Source: Charlotte Forten, "Life on the Sea Islands," *Atlantic Monthly*, Volume 13, May and June 1864.

O Captain! My Captain!

by Walt Whitman, 1865–1866

The assassination of President Lincoln, just days after the Union victory, shocked and grieved many Americans. In "O Captain! My Captain," the poet Walt Whitman (1819–1892) described the devastation of the war and his keen feelings of sorrow for the slain President. Whitman, a writer, teacher, and journalist (among other professions) had served as an army nurse during the Civil War. He knew firsthand the price the United States had paid for the preservation of the Union. In the poem the Union is a ship and the late President its captain. How might you interpret the line, "From fearful trip the victor ship comes in with object won"?

O Captain! my Captain, our fearful trip is done,
The ship has weather'd every rack, the prize we sought is won,
The port is near, the bells I hear, the people all **exulting**,
While follow eyes the steady keel, the vessel grim and daring;
    But O heart! heart! heart!
        O the bleeding drops of red,
           Where on the deck my Captain lies,
              Fallen cold and dead.

exulting: rejoicing

O Captain! my Captain! rise up and hear the bells;
Rise up—for you the flag is flung—for you the bugle trills,
For you **bouquets** and ribbon'd **wreaths**—for you the shores
    a-crowding,
For you they call, the swaying mass, their eager faces turning;
    Here Captain! dear father!
        The arm beneath your head!
           It is some dream that on the deck,
              You've fallen cold and dead.

bouquets: bunches of flowers

wreaths: flowers arranged in a ring

My Captain does not answer, his lips are pale and still,
My father does not feel my arm, he has no pulse nor will,
The ship is anchor'd safe and sound, its voyage closed and done,
From fearful trip the victor ship comes in with object won;
    Exult O shores, and ring O bells!
        But I with mournful tread,
           Walk the deck my Captain lies,
              Fallen cold and dead.

Whitman privately printed and distributed his first book of poems, Leaves of Grass, *in 1855. Many modern and contemporary poets have acknowledged their debt to Whitman, who is now considered one of our finest American poets. Whitman continued to revise* Leaves of Grass *throughout his life.*

Source: George Gesner, ed., *Anthology of American Poetry.* New York: Avenel Books, 1983.

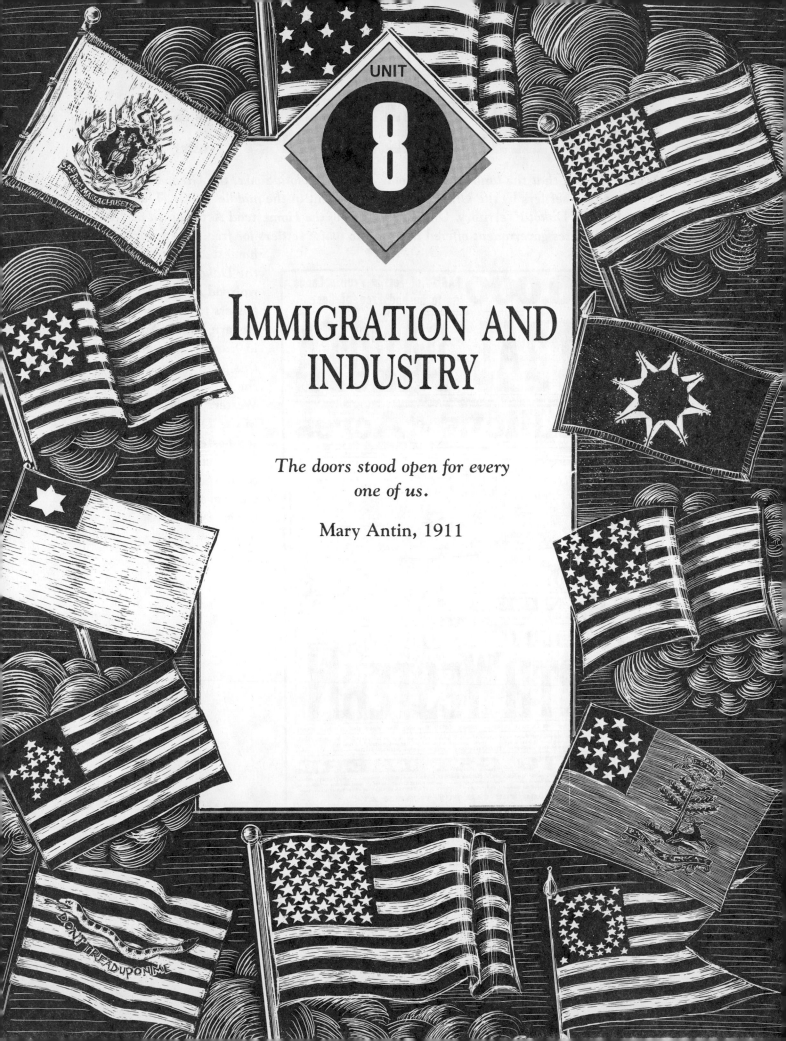

UNIT

8

IMMIGRATION AND INDUSTRY

The doors stood open for every one of us.

Mary Antin, 1911

RESETTLING THE GREAT PLAINS
Poster, 1870s

Despite the fact that the land was the home of many Lakota Sioux, the Great Plains was opened to new settlers by the United States government in the middle 1800s. This area was called the Dakota Territory. Under the terms of the Homestead Act, passed in 1862, the United States government offered this land to white settlers for free. To encourage homesteaders to move to the Dakota Territory, railroad companies put up posters throughout the eastern United States and in Europe. The poster on this page was used by the Chicago and North-Western Railway Company in the 1870s. How does the poster try to attract homesteaders? Why do you think the railroad company was eager for new settlers to come west?

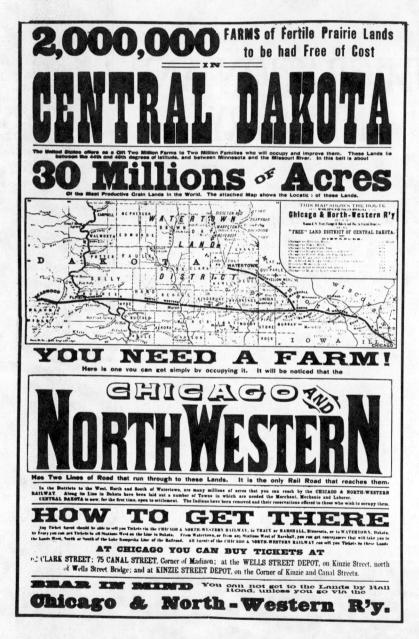

Attracted by posters such as the one above, thousands of people headed west to the Great Plains in the 1870s and 1880s. Some of these posters were aimed at people called Exodusters. To learn about Exodusters, read the document on page 125.

Don't Fence Me In

by Cole Porter, 1944

Few other countries on Earth stretch across an entire continent or border two different oceans. Although the life of a cowhand in the 1800s was often hard, many cowhands loved traveling across our country's wide open spaces and having the freedom to move about as they pleased. Songwriter Cole Porter (1893–1964) captured such feelings in the song below. Which regions of the country might the cowhand in this song be describing?

Wild Cat Kel-ly,   look-ing might-y pale, was stand-ing by the sher-iff's
Wild Cat Kel-ly,   back a - gain in town, was   sit-ting by his sweet-heart's

side_____   and when that she - riff said "I'm   send-ing you to jail,"
side_____   and when his sweet-heart said "Come on, let's set - tle down,"

Refrain

Wild Cat raised his head and   cried: } Oh, give me   land, lots of land un - der
Wild Cat raised his head and   cried:

star-ry skies a-bove,   don't fence me in._____ Let me   ride thru the wide o-pen coun - try that I love, don't fence me in. Let me be by my-self in the

eve - ning breeze,___ lis - ten to the mur - murs of the cot - ton-wood trees.___

Send me off for - ev - er, but I ask you please,___ don't fence me in.___

___ Just turn me loose, let me strad - dle my old sad - dle un - der - neath the west - ern

skies. _____ On my cay - use, let me wan - der o - ver

yon - der till I see the moun - tains rise. _____ I want to

ride to the ridge where the West com - menc - es, gaze at the moon till I

lose my sens - es. Can't look at hob - bles and I can't stand fenc - es,

1.
don't fence me in.___ Oh, give me___
2.

Source: Cole Porter, *Don't Fence Me In*. Secaucus, NJ: Warner Bros. Publications, 1944.

EXODUSTERS

Poster, 1877

As a result of the Civil War, slavery was ended in the United States in 1865. Although free, African Americans faced many hardships. With little money to buy land, many African Americans in the South became sharecroppers and fell deeply into debt. Unfair laws denied them equal rights, and secret groups such as the Ku Klux Klan attacked and killed them throughout the South. To escape these conditions, many African Americans moved west to the Great Plains. A large migration, or movement, of people is called an exodus, and the African Americans from the South who moved west after the Civil War were called Exodusters.

Most Exodusters headed to Kansas because it had been one of the first free states in the Great Plains to enter the Union. This is a poster from 1877 encouraging African Americans to move to Kansas. Why do you think the poster is urging Exodusters to move in colonies, or groups?

All Colored People

THAT WANT TO

GO TO KANSAS,

On September 5th, 1877,

Can do so for $5.00

IMMIGRATION.

WHEREAS, We, the colored people of Lexington, Ky,. knowing that there is an abundance of choice lands now belonging to the Government, have assembled ourselves together for the purpose of locating on said lands. Therefore,

BE IT RESOLVED, That we do now organize ourselves into a Colony, as follows:— Any person wishing to become a member of this Colony can do so by paying the sum of one dollar ($1.00), and this money is to be paid by the first of September, 1877, in installments of twenty-five cents at a time, or otherwise as may be desired.

RESOLVED, That this Colony has agreed to consolidate itself with the Nicodemus Towns, Solomon Valley, Graham County, Kansas, and can only do so by entering the vacant lands now in their midst, which costs $5.00.

RESOLVED, That this Colony shall consist of seven officers—President, Vice-President, Secretary, Treasurer, and three Trustees. President—M. M. Bell; Vice-President —Isaac Talbott; Secretary—W. J. Niles; Treasurer—Daniel Clarke; Trustees—Jerry Lee, William Jones, and Abner Webster.

RESOLVED, That this Colony shall have from one to two hundred militia, more or less, as the case may require, to keep peace and order, and any member failing to pay in his dues, as aforesaid, or failing to comply with the above rules in any particular, will not be recognized or protected by the Colony.

Spurred on by the hope of cheap land and a freer life, thousands of Exodusters left the South and settled in Kansas in the 1870s and 1880s. Farming in the Great Plains, however, was anything but easy. To learn about some of the challenges facing new settlers—whether they were black or white—read the story on pages 126–129.

GRASSHOPPER SUMMER

by Ann Turner, 1989

After the Civil War, posters like those on pages 122 and 125 helped persuade thousands of homesteaders to head west and settle on the Great Plains. Turning the vast, treeless prairies into productive farmland, however, took years of hard work. Homesteaders had to dig deep wells for water, build houses out of sod, and endure long, harsh winters. Grasshopper Summer, a novel by Ann Turner, is about a homesteading family that leaves Kentucky and settles in the Dakota Territory in 1874. When they first arrive, 11-year-old Sam White and his younger brother Billy help to build their family's house and to plant a field of corn. Sam's parents, Walter and Ellen, hope that they have made the right decision in coming west. But suddenly, during their first summer on the Great Plains, something happens that they never expected. As you read the following excerpt from Turner's novel, note the fear that grips the White family. How do they try to protect themselves?

Billy made a face at me. "Want to go fishing?"

"Nope. Too hot. Too many flies." Down by the creek it would be cooler, but the bugs'd be worse.

Billy flicked at the flies with one hand. "Poor horses," he sighed. We watched Pa **tethering** Ham and Duke in the shade of the sod barn. Their tails swished back and forth. They stamped, and Ham's big sides shuddered to keep the flies off.

tethering: tying

Pa came and flopped down beside us. "It's too hot to work today. Hope it won't hurt the corn," he worried.

"Now, Walter, the corn can survive a little heat. As long as we keep getting some rain."

126

"Haven't had much of *that!*" Pa said.

None of us said any more. It felt like bad luck to talk too much about the corn crop and what might go wrong. It was like looking backward over your shoulder when you went past a graveyard; as long as you *didn't* look, no ghosts could get you.

"Everything'll be just fine," **Mrs. Grant** said. I wanted to hush her, not to say more, but she went on. "We'll harvest the crops and get a good price, **Pete** says. Then we'll all be riding in **buggies** and dressing in silks, isn't that so, Ellie?"

"I hope so, Mary." She pushed at her wet hair and fanned baby **Ben**. He lay on the grass, looking up at the sky and played with his toes.

Allan and I had it all worked out. Once the crops were sold, we were both going to get rifles and go hunting together—maybe for coyotes. With what we could shoot and trap come winter, we'd have money of our own next spring.

Then the baby began to cry, a high, **fretful** sound. Mrs. Grant picked him up and **joggled** him back and forth.

"Here." Ma handed her a wet cloth, and Mrs. Grant patted Ben's face. He just cried harder.

Then the horses began to stamp and shy. First Ham—the nervous one—then Duke. Pa pointed to the sky. It was dark and smoky.

"Must be a storm coming. Quick, boys, help with the horses." We ran to the barn and Pa got Ham inside while Billy and I untethered Duke and put him in the barn. Once inside, they calmed down a bit, but Ham still tossed his head and rolled his eyes.

"They're spooked," Pa said, wiping his brow. "Don't know why, but something's got into them. I don't like the look of that sky. Maybe there's a thunderstorm coming."

We went back to the **dugout**, and Ma gave us water in a tin cup. The baby still cried.

"Shhh, let me have Ben," Billy said. Mrs. Grant hesitated, then handed him over. Billy snuggled the baby against his shoulder and walked up to the top of the dugout. "Maybe there's a breeze up here," he called down. The baby's head bobbed against his shoulder, and the crying stopped.

Billy watched the sky, and I watched him. He looked nervous, too, like the horses. The sun dimmed as the clouds came up. Suddenly, Billy cricked his neck back and shouted. He ran downhill to us, holding tight to the baby.

"There's something in those clouds, Pa, can't you see?" He pointed.

The clouds rolled toward us, like a big wind pushed them. The light was a strange, hard gray. At first they looked like everyday clouds, but then I began to see things in them.

Mrs. Mary Grant: a neighbor

Pete: Mrs. Grant's husband

buggies: carriages

Ben: Mrs. Grant's baby

Allan: Sam's friend

fretful: worried

joggled: rocked

dugout: sod house

"There's something moving in them!" Mrs. Grant yelled. "Small things."

"Insects!" Pa said in an awful voice. "**Locusts!**" They began to fall from the sky. Brown things falling, *plunk!* on Ma's bonnet. *Plunk!* on the baby's head and on Mrs. Grant's striped dress. *Thunk!* they landed on the garden.

locusts: grasshoppers

We just stood there a moment, frozen, then Ma shouted, "My garden!" She ran into the dugout and came back with **gunnysacks**. Mrs. Grant took her baby from Billy, rushed him into the dugout, tied him to the bedpost, and shut the door. They ran to the garden and ripped out the rows of lettuce and tiny, new carrots. The grasshoppers rained down on us, and it was hard to see. Ma and Mrs. Grant looked like people working in clouds of smoke.

gunnysacks: sacks made of gunny, a rough, heavy fabric

Pa shouted. "My rifle! Boys, you grab shovels, anything you can find from the barn and get out to the cornfield!"

Billy and I ran to the barn and grabbed rakes and shovels and raced out to the cornfield. Pa ran around the edge, shooting his rifle.

Capow! A small cloud lifted, then settled. He threw his hat on the ground and set off another volley. *Capow! Capow! Capow!*

I hit at them with the shovel, but for every ten I squished, another twenty fell from the sky. Brown bodies hanging on green leaves. Brown jaws tearing into the unripe corn. Billy struck at them with the spade, but nothing made any difference. All the time we raced around, trying to scare them off, no one said a word. Their crunching filled our ears.

Pa fired until all his bullets were gone. Then he shouted, "Sam, we'll dig a **trench** as far as we can in the plowed edge of the field. Billy, grab all the grass and twigs you can find. Pile them in the trench."

trench: ditch

Pa and I dug as fast as we could in the hard ground. The dirt flew to the side, and the grasshoppers fell on my hat, chewed on my collar. Their **raspy** claws poked through my shirt, but I couldn't stop digging.

raspy: scratchy

Billy ran up with arms full of grass and threw it into the trench. Pa pulled out his matches and lit the grass. It flared and caught, sending smoke up in dark clouds. The grasshoppers seemed to rise over the smoke for a moment. Pa put his hat on and cheered.

clamped: shut

Then the grasshoppers fell into the trench, *plunk!* They fell on top of each other, again and again. The fire sputtered and died. Pa just looked at it. He turned but did not see us.

"It's no use. Nothing will scare them. There's too many." He picked up his hat, wiped the grasshoppers off, and jammed it on his head. "Come back to the dugout, boys."

He turned, and we followed, Billy dragging the shovel behind. His face looked green, and his jaws were **clamped** tight. I clamped mine, too, afraid that I'd eat one of them if I breathed through my mouth. I felt sick and greasy inside, with those little claws clutching at my shirt and back and their bodies squishing under my feet. They were so deep now, it was like walking through a pile of leaves—brown, moving leaves.

Mrs. Grant and Ma were still outside, flapping at the garden with those sacks. Pa yelled, "Come inside! It's no good, Ellen."

I went to help carry in the sacks of vegetables they'd picked, when Mrs. Grant began to scream.

"Ellen! Ellen! They're eating my dress. Get them off me!"

All along the green stripes of her dress, the grasshoppers were chewing. Pieces of white cloth fell to the ground. Pa ran into the dugout, and brought out Grandma's quilt. He wrapped it tight around her and pulled it off, taking most of the grasshoppers with it. She yelled, with loud, rising screams, and Pa hurried her inside. I slammed the door shut behind us. We brushed the grasshoppers off each other and stamped them dead.

"Ooooh, ooooh, get them off me!" Mrs. Grant beat at her tattered dress. "Get them off me!"

"They're off, Mary, it's all right," Ma soothed her, brushing the last grasshoppers from her and squishing them with a shovel. . . .

Billy went over and untied Ben, holding him tight against his chest. His eyes, over Ben's shoulder, looked . . . wide and scared. Pa stood in the middle of the room as wet as if he'd been in a rainstorm. Ma dabbed at her face with a handkerchief and kept repeating, "My heavens. Who would've ever thought. Who!" She shook herself, patted Mrs. Grant's hand, and drew out the water pail from under the table. She skimmed grasshoppers from it and filled a tin cup.

"Here. Drink this, Mary." Mrs. Grant hiccupped and drank.

"Ooooh, ooooh," she kept sighing. "Ooooh, their little feet." Ma drank some water, then Pa, and Billy, and I swallowed it down. Just to make the taste of them go away.

Bits of white clung to the seams around Mrs. Grant's shoulders and waist, along with a few ragged pieces of green. . . .

She blew her nose, and I could see she was trying hard not to cry. Suddenly, she buried her face in her arms and began to sob. "We have nothing, Ellen, nothing at all. We borrowed to buy the seed. Don't you see what this means?" She turned a terrible face toward Ma.

Quietly, Ma took a deep breath and said, "'The locusts have no king, yet go they forth all of them by bands.' Oh, Mary, I am so sorry."

My mouth felt dusty and raw. My stomach hurt. I couldn't even look at Billy. We sat in that dugout, and even the thick walls could not keep out the sound of them chewing, eating up all we'd worked for.

The grasshoppers destroy the Whites' crops and force the family to borrow money to survive the following winter. The grasshoppers attack of 1874, along with drought, tornadoes, hailstorms, and blizzards, forced thousands of homesteaders to give up farming on the Great Plains. Many stayed, however, and through hard work helped to turn this vast region into the nation's breadbasket.

Source: Ann Turner, *Grasshopper Summer.* New York: Macmillan Publishing Company, 1989.

Battling with the Sioux

by George Armstrong Custer, 1873

During the middle 1800s white settlers and Native Americans on the Great Plains clashed many times. Although the Native Americans, expecially the Lakota Sioux, were skilled warriors and noted for their fine horsemanship, they often lost these battles. Why do you think this was so? Following is an excerpt from a firsthand account by George Armstrong Custer of one of these battles. In this excerpt, Custer's negative attitude toward Native Americans can be seen. The "Colonel Custer" he refers to is his brother.

Scarcely had the long line of splendidly mounted [Sioux] warriors rushed from their hiding place before Colonel Custer's voice rang out sharp and clear, "Prepare to fight on foot." This order required three out of four troopers to leap from their saddles and take their position on the ground, where by more deliberate aim, and being freed from the management of their horses, a more effective resistance could be opposed to the rapidly approaching warriors. The fourth trooper in each group of "fours" remained on his horse holding the reins of the horses of his three comrades.

Quicker than words can describe, the fifteen cavalrymen now on foot, and acting as **infantry**, rushed forward a few paces in advance of their horses, **deployed** into open order, and dropping on one or both knees in the low grass, waited with loaded **carbines**—with finger gently pressing the trigger—the approach of the Sioux, who rode boldly down as if apparently unconscious that the small group of troopers were on their front.... The victory was almost within the grasp of the **redskins**. It seemed that but a moment more, and they would be trampling the kneeling troopers beneath the feet of their fleet-limbed ponies; when, "Now, men, let them have it!" was the signal for a well-directed **volley**, as fifteen cavalry carbines poured their contents into the ranks of the **shrieking savages**. Before the latter could recover from the surprise and confusion which followed, the carbines—thanks to the invention of **breech-loaders**—were almost instantly loaded, and a second carefully aimed **discharge** went whistling on its deadly errand. Several warriors were seen to **reel** in their saddles, and were only saved from falling by the quickly extended arms of their fellows.... But more quickly than my sluggish pen has been able to record the description of the scene, the battle line of the warriors exhibited signs of **faltering** which soon degenerated into an absolute **repulse**.

infantry: foot soldiers

deployed: arranged themselves

carbines: type of rifle

redskins: negative term for Native Americans

volley: burst of gun fire

shrieking savages: negative term for Native Americans

breech-loaders: a kind of rifle

discharge: shooting of the guns

reel: fall back

faltering: failing

repulse: turning back of the Sioux

Although George Armstrong Custer had led his troops to many victories in the Plains Wars, on June 25, 1876 he was caught in a trap set by the Lakota Sioux leader Crazy Horse. Custer and his men were killed in this battle—the Battle of Little Bighorn—which was to be the last Lakota Sioux victory on the Great Plains.

Source: Paul Andrew Hutton, ed., *The Custer Reader.* Lincoln, NE: University of Nebraska Press, 1992.

The Battle of Little Bighorn

by Two Moon, 1898

In 1868 the United States government signed a treaty giving the Lakota Sioux ownership of the Black Hills region of what is today South Dakota. (You can see a record of this treaty in Lone Dog's Winter Count on pages 12–14.) When gold was discovered in the Black Hills in 1874, the United States government demanded that the Lakota Sioux sell their land. When the Lakota Sioux refused, the United States went to war against them and their neighbors, the Cheyenne. The first major battle, in the spring of 1876 on the Rosebud River in present-day Montana, resulted in defeat for the United States Army. An even larger battle, known as the Battle of Little Bighorn, or Custer's Last Stand, took place on June 25, 1876, along the banks of the nearby Little Bighorn River. Chief Two Moon (1847–1917) of the Cheyenne—who is pictured on page 133—fought in these two battles. More than 20 years later, in 1898, he described these battles to a magazine reporter. As you read an excerpt from this article, think about the scenes Chief Two Moon describes. What did the Lakota Sioux and the Cheyenne think about the fighting? How did that change after the Battle of Little Bighorn?

*T*hat spring [1876] I was camped on **Powder River** with fifty lodges of my people—Cheyennes. . . . One morning soldiers charged my camp. . . . We were surprised and scattered, leaving our ponies. The soldiers ran all our horses off. That night the soldiers slept, leaving the horses [on] one side; so we crept up and stole them back again, and then we went away.

We traveled far, and one day we met a big camp of Sioux at **Charcoal Butte**. We camped with the Sioux, and had a good time, plenty [of] grass, plenty [of] game, [and] good water. **Crazy Horse** was head chief of the camp. **Sitting Bull** was camped a little ways below, on the **Little Missouri River**.

Crazy Horse said to me, "I'm glad you [have] come. We are going to fight the white man again."

The camp was already full of wounded men, women, and children.

I said to Crazy Horse, "All right. I am ready to fight. I have fought already. My people have been killed, my horses stolen; I am satisfied to fight." . . .

Powder River: river in southeast Montana

Charcoal Butte: steep-sided flat hill in southeast Montana

Crazy Horse: a Lakota Sioux leader

Sitting Bull: a Lakota Sioux leader

Little Missouri River: river in southeast Montana

About May, when the grass was tall and the horses strong, we broke camp and started [west] across the country to the mouth of the **Tongue River**. Then Sitting Bull and Crazy Horse and all went up the **Rosebud [River]**. There we had a big fight with **General [George] Crook**, and whipped him. Many soldiers were killed—few Indians. It was a great fight, much smoke and dust.

From there we all went over the divide, and camped in the valley of [the] **Little [Bighorn River]**. Everybody thought, "Now we are out of the white man's country. He can live there, we will live here." After a few days, one morning when I was in camp north of Sitting Bull, a Sioux messenger rode up and said, "Let everybody paint up, cook, and get ready for a big dance."

Cheyennes then went to work to cook, cut up tobacco, and get ready. We all thought to dance all day. We were very glad to think we were far away from the white man.

I went to water my horses at the creek, and washed them off with cool water, then took a swim myself. I came back to the camp afoot. When I got near my lodge, I looked up the Little [Bighorn] towards Sitting Bull's camp. I saw a great dust rising. It looked like a whirlwind. Soon [a] Sioux horseman came rushing into camp shouting: "Soldiers come! Plenty [of] white soldiers."

I ran into my lodge, and said to my brother-in-law, "Get your horses; the white man is coming. Everybody run for horses."

Outside, far up the valley, I heard a battle cry, *Hay-ay, hay-ay!* I heard shooting, too. . . . I couldn't see any Indians. Everybody was getting horses and saddles. After I had caught my horse, a Sioux warrior came again and said, "Many soldiers are coming."

Then he said to the women, "Get out of the way, we are going to have [a] hard fight."

I said, "All right, I am ready."

I got on my horse, and rode out into my camp. I called out to the people all running about: "I am Two Moon, your chief. Don't run away. Stay here and fight. You must stay and fight the white soldiers. I shall stay even if I am to be killed."

I rode swiftly toward Sitting Bull's camp. There I saw the white soldiers fighting in a line. Indians covered the **flat**. They began to drive the soldiers all mixed up—Sioux, then soldiers, then more Sioux, and all shooting. The air was full of smoke and dust. I saw the soldiers fall back and drop into the river-bed like buffalo fleeing. They had no time to look for a crossing. The Sioux chased them up the hill, where they met more soldiers in wagons, and then messengers came saying more soldiers were going to kill the women, and the Sioux turned back. **Chief Gall** was there fighting, Crazy Horse also.

I then rode toward my camp. . . . While I was sitting on my horse I saw flags come up over the hill to the east. . . . Then the soldiers

Tongue River: Montana river west of the Powder and Little Missouri rivers

Rosebud River: Montana river west of the Tongue River

General George Crook: a United States army officer

Little Bighorn River: Montana river west of the Rosebud River

flat: valley

Chief Gall: a Lakota Sioux leader

rose all at once, all on horses. . . . They formed into three bunches with a little ways between. Then a bugle sounded, and they all got off horses, and some soldiers led the horses back over the hill.

Then the Sioux rode up the ridge on all sides, riding very fast. The Cheyennes went up the left way. Then the shooting was quick, quick. Pop—pop—pop very fast. Some of the soldiers were down on their knees, some standing. Officers all in front. The smoke was like a great cloud, and everywhere the Sioux went the dust rose like smoke. We circled all round them—swirling like water round a stone. We shoot, we ride fast, we shoot again. Soldiers drop, and horses fall on them. Soldiers in line drop, but one man rides up and down the line—all the time shouting. He rode a **sorrel** horse. . . .

sorrel: light brown

Indians keep swirling round and round, and the soldiers killed only a few. Many soldiers fell. At last all horses [were] killed but five. Once in a while some man would break out and run toward the river, but he would fall. At last about a hundred men and five horsemen stood on the hill all bunched together. All along the bugler kept blowing his commands. He was very brave. . . . Then a chief was killed. I hear it was **Long Hair**, I don't know; and then the five horsemen and the bunch of men, may be . . . forty, started toward the river. The man on the sorrel horse led them, shouting all the time. He wore a **buckskin** shirt, and had long black hair and [a] mustache. He fought hard with a big knife. His men were all covered with white dust. I couldn't tell whether they were officers or not. One man all alone ran far down toward the river, then round up over the hill. I thought he was going to escape, but a Sioux fired and hit him in the head. He was the last man. . . .

Long Hair: nickname for Colonel George Armstrong Custer, a United States army officer

buckskin: antelope or deer hide

All the soldiers were now killed, and the bodies were stripped. After that no one could tell which were officers. The bodies were left where they fell. We had no dance that night. We were sorrowful.

Next day four Sioux chiefs and two Cheyennes and I, Two Moon, went upon the battlefield to count the dead. One man carried a little bundle of sticks. When we came to dead men, we took a little stick and gave it to another man, so we counted the dead. There were 388. There were thirty-nine Sioux and seven Cheyennes killed, and about a hundred wounded.

The Battle of Little Bighorn in 1876 marked the greatest military victory by Native Americans against the United States Army. It would also be one of their last triumphs. In 1877 the army defeated the Lakota Sioux and the Cheyenne and forced them onto reservations. One of those forced to surrender was Chief Two Moon, who later served as a scout for the United States Army.

Source: Hamlin Garland, "General Custer's Last Fight as Seen by Two Moon," *McClure's Magazine*, September 1898.

For SALE By MAIL

Advertisements from the *Sears, Roebuck Catalogue*, 1897

In the late 1800s factories in the United States were producing more goods than ever before. But factory owners had a problem. Two out of three Americans lived in rural areas, far from stores and businesses. Getting into town to buy goods was often hard and time-consuming. In the 1890s business leaders came up with a new way to reach customers—by mail. Large companies such as Sears, Roebuck began printing huge catalogs—some of them over 1,000 pages—filled with products for sale. These catalogs featured new items such as refrigerators and "magic lanterns." Look at some of the items advertised in the 1897 Sears, Roebuck Catalogue. Why might people have wanted these products? How do the advertisements try to encourage shoppers to buy the products? How do these advertisements compare with advertisements today?

No. 65011.
CALENDAR WATCH.
If you own one of these watches you will not find it necessary to consult an almanac or ask some one to tell you the day of the month.

The case is nickel plated, and fitted with a heavy beveled edge glass.

The movement is imported, stem wind and stem set, jeweled, cylinder escapement, hard enameled dial, and in addition to being complete in every respect as a timekeeper, it has a complete calendar, which works automatically, always indicating correctly the day of the month.

Price...$4.45

OUR $58.00 B GRADE COLUMBUS PHAETON.

This is a Genuine Columbus, O. Phaeton,

With care they will Last a Lifetime.

MADE BY

One of the Oldest and Most Reliable Manufacturers in Columbus, Ohio.

A BINDING TWO YEAR'S GUARANTY GOES WITH EVERY PHAETON.

OUR REGULAR B GRADE

Guaranteed

Work

We Offer a Cheap Special B Grade Phaeton at $39.90.

No. 92816. Order by Number.

We have many other grades of Phaeton's in our Special Vehicle Catalogue which will be mailed free to any Address upon application.

Juvenile Magic Lanterns and Outfit.
We believe that money cannot be spent to better advantage for the amusement of children than for a magic lantern and outfit. They derive a great deal of pleasure from giving magic lantern exhibitions, posting circulars, and all of the detail connected with an amateur entertainment.

No. 61000.

No. 61000. The "Home" Magic Lantern for parlor entertainments; has metal body, handsomely japanned, with gilt decorations, and has kerosene lamp with six colored slides, with views 1½ inches wide, magnifying picture to about one foot. Each..................75c

PRESERVED MEATS.

No family should be without a nice supply of these preserved meats. Handy for quick lunches, outings, traveling and very palatable. As usual, we keep only the best, and you must be sure to include some in your freight order.

Tongue.
                                    Doz.   Each.
G 1472 1-lb. Lunch
        Tongue $2 75 $0 25

Ham.
G 1473 Potted, ½-
        lb. tins.........$1 00 $0 10

POTTED HAM
SEARS ROEBUCK & CO.
CHICAGO

Boys' Blouse Waists.

Sizes 4 to 12 Years.
EVERY ONE A GREAT BARGAIN. New and Handsome Patterns; Nobby Effects and Rich Colorings. You cannot afford to overlook them.
No. 21471 Boys' Extra Quality Fast Colored Percale Blouse, with large ruffled sailor collar, ruffled front and cuffs. Assorted colors and patterns; pinks, blues, etc. All combination colors. Sizes 4 to 12 years.
Price each...$0.43
Three for.... 1.20

SPALDING'S BASEMEN'S AND INFIELDERS' MITTS.

No. 8924. Mitt, made of the very best and softest light tanned buckskin; the thumb and at wrist are extra well padded with the highest quality felt, making it a very safe and easy fitting mitt combined with strength and durability. The mitt throughout is of the best workmanship, as indicated by our "Highest Quality" trade mark. Made in rights and lefts. Each.....................$2.55

No. 8924.

...stained and polished, and decorated with gilt stripe. Extra value and worth double the money. Each...$0.10

No. 8910. Spalding's Black End, Boys' Maple Bat, plain finish with gilt stripes, a dandy bat for a few pennies. Each...............$0.04   Per dozen..........$0.45

D 184 Worm Cakes. This is a very satisfactory remedy for destroying worms and removing them from the system. It is in convenient form for children to take, thinking they readily do, thinking it is a candy. Full instructions how to give them, and other useful information in each box. Price 20c; Doz.................$2.25

Our $1.99 Leader.

No. 23469 A style made Hat, one of the lovely productions of '97. Wire frames entirely covered with handsome lace, finished with a jet edge and a very pretty jet crown, trimmed on right side with loops of lace and on left side with a handsome bunch of flowers and loops...red lace...

Tricycles and Velocipedes.

Notwithstanding the immense popularity of the bicycle, the tricycle and velocipede still remain in favor. Many parents prefer them for their children by reason of their safety, convenience and the ease with which they can be run by the little girl or boy. The tricycle, which we illustrate, is made for girls or boys from two to fifteen years. They are constructed with especial care and will stand the abuse they very frequently receive. They are very easy running and handsomely finished. The improved spring seat takes all vibration, and being upholstered in plush and furnished with back makes riding easy and comfortable. Frame is enameled black. Quoted with iron tire wheels or C plate rubber tire wheels. The illustration shows the tricycle with fenders. We quote without fenders. The following are our special prices with iron tire wheels:

No. 85018 Rear wheels 18 inch, for girls 2 to 4 years	$3.35
No. 85019 Rear wheels 20 inch, for girls 3 to 5 years	4.45
No. 85020 Rear wheels 22 inch, for girls 4 to 7 years	5.30
No. 85021 Rear wheels 26 inch, for girls 7 to 10 years	6.35
No. 85022 Rear wheels 30 inch, for girls 10 to 15 years	7.35

Kazoos.

No. 7778. The Kazoo is the simplest musical instrument made. No trouble to learn. Insert some noise at the one end, the pleasing music is emitted from the other. Made of maple with metal ring.
Each $0.08
Per dozen 0.85

..Perfection in Fine Footwear..

No. 3607 THIS ELEGANT BOOT is the very latest production in fine footwear, and is one of the most popular shoes we have ever sold. Made from finest selection of VICI KID, Coin Toe with Patent Leather Tips. Patent Leather Lace Stay, fancy vamp and heel foxing. AND NEVER WAS EQUALED FOR THIS PRICE.

SIZES: 2 1-2 to 7.
WIDTHS: B, C, D, E and EE.

OUR SPECIAL PRICE, PER PAIR.... $2.85

Rich's Patent "Julia Marlowe" Lace Boot

THE RICH SHOE CO.

NONE GENUINE Unless bearing this Stamp on every Sole.

Pat. Aug 11 -96.

A FEW OF ITS GOOD POINTS.....

Produced Through Having.......
Elastic Coring Over the Instep.
FITS like a glove. IT IS BEAUTIFUL.
IT NEVER PINCHES the foot.
either high or low instep. IT YIELDS
action of the foot.
CONFORMS in vital points to the shape of
foot instead of pressing the foot

Our Combined Acme Dry Air Refrigerator and Sideboard at from $11.47 to $18.67.

One of our very finest ..

REFRIGERATORS

It is made of solid oak.

Finished antique, highly polished, heavily paneled on front, sides, back and bottom; is fitted with a sideboard attachment with a heavy beveled French plate mirror. The whole is beautifully carved and decorated with raised carved ornamentations. This is a very large refrigerator and one of the most popular styles we have. All but the two smaller sizes have an ice chest large enough to take artificial ice.

Has lift-out Ice Reservoir.

Ice Rack is made entirely of metal.

Sears, Roebuck quickly became the biggest mail-order company in the world. Goods that had once been available only in towns and cities could now be bought anywhere in the United States. In this way, mail-order catalogs helped to bridge the gap between country and city. How might these new products have changed people's lives?

Source: *Sears, Roebuck Catalogue.* Chicago, 1897.

THE INDUSTRIAL PROBLEM

by Andrew Carnegie, 1903–1911

By the end of the 1800s, the United States had become an industrial giant. Andrew Carnegie, who came to the United States as a poor immigrant from Scotland, became a millionaire businessman by using new technologies to make steel cheaply. The rise of big business, however, created problems between owners of factories, such as Carnegie, and labor, the workers in the factories. Read the excerpt from Carnegie's essays below. What solutions does he propose?

We did not fail to see, as the **works** enlarged, how much success depended upon the mechanical men, the superintendents and **foremen**, yet not one of these had up to that time been admitted as partner. The business and the mechanical men—office and mill—were still widely separated. Well do I remember the first attempt to bring these two departments into closer relations. It was made with our Captain Jones, one of your members, well known and appreciated by many of you as in the foremost rank of managers, perhaps the foremost of his day in America. He came to us as a working mechanic at eight shillings per day. I explained to the Captain how several of the younger men in the business department had been made partners and were actually receiving much greater rewards than he, while his services were at least equally valuable, and informed him that we wished to make him a partner. I shall never forget his reply. "Mr. Carnegie, I am very much obliged, but I know nothing about business, and never wish to be troubled with it—I have plenty to trouble me here in these works. Leave me as I am, and just give me a **thundering** salary." "Henceafter," I said, "the salary of the President of the United States is yours, Captain," and so it remained until the sad day of his death. My seniors, the presidents of the other manufacturing concerns, did not fail to take me to task for ruining the steel business by paying a mechanic more salary than any of them received. Being much the youngest of these great **dignitaries**, I humbly confessed my wrongdoing, not, however, failing to inquire if they knew where we could find two or three more Captain Joneses at double the price....

Unsuspected powers lie **latent** in willing men around us which only need appreciation and development to produce surprising results. Money rewards alone will not, however, insure these, for to the most sensitive and ambitious natures there must be the note of sympathy, appreciation, friendship. Genius is sensitive in all its forms, and it is unusual, not ordinary, ability that **tells** even in practical affairs. You must capture and keep the heart of the original and supremely able man before his brain can do its best. Indeed this

works: factory

foremen: supervisors

thundering: huge

dignitaries: important people

latent: sleeping

tells: shows up

law has no limits. Even the mere laborer becomes more efficient as regard for his employer grows. Hand service or head service, it is heart service that counts.

On the other hand, the precious example of the **United States Steel Corporation**, under the direction of Judge Gary, in offering advantageous terms upon which its workmen can become shareholders, of which they have availed themselves so freely; in providing eight millions of dollars as **pension fund** for its employees and uniting it with the four millions given by **the writer** upon his retirement from business, for a relief and pension fund for workmen in the Carnegie Works, and its generous treatment of men injured, are gratifying proofs that **labor and capital** are drawing closer together. This most desirable feature must not be overlooked. Instead of a few partners under the old system, we have in one company the cheering spectacle of more than a hundred thousand shareholders, and *no less than thirty thousand of these employees*. Judge Gary and Mr. Perkins are to rank as the great pioneers in this noble advance. It is advisable that in our day at least workmen shareholders should be guaranteed against actual loss upon their shares as small homesteads are **exempt** from **mortgages**.

It is to this feature I wish especially to call attention, as it contains, in my opinion, the germ of the future peaceful **consolidation**, through partnership, of labor and capital. Many a time since the writer's retirement from business he has felt that if he were induced to return thereto, his chief aim would be to address many thousands of workmen as "fellow-shareholders." He envies Judge Gary, chairman of the Steel Company, who has this privilege today. The Harvester Company has been another pioneer in this **beneficent** movement, and today we hear of it creating a large pension fund for employees. The work goes bravely on. Capital is steadily awakening to a keener sense of its responsibilities to labor, and labor's hearty response will soon be seen in closer relations with employers than ever before. We may expect a great and continual advance in this direction, for it's not only just, it will prove highly profitable to both parties. Capital, labor, ability, constitute a three-legged stool, each member indispensable; neither first, second, nor third, but all equal.

United States Steel Corporation: company founded and run by Carnegie until his retirement in 1901

pension fund: money that is saved and invested to pay for retirement

the writer: Carnegie

labor and capital: workers and owners

exempt: freed from, excused

mortgages: bank loans used to buy property

consolidation: joining together

beneficent: positive, helpful

Carnegie believed in paying workers good salaries and involving them in the management of the company. He felt that this would create a strong workforce that would strive to make his business profitable. Not all business owners agreed with Carnegie. So many workers organized themselves into labor unions to fight for the benefits that the workers in Carnegie's factories already had.

Source: Burton J. Hendrick, ed., *Miscellaneous Writings of Andrew Carnegie*, Vol. II. Garden City, NY: Doubleday, Doran & Company , Inc., 1933.

Eight Hours

Words by I. G. Blanchard and Music by Jesse H. Jones, 1866

During the late 1800s and early 1900s, children often worked in mines and factories for 10 hours a day. Adults worked even longer—as many as 16 hours a day. Workers formed labor unions to gain better working conditions and a shorter workday. In 1866 a newspaper called the Workingman's Advocate printed a poem by I. G. Blanchard called Eight Hours. A minister named Jesse H. Jones later set the words to music. How does this song express some of the hopes, goals, and accomplishments of American workers and unions?

1. We mean to make things o-ver, we are tired of toil for naught,
2. Hur-rah, hur-rah, for La-bor! for it shall a-rise in might;

With___ bare-ly e-nough to live up-on, and nev-er an hour for thought;___
It has filled the world with plen-ty, it shall fill the world with light;____

We want to feel the sun-shine, and we want to smell the flowers,
Hur-rah, hur-rah, for La-bor! it is muster-ing all its powers,

We are sure that God has will'd it, and we mean to have eight hours.___
And shall march a-long to vic-tor-y with the ban-ner of Eight Hours!__

We're sum-mon-ing our for-ces from the ship-yard, shop and mill,
Shout, shout the ec-ho-ing ral-ly till all the hea-vens thrill,

Eight hours for work, eight hours for rest, eight hours for what we___ will!

Eight hours for work, eight hours for rest, eight hours for what we will!____

Source: Adapted from the *Workingman's Advocate*, August 18, 1866, reprinted in Philip S. Foner, *American Labor Songs of the Nineteenth Century*. Chicago: University of Illinois Press, 1975.

The Promised Land

by Mary Antin, 1911

In one of the greatest waves of immigration in history, more than 28 million people from all over the world came to the United States between 1860 and 1920. Many immigrants came for freedom and for opportunity, and they called America "the promised land." One of these immigrants was a 13-year-old Russian Jew named Mary Antin (1881–1949). Speaking no English, she and her family arrived in Boston, Massachusetts, in 1894 to join Mary's father, who had come to the United States three years earlier. In 1911 she wrote her autobiography, which she titled The Promised Land. *In the following excerpt, Antin describes her first days in the United States. How does she feel about her new country? What are her first thoughts about going to school?*

Our **initiation** into American ways began with the first step on the new soil. My father found occasion to instruct or correct us even on the way from the pier to **Wall Street**, which journey we made crowded together in a rickety cab. He told us not to lean out of the windows, [and] not to point. . . .

The first meal was an object lesson of much variety. My father produced several kinds of food, ready to eat, without any cooking, from little tin cans that had printing all over them. He attempted to introduce us to a queer, slippery kind of fruit, which he called [a] "banana," but [he] had to give it up for the time being. After the meal, he had better luck with a curious piece of furniture on runners, which he called [a] "rocking-chair." There were five of us newcomers, and we found five different ways of getting into the American machine of **perpetual** motion, and as many ways of getting out of it. One born and **bred** to the use of a rocking-chair cannot imagine

initiation: introduction

Wall Street: street in Boston

perpetual: constant
bred: raised

how **ludicrous** people can make themselves when attempting to use it for the first time. We laughed **immoderately** over our various experiments with the **novelty**, which was a **wholesome** way of letting off steam after the unusual excitement of the day.

In our **flat** we did not think of such a thing as storing the coal in the bathtub. There was no bathtub. So in the evening of the first day my father conducted us to the **public baths**. As we moved along in a little **procession**, I was delighted with the **illumination** of the streets. So many lamps, and they burned until morning, my father said, and so people did not need to carry lanterns. In America, then, everything was free, as we had heard in Russia. Light was free; the streets were as bright as a **synagogue** on a holy day. Music was free; we had been **serenaded**, to our gaping delight, by a brass band of many pieces, soon after our **installation** on **Union Place**.

Education was free. That subject my father had written about repeatedly, as **comprising** his chief hope for us children, the **essence** of American opportunity, the treasure that no thief could touch, not even misfortune or poverty. It was the one thing that he was able to promise us when he sent for us; surer, safer than bread or shelter. On our second day I was thrilled with the **realization** of what this freedom of education meant. A little girl from across the alley came and offered to **conduct** us to school. My father was out, but we five between us had a few words of English by this time. We knew the word school. We understood. This child, who had never seen us till yesterday, who could not pronounce our names, who was not much better dressed than we, was able to offer us the freedom of the schools of Boston! No application made, no questions asked, no **examinations**, rulings, **exclusions**; no **machinations**, no fees. The doors stood open for every one of us. The smallest child could show us the way.

This incident impressed me more than anything I had heard in advance of the freedom of education in America. It was a concrete proof—almost the thing itself. One had to experience it to understand it.

ludicrous: silly, ridiculous
immoderately: very much
novelty: new item
wholesome: healthy
flat: apartment

public baths: places where people can bathe
procession: group
illumination: lighting

synagogue: Jewish house of worship
serenaded: sung to
installation: settling in
Union Place: street in Boston
comprising: making up
essence: heart, basis

realization: understanding

conduct: lead

examinations: tests
exclusions: keeping people out
machinations: tricks

As was the case in many immigrant families, Mary Antin's older sister could not go to school because she needed to work to help the family earn money. Because of the sacrifices of both her sister and her parents, Mary was able to attend school and go to college. She later became a poet and an author and worked for women's rights. Antin never forgot her immigrant roots, and she later fought against efforts to limit the number of immigrants to the United States. For an account of some immigrants' very different experiences in our country, read the next document on pages 141–142.

Source: Mary Antin, *The Promised Land*. Boston: The Atlantic Monthly Company, 1911; reprinted Boston: Houghton Mifflin Company, 1969.

From the Walls of Angel Island

Poems by Unknown Chinese Immigrants, 1910–1940

Congress passed a law in 1882 limiting immigration from China. But many Chinese, seeking a better life, still tried to come. In 1910 the United States opened a new immigration center for Chinese immigrants on Angel Island in San Francisco Bay. As soon as their boats docked, Chinese men and women were separated from each other and taken to a wooden building on Angel Island. On this island, Chinese immigrants had to take medical tests and answer many questions before they could leave. Some were forced to stay on Angel Island for a few weeks, others for as long as three years. This lack of freedom, along with poor food, poor health care, and lack of privacy, made Angel Island seem like a prison. During their long hours of waiting, many of the immigrants wrote poems on the walls of the building expressing their feelings about their condition. Most of these poems were written by teenage boys and young men who did not sign their names. Five of their poems are printed below in the original Chinese and in English translation. In what ways do these poems describe how the immigrants felt about their treatment in America?

困因木屋常愁悶：
憶別家鄉月幾圓。
家人倚望音書切：
憑誰傳語報平安？

Imprisoned in this wooden building,
   I am always sad and bored.
I remember since I left my native village,
   it has been several **full moons**.   **full moons: months**
The family at home is leaning on the
   door, urgently looking for letters.
Whom can I count on to tell them I
   am well?

141

美有強權無公理，　　America has power, but not justice.
囹圄吾人也罹辜。　　In prison, we were **victimized** as if we were guilty.　　**victimized:** treated badly
不由分說真殘酷，　　Given no opportunity to explain, it was really brutal.
俯首回思莫奈何。　　I bow my head in **reflection** but there is nothing I can do.　　**reflection:** deep thought

凤慕花旗幾優哉，　　I used to admire the **land of the Flowery Flag** as a country of **abundance**.　　**land of the Flowery Flag:** Chinese term for the United States
即時籌款動程來。　　I immediately raised money and started my journey.　　**abundance:** plenty
風波閱月已歷盡。　　For over a month, I have experienced enough winds and waves.
監牢居所受災磨。　　Now on an extended **sojourn** in jail, I am subject to the **ordeals** of prison life.　　**sojourn:** stay
仰望屋崙相咫尺，　　I look up and see **Oakland** so close by.　　**ordeals:** struggles
願回祖國負耕鋤。　　I wish to go back to my motherland to carry the farmer's hoe.　　**Oakland:** city near San Francisco
滿腹牢騷難寢寐，　　Discontent fills my belly and it is difficult for me to sleep.
聊書數句表心裁。　　I just write these few lines to express what is on my mind.

壁上題詩過百篇，　　Over a hundred poems are on the walls.
看來皆是嘆迍邅。　　Looking at them, they are all **pining** at the delayed progress.　　**pining:** suffering
愁人曷向愁人訴，　　What can one sad person say to another?
自古英雄每厄先。　　Unfortunate travellers everywhere wish to **commiserate**. . . .　　**commiserate:** share their feelings of sadness
　　　　　　　　　　From ancient times, heroes often were the first ones to face **adversity**.　　**adversity:** hardship

埃屋三椽聊保身，　　The low building with three **beams** merely shelters the body.　　**beams:** heavy pieces of lumber
崙麓積懷不堪陳。　　It is unbearable to relate the stories **accumulated** on the Island slopes.　　**accumulated:** gathered
待得飛騰順遂日，　　Wait till the day I become successful and fulfill my wish!
劃除關稅不論仁。　　I will not speak of love when I **level** the immigration station!　　**level:** destroy

Between 1910 and 1940, about 100,000 Chinese passed through Angel Island. Some were allowed to enter the United States but many were forced to return to China. Some of the Chinese imprisoned on the island banded together and successfully fought for better conditions. Angel Island was closed in 1940. Today Angel Island is a state park open to the public and the poems can still be seen on the building's walls.

Source: Him Mark Lai, Genny Lim, and Judy Yung, *Island: Poetry and History of Chinese Immigrants on Angel Island, 1910–1940*. Seattle, WA: University of Washington Press, 1980.

Jane Addams and Hull House

by Navidad O'Neill, 1996

In the early 1900s many immigrants came to the United States to find a better way of life. Unfortunately, the way was not always easy for them. Many were poor and did not speak English. Others worked long hours in factories and mines for very little pay. Jane Addams decided that she had to do something for the poor. At first she decided to share her knowledge of art and literature, but soon she realized that they had more basic needs that had to be met. She and her friend, Ellen Starr, opened Hull House, the first settlement house in our country. Why do you think Jane Addams and her friend wished to help the poor?

CAST OF CHARACTERS:

Narrator
Jane Addams
Ellen Gates Starr, her friend
George, John, Charles, Alice, Mary and Julia, all Hull House volunteers.
Marie and Helen, German immigrants
John and Joseph, Italian immigrants

Jane Addams should be alone at the beginning of the play. Either the playing area can be set with empty chairs or each character can bring in a chair when entering. The narrator serves the tea, either by miming it, or by bringing in new tea cups for each character. The effect should be of the play beginning with one person and then accumulating and expanding throughout until the end.

Narrator: Jane Addams sits down to tea and ponders her future—and that of others.

Jane: In Chicago, there are people who sit in their large comfortable homes and drink tea. But in the slums of Chicago there are many people who live in small, crowded apartments. Sometimes 9 people live in one room. There is no time to sit down and rest because many of them work 16 hours a day. I wish I could do something to help them. But what? And how? What should I do with my life that would help change people's lives for the better?

Narrator: *(A doorbell rings off-stage, or the narrator rings a bell to indicate each new arrival.)* Jane is joined by Ellen Gates Starr, her friend from college, who sits down with her for tea.

Jane: I am sick of asking myself what I am and what I ought to be, Ellen.

Ellen: You haven't been happy since our return from England.

Jane: Ahhh. England. Remember Toynbee Hall, Ellen? Wasn't it inspiring? There in the middle of the London slums is a place where educated men and women share their knowledge and their lives with those around them. There they teach people how to read, how to paint, how to write, and how to sing. They help them get jobs and live full lives.

Ellen: Yes, I remember our visit there. The young men and women of Toynbee Hall live and work among the poor. They don't simply hand out food on holidays.

Jane: Do you think we could create a "Settlement" house like Toynbee Hall, here in Chicago where surely it is needed?

Ellen: Jane, I think you could create anything. You never think anything is too difficult, once you set your mind to it.

Jane: Would you help me?

Ellen: What do we do first?

Jane: Find a large table. And a large house in which to place it.

Narrator: *(Doorbell rings.)* Jane and Ellen are joined by George, John, Charles, Alice, Mary, and Julia, who discuss how they can volunteer their time to make Hull House work.

Jane: So do we all know our assignments for today?

George: I'm trying to locate more books for our library. We have the complete works of Shakespeare, but I think we could use more Greek classics and drama. We have many people from Greece in the neighborhood who would appreciate such literature.

Mary: I've purchased the paints and will set up the easels in the sunroom for the art classes that begin tonight.

John: The cribs for the child care room will be delivered this afternoon. I'll need help putting them together.

Ellen: I'll help you with that.

John: Great. There are 12 of them. There is a desperate need for a place where babies can be cared for while their parents are at work.

Julia: I'm going to find out how many children are actually working in factories 12 hours a day. I believe some are as young as five years old.

Jane: Do you want my help with that?

Julia: Not just yet. I'll let you know when it's time to present our findings to the American public. Then, when they know the facts, hopefully we can start to change this situation.

Charles: I'll see if I can get a doctor to volunteer to give the babies the shots they need.

Jane: Great. Try Dr. Alice Hamilton. She said she wanted to help.

Charles: Jane, what about the problem of garbage on the streets?

Ellen: It's not collected on a regular schedule and when the workers do collect it, they often dump it a block away. Last week a horse died in the middle of the street, and it's still there.

Julia: This is a serious problem. It's unhealthy for everyone who lives nearby.

Jane: I'll see what I can do. If I have to, I'll follow the garbage wagons all the way to the city dump to make sure the garbage is properly disposed of.

John: Would you really do that?

Jane: Why not? That's our job, to do anything it takes to make things better in our community.

Mary: Oh, and another thing. Jane, I think we need to buy more tables. (*Everyone freezes in action.*)

Narrator: (*Doorbell rings again. Marie and Helen enter.*) The neighborhood comes to Hull House for tea, and finds many reasons to stay.

Marie: I'm bringing my embroidered curtains. Miss Addams wants us to display our best work.

Helen: But Marie, what will you put on your windows in the meantime?

Marie: Plain, ordinary curtains. I want to save my best work for the Labor Museum, where all of the neighborhood can see it. What are you bringing, Helen?

Helen: You know the church I made from cookies and sweets?

Marie: With the steeple of cookies and the sugar-stained glass?

Helen: Yes. We will put that on display, on a high shelf where little hands won't be able to reach it and take a bite!

Marie: This Labor Museum is a good idea. Miss Addams said she noticed some of the young people thinking that the new ways people do things in the United States are better than what they call the old-fashioned ways of their parents.

Helen: We'll show them "old-fashioned"! We'll teach them to be proud of their culture and of what good things the "old folks" can make.

Marie: Miss Addams said there will be many guests at the opening of the Labor Museum. Even the newspaper reporters will be there.

Helen: We should tell Elsa to bring her needlepoint.

Marie: And Hubert should display his clocks.

Helen: Let's tell all of our neighbors.

(*The narrator rings the doorbell. Marie and Helen freeze in action.*)
Joseph and John enter.)

John: Someone told me that Miss Addams got the idea for her Labor Museum from you. Is that true?

Joseph: I don't know if it's true, but I do know that she came to visit my wife and I one night and stood admiring the stairpost I had carved in our hallway.

John: The one with the angels?

Joseph: Yes, that's the one. She said, "This should be on display for the whole neighborhood to see." And then she asked me if I would bring something else I had carved.

John: My wife told me that Miss Addams wanted me to bring in one perfect tomato to show in this museum of our labors.

Joseph: And look at all the wonderful work everyone in the neighborhood is bringing. I'm glad we have a place where we can all gather together to celebrate what we give to America.

Narrator: *(Doorbell rings. Jane Addams and the volunteers unfreeze.)* Many people came to Hull House for help.

Mary: We must work to get the country to agree to an eight-hour work day. Only then will everyone have enough time to take care of their families and stay healthy.

Julia: Adults should earn enough so that their children don't have to work and can go to school.

Ellen: Jane, can we really do all that needs doing?

Jane: Why not? That's our job—to do anything it takes to make things better.

(The narrator rings the doorbell seven times in a row. Everyone is arranging their seats in a semicircle facing the audience. All together everyone applauds. In the middle of clapping they freeze and the narrator speaks.)

Narrator: Children in the neighborhood put on plays quite often at Hull House. Jane Addams helped to make costumes and direct scenes. Parents and friends attended the performances after work.

(The other characters unfreeze.)

Marie: What a lovely play!

Joseph: I wish there were more things like this for the children to do.

John: Yes, me too.

Jane: We've been talking to City Hall about the need for public spaces where children can play safely.

Ellen: They agreed to clear out an empty lot on the next block, and help create a ballfield where the children can play. They will build a jungle gym, too.

Jane: This way the children will get exercise in the fresh air.

Joseph: Will the city really go along with this plan?

Jane: Why not?

Narrator: And it did happen. Jane Addams started the country's first public playground in Chicago, because she set her mind to it and worked hard for it.

(The group applauds.)

In 1931, Jane Addams was awarded the Nobel Peace Prize. She donated her prize money of $16,000 plus $10,000 more of her own funds to it to the Women's International League of Peace and to Hull House.

(The group applauds, louder this time, and rises to give Jane Addams a standing ovation.)

THE END

Hull House served as a model for other settlement houses in the United States. At the settlement houses, people could learn English, receive care for their children, and get help in becoming American citizens. Many immigrants went on to start their own self-help organizations.

Building the Panama Canal

by Theodore Roosevelt, 1910

Theodore Roosevelt, who became President of the United States in 1901, did much to help the United States become a major world power. Roosevelt, who had been a Rough Rider in the Spanish-American War in 1898, was convinced that a canal across the Isthmus (IS mus) of Panama would be beneficial to the United States. Such a canal would cut the distance of a sea voyage between the Atlantic and the Pacific by 7,000 miles. The French had already tried to dig a canal in Panama, but had failed. Why do you think the job might have been so difficult? In this excerpt from a speech he gave at Harvard University in Massachusetts, Roosevelt praises the United States effort to build the Panama Canal.

The digging of the Panama Canal, the success with which it has been dug, has curiously enough, made, I think, a deeper impression abroad than at home. Unfortunately—and with a certain amount of justification—there has grown up a feeling that there is danger of corruption in work undertaken among us by the government for the public, and the total failure of all previous efforts by other nations, to accomplish anything on the Panama Canal had given rise in Europe to much cynical disbelief in our power to do the work. But it has been done; the success is literally astounding. It has been done with as near absolute cleanness, as near absolute honesty, as it is humanly possible to do any work, public or private. We have put down there men at small salaries—improperly small salaries—who have handled hundreds of millions of dollars, without the slightest suspicion of financial corruption on the part of any government servant holding a position of any importance in connection with the work. Moreover, the work has been done with the utmost efficiency.

It took ten years to complete the Panama Canal, which opened in 1914. Swamps had to be drained so that the mosquitoes that carried yellow fever and malaria would have no place to lay their eggs. Huge mounds of dirt had to be moved, and mountains of solid rock had to be blasted. In the end Theodore Roosevelt's plan was accomplished through the use of new American technologies such as steam shovels.

Source: Albert Bushnell Hart and Herbert Ronald Ferleger, eds., *Theodore Roosevelt Cyclopedia*, rev. 2nd ed. New York: Theodore Roosevelt Association, 1989.

EXPLOSION OF THE *MAINE*

from the *New York Journal*, 1898

In 1895 Cuban colonists began fighting for their independence from Spain. For the next three years many newspapers in the United States reported shocking stories of bloody battles and Spanish cruelty in Cuba. Not all these stories were true, but they sold newspapers. They also helped to increase tensions between the United States and Spain, and some Americans wanted the United States to declare war. Suddenly, on February 15, 1898, the American battleship Maine mysteriously blew up in Cuba's port city of Havana, killing 260 sailors. Was the explosion an accident or did someone plan it? No one knew for sure, but some newspapers rushed to assign blame. Take a close look at the front page of the New York Journal, which was printed two days after the explosion. According to the newspaper, what caused the disaster? How do the headlines try to shape readers' opinions?

In April 1898, two months after the explosion of the Maine, the United States declared war on Spain. By summertime the Spanish-American War was over. By defeating Spain, the United States gained control of the Philippines, Puerto Rico, and Guam, and Cuba gained its independence. For many years the United States maintained control over Cuba. No one ever discovered why the Maine blew up. To this day the cause of the explosion remains a mystery.

Source: *New York Journal*, February 17, 1898.

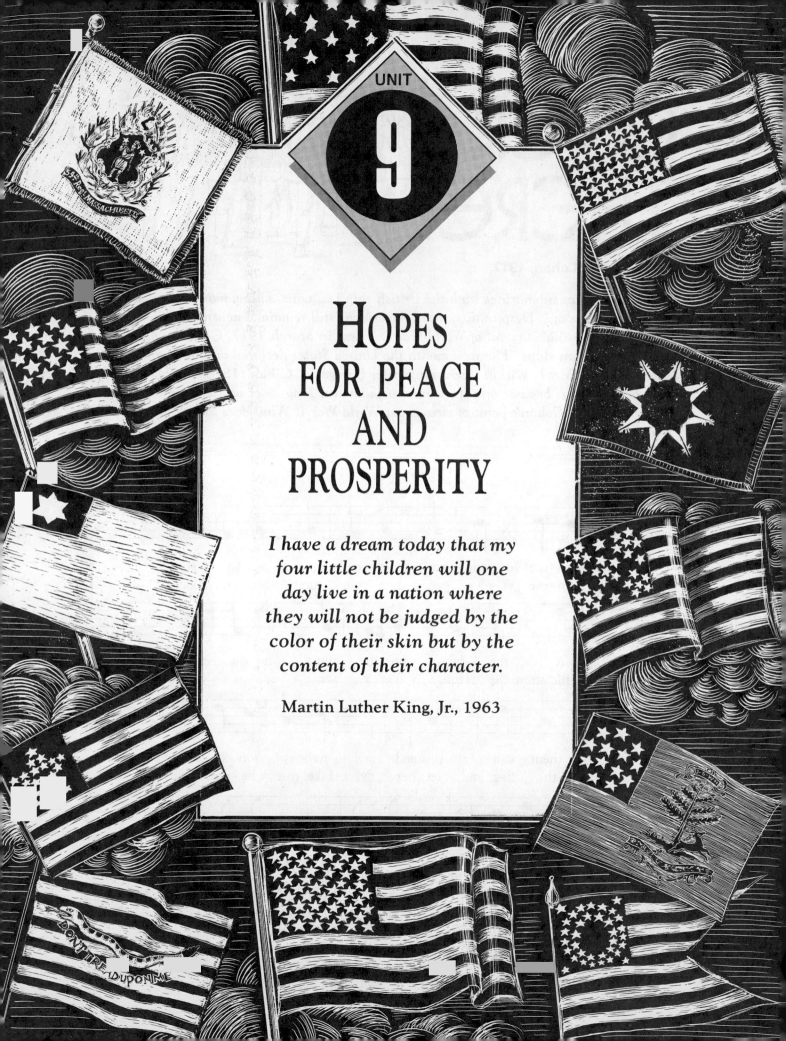

UNIT

9

HOPES FOR PEACE AND PROSPERITY

I have a dream today that my four little children will one day live in a nation where they will not be judged by the color of their skin but by the content of their character.

Martin Luther King, Jr., 1963

OVER THERE

by George M. Cohan, 1917

In 1915 German submarines sank the British ship Lusitania, killing many American passengers on board. Despite this, many Americans still remained neutral and hoped the United States would stay out of World War I. Then, in March 1917, Germany began sinking American ships. The next month the United States declared war on Germany and entered World War I. Within weeks songwriter George M. Cohan (1878–1942) wrote the song below, which became one of the most popular war songs ever written. As you read this song, notice Cohan's point of view about World War I. What does he ask American soldiers to do?

1. John - nie get your gun, get your gun, get your gun,
2. John - nie get your gun, get your gun, get your gun,

Take it on the run, on the run, on the run;
John - nie show the Hun, you're a son - of - a - gun,

Hear them call - ing you and me; Ev - 'ry son of lib - er - ty.
Hoist the flag and let her fly, Like true he - roes do or die.

Hur - ry right a - way, no de - lay, go to - day,
Pack your lit - tle kit, show your grit, do your bit,

Make your dad - dy glad, to have had such a lad,
Sol - diers to the ranks from the towns and the tanks,

THE GREAT MIGRATION

by Jacob Lawrence, 1992

Jacob Lawrence (1917–) is one of the leading American painters of our time. His work is known for its flat, outlined shapes, bright colors, and strong geometric patterns. Many of his paintings deal with important people and events in African American history. Following is an excerpt from Lawrence's introduction to his book The Great Migration. *The book is a series of paintings by Lawrence with captions that describe the Great Migration. On this page you can see one of his paintings. Why do you think Lawrence cared so much about this historical event?*

This is the story of an **exodus** of African-Americans who left their homes and farms in the South around the time of World War I and traveled to northern industrial cities in search of better lives. It was a momentous journey. Their movement resulted in one of the biggest population shifts in the history of the United States, and the migration is still going on for many people today.

exodus: mass departure of people

The great migration is a part of my life. I grew up knowing about people on the move from the time I could understand what words meant. There was always talk in my house of other families arriving from the South. My family was part of the first big wave of the migration, which occurred between the years 1916 and 1919. My mother was born in Virginia, and my father was born in South Carolina. Somehow they met on their way north, and I was born in Atlantic City, New Jersey, in 1917. We settled for a while in Philadelphia. Many other families settled there, too, but many traveled even farther, to Pittsburgh, New York, Chicago, Detroit, Cleveland, and St. Louis.

I arrived in New York City's Harlem community in 1930, when I was thirteen years of age. Harlem was crowded with newcomers, but we all settled in somehow. I went to school, and after school I went to an arts-and-crafts program at the Utopia Children's House, which my mother enrolled me in to keep me busy while she was at work. I decided then that I wanted to be an artist. When I first started painting, I was just making designs. The colors and patterns that decorated my mother's apartment influenced my pictures. Later I started painting street scenes. I painted peddlers, parades, fire escapes, apartment houses—all that was new to me.

Eventually, teachers, friends, even actors on the street corners helped me to understand how my own experiences fit into a much larger story—the history of African-Americans in this country. It seemed almost inevitable that I would tell this story in my art. I spent many hours at the Schomburg Library in Harlem reading books about the great migration, and I took notes. Soon my research gave me the images I needed to tell the story of the great migration. Many of the images were new for me—along with my street scenes, I would now need to paint rural landscapes, images of violence, and interiors, like the inside of a schoolroom. . . .

To me, migration means movement. While I was painting, I thought about trains and people walking to the stations. I thought about **field hands** leaving their farms to become factory workers, and about the families that sometimes got left behind. The choices made were hard ones, so I wanted to show what made the people get on those northbound trains. I also wanted to show just what it cost to ride them. Uprooting yourself from one way of life to make your way in another involves conflict and struggle. But out of the struggle comes a kind of power, and even beauty. I tried to convey this in the rhythm of the pictures, and in the repetition of certain images.

"And the migrants kept coming" is a refrain of triumph over adversity. My family and others left the South on a quest for freedom, justice, and dignity. If our story rings true for you today, then it must still strike a chord in our American experience.

field hands: people who work on the land doing farmwork

Many African Americans who moved to the North during the Great Migration improved their lives and made valuable contributions to the cities in which they settled. Today some African Americans are returning to the Southeast because of new economic opportunities.

Source: Jacob Lawrence, *The Great Migration*. New York: HarperCollins Publishers, 1993.

Let America Be America Again

by Langston Hughes, 1936

Although greater opportunities were available to African Americans during World War I and the period of prosperity that followed, many still faced discrimination and had to struggle to make ends meet. Langston Hughes (1902–1967) was one of the great poets of the Harlem Renaissance. He wrote the poem below during the Great Depression of the 1930s. During this time of great economic hardship, conditions worsened for many Americans. In the poem Hughes describes the ongoing struggle of all the people who have worked to make our country a land of freedom and opportunity. Who are some of these people, and what role have they played in our country's history?

Let America be America again.
Let it be the dream it used to be.
Let it be the pioneer on the plain
Seeking a home where he himself is free.

(America never was America to me.)

Let America be the dream the dreamers dreamed—
Let it be that great strong land of love
Where never kings **connive** nor tyrants scheme   **connive:** plot
That any man be crushed by one above.

(It never was America to me.)

O, let my land be a land where Liberty
Is crowned with no false patriotic **wreath**,   **wreath:** circular bouquet
But opportunity is real, and life is free,   of flowers
Equality is in the air we breathe.

(There's never been equality for me,
Nor freedom in this "homeland of the free.")

Say who are you that mumbles in the dark?
And who are you that draws your veil across the stars?

I am the poor white, fooled and pushed apart,
I am the Negro bearing slavery's scars.
I am the **red man** driven from the land,
I am the immigrant clutching the hope I seek—
And finding only the same old stupid plan
Of dog eat dog, of mighty crush the weak.

red man: Indian, Native American

I am the young man, full of strength and hope,
Tangled in that ancient endless chain
Of profit, power, gain, of grab the land!
Of grab the gold! Of grab the ways of satisfying need!
Of work the men! Of take the pay!
Of owning everything for one's own greed!

I am the farmer, **bondsman** to the soil.
I am the worker sold to the machine.
I am the Negro, servant to you all.
I am the people, worried, hungry, mean—
Hungry yet today despite the dream.
Beaten yet today—O, Pioneers!
I am the man who never got ahead,
The poorest worker **bartered** through the years.

bondsman: servant

bartered: traded

Yet I'm the one who dreamt our basic dream
In that Old World while still a **serf** of kings,
Who dreamt a dream so strong, so brave, so true,
That even yet its mighty daring sings
In every brick and stone, in every **furrow** turned
That's made America the land it has become.
O, I'm the man who sailed those early seas
In search of what I meant to be my home—
For I'm the one who left dark Ireland's shore,
And Poland's plain, and England's grassy **lea**,
And torn from Black Africa's **strand** I came
To build a "homeland of the free."
The free?

serf: slave

furrow: plowed field

lea: pasture
strand: shore

A dream—
Still **beckoning** to me!

beckoning: reaching out

O, let America be America again—
The land that never has been yet—
And yet must be—
The land where *every* man is free.
The land that's mine—
The poor man's land, Indian's, Negro's, ME—
Who made America,
Whose sweat and blood, whose faith and pain,
Whose hand at the **foundry**, whose plow in the rain,   **foundry:** metal factory
Must bring back our mighty dream again.

Sure, call me any ugly name you choose—
The steel of freedom does not stain.
From those who live like **leeches** on the people's lives,   **leeches:** worms that suck
We must take back our land again,   blood
America!

O, yes,
I say it plain,
America never was America to me,
And yet I swear this oath—
America will be!
An ever-living seed,
Its dream
Lies deep in the heart of me.

We, the people, must **redeem**   **redeem:** free, win back
Our land, the mines, the plants, the rivers,
The mountains and the endless plain—
All, all the stretch of these great green states—
And make America again!

This poem by Langston Hughes reminds us that American history is an ongoing story in which we all play a part. The poem also reminds us that the struggles of people who lived before us must never be forgotten. Many challenges lie ahead, and it is up to all of us to work together to help our country achieve its great ideals.

Source: Langston Hughes and Arna Bontemps, eds., *The Poetry of the Negro, 1746-1949.* Garden City, NY: Doubleday & Company, Inc., 1949.

The Trial of Susan B. Anthony

Trial Transcript, 1873

In the early 1900s women's suffrage leaders worked hard to gain women the right to vote. As you have read, the fight for women's suffrage had actually begun many years earlier when women had gathered for the Seneca Falls Convention in 1848. One of the most important suffrage leaders in the late 1800s was a former schoolteacher named Susan B. Anthony (1820–1906). On November 5, 1872, Anthony did something that shocked people—she voted in an election in Rochester, New York! She was arrested and put on trial in June 1873. The judge denied Anthony the right to have a trial by jury. He decided the case himself and found her guilty. Just as he was about to announce her punishment for breaking the law, Anthony stood up to defend herself. Below is an excerpt of Anthony's comments and the judge's response. Their statements are taken from a transcript, or written record, of the trial. As you read this transcript, notice why Anthony believes her trial has been unfair. Why does she think she has the right to vote? How does she compare the condition of women to the enslavement of African Americans before the Civil War?

Judge: The prisoner will stand up. Has the prisoner anything to say why **sentence** shall not be pronounced?

Anthony: Yes, your honor, I have many things to say; for in your ordered **verdict** of guilty, you have trampled underfoot every **vital** principle of our government. My natural rights, my civil rights, my political rights, are all alike ignored. Robbed of the **fundamental** privilege of citizenship, I am **degraded** from the status of a citizen to that of a **subject**; and not only myself individually, but all of my sex, are, by your honor's verdict, doomed to political **subjection**. . . .

Judge: The Court can not listen to . . . arguments [that] the prisoner's **counsel** has already **consumed** three hours in presenting.

Anthony: May it please your honor, I am not arguing the question, but simply stating the reasons why sentence can not, in justice, be pronounced against me. Your denial of my citizen's right to vote is the denial of my right of consent as one of the governed, the denial of my right of representation as one of the taxed, the denial of my right to a trial by a jury of my **peers** as an offender against law, therefore, the denial of my sacred rights to life, liberty, property, and—

Judge: The Court can not allow the prisoner to go on.

Anthony: But your honor will not deny me this one and only poor privilege of protest against this **high-handed** outrage upon my

sentence: punishment

verdict: decision
vital: important
fundamental: basic
degraded: reduced
subject: person ruled by others
subjection: second-class citizenship
counsel: lawyer
consumed: spent

peers: equals

high-handed: harsh, overwhelming

citizen's rights. May it please the Court to remember that since the day of my arrest last November, this is the first time that either myself or any person of my **disfranchised** class has been allowed a word of defense before judge or jury—

Judge: The prisoner must sit down; the Court can not allow it.

Anthony: All my **prosecutors**, from the [neighborhood] politician, who **entered** the complaint [against me], to the United States Marshal, Commissioner, District Attorney, District Judge, [and] your honor on the bench, not one is my peer, but each and all are my political **sovereigns**; and had your honor submitted my case to the jury, as was clearly your duty, even then I should have had just cause of protest, for not one of those men was my peer; but, native or foreign, white or black, rich or poor, educated or ignorant, awake or asleep, sober or drunk, each and every man of them was my political superior; hence, in no sense, my peer. . . . Precisely as no disfranchised person **is entitled** to sit upon a jury, and no woman is entitled to the **franchise**, so, none but a regularly **admitted** lawyer is allowed to practice [law] in the courts, and no woman can gain admission to the **bar**—hence, jury, judge, counsel, must all be of the superior class.

Judge: The Court must insist—the prisoner has been tried according to the established forms of law.

Anthony: Yes, your honor, but by forms of law all made by men, interpreted by men, administered by men, in favor of men, and against women; and hence, your honor's ordered verdict of guilty, against a United States citizen for the exercise of "that citizen's right to vote," simply because that citizen was a woman and not a man. But, yesterday, the same man-made forms of law declared it a crime punishable with $1,000 fine and six months' imprisonment, for you, or me, or any of us, to give a cup of cold water, a crust of bread, or a night's shelter to a panting fugitive [slave] as he was tracking his way to Canada. And every man or woman in whose veins **coursed** a drop of human sympathy violated that wicked law, **reckless** of consequences, and was justified in so doing. As then the slaves who got their freedom must take it over, or under, or through the unjust forms of law, precisely so now must women, to get their right to a voice in this Government, take it; and I have taken mine [my rights], and mean to take it at every possible opportunity.

Judge: The Court orders the prisoner to sit down. It will not allow another word.

Anthony: When I was brought before your honor for trial, I hoped for a broad and **liberal** interpretation of the Constitution . . . that should declare all United States citizens under its protecti[on] . . . equality of rights [which is] the national guarantee to all persons born or **naturalized** in the United States. But failing to get this justice—failing, even, to get a trial by a jury *not* of my peers—I ask not **leniency** at your hands—but rather the full **rigors** of the law.

disfranchised: denied the right to vote

prosecutors: accusers
entered: filed

sovereigns: rulers

is entitled: has the right
franchise: vote
admitted: qualified
bar: court system

coursed: flowed
reckless: regardless

liberal: open-minded

naturalized: made citizens
leniency: easy treatment
rigors: force

Judge: The Court must insist—(Here the prisoner sat down.) The prisoner will stand up. (Here Miss Anthony arose again.) The sentence of the Court is that you pay a fine of one hundred dollars and the costs of the **prosecution**.

Anthony: May it please your honor, I shall never pay a dollar of your unjust penalty. All . . . I possess is a $10,000 debt, **incurred** by publishing my [news]paper—[named] *The Revolution*—. . . the sole object of which was to educate all women to do precisely as I have done, rebel against your man-made, unjust, unconstitutional forms of law, that tax, fine, imprison, and hang women, while they deny them the right of representation in the Government; and I shall work on with **might and main** to pay every dollar of that honest debt, but not a penny shall go to this unjust claim. And I shall earnestly and **persistently** continue to urge all women to the practical recognition of the old revolutionary maxim, that "Resistance to **tyranny** is obedience to God."

prosecution: trial

incurred: brought about

The Revolution: newspaper on women's rights, started by Anthony in 1868

might and main: all my strength

persistently: constantly

tyranny: oppressive rule

Susan B. Anthony never paid the $100 fine charged by the judge. Six years later, in 1878, Anthony persuaded the United States Senate to debate an amendment to the Constitution granting women the right to vote. Although the amendment failed, Anthony spent the rest of her life fighting for it. Her bold actions inspired millions of women to fight for women's suffrage in the late 1800s and early 1900s. Finally, in 1920, the Nineteenth Amendment to the Constitution was approved, granting women the right to vote. In honor of her lifelong efforts, many people have called this the "Anthony Amendment."

Source: Elizabeth Cady Stanton, Susan B. Anthony, and Matilda Joslyn Gage, eds., *History of Woman Suffrage*, Volume 1. New York: Fowler & Wells, 1881.

DUST STORM DISASTER

by Woody Guthrie, 1935

During the Great Depression many people across the United States struggled to survive. Farmers on the Great Plains faced another kind of disaster in the 1930s—the Dust Bowl. For many years little rain had fallen on this region of the country. Crops died and the farmland became very dry. Then huge winds began blowing across the Great Plains. These winds picked up the loose topsoil and created massive black clouds of dust and dirt that stretched for miles. The Dust Bowl was born. Woody Guthrie (1912–1967), one of the country's best-known songwriters, experienced the Dust Bowl firsthand. As you read this song, notice all the different places he mentions. According to Guthrie, what were the dust storms like? How did farmers on the Great Plains react?

1. On the four - teen day of A - pril___ Of
(3. From)___ O - kla - ho - ma Cit - y___ To the
(5. The)___ ra - di - o re - port - ed___ We

nine - teen thir - ty - five___ There struck the worst of
Ar - i - zo - na line___ Da - ko - ta and Ne -
lis - tened with a - larm___ The wild and wind - y

dust - storms___ That ev - er filled the sky.___ 2. You could
bras - ka___ To the la - zy Ri - o Grande.___ 4. It
ac - tions___ Of this great mys - ter - ious storm. 6. From___

162

see that dust storm com - ing _____ The cloud looked death - like
fell a - cross our cit - y _____ Like a cur - tain of black rolled
Al - bu - quer-que and Clo - vis And all New Mex - i -

black _____ And through our might - y na - tion _____ It
down _____ We thought it was our judg - ment _____ We
co _____ They said it was the black - est _____ That

left a dread - ful track. _____ 3. From gain. _____
thought it was our doom. _____ 5. The
ev - er they had saw. _____ (7. From)

7. From old Dodge City, Kansas,
   The dust had rung their knell,
   And a few more comrades sleeping
   On top of old Boot Hill.

8. From Denver, Colorado,
   They said it blew so strong,
   They thought that they could hold out,
   They didn't know how long.

9. Our relatives were huddled
   Into their oil-boom shacks,
   And the children they were crying
   As it whistled through the cracks.

10. And the family, it was crowded
    Into their little room,
    They thought the world had ended,
    And they thought it was their doom.

11. The storm took place at sundown.
    It lasted through the night.
    When we looked out next morning
    We saw a terrible sight.

12. We saw outside our window
    Where wheatfields they had grown,
    Was now a rippling ocean
    Of dust the wind had blown.

13. It covered up our fences,
    It covered up our barns,
    It covered up our tractors
    In this wild and dusty storm.

14. We loaded our jalopies
    And piled our families in,
    We rattled down that highway
    To never come back again.

Source: Woody Guthrie, "Dust Storm Disaster," in Harold Levanthal and Marjorie Guthrie, eds., *The Woody Guthrie Songbook.* New York: Grosset & Dunlap, 1976.

The Four Freedoms

by Franklin Delano Roosevelt, 1941

Each year in January the President of the United States gives a State of the Union address. In January 1941 when President Franklin Delano Roosevelt made his State of the Union address, World War II had begun in Europe. France had already fallen to Hitler's forces, and Great Britain was in the midst of resisting Nazi air attacks. President Roosevelt knew that the American people needed to be prepared for the possibility of entering the war. In this excerpt from his speech, what reasons does he offer the American people for helping the Allies?

In the future days which we seek to make secure, we look forward to a world founded upon four essential human freedoms.

The first is freedom of speech and expression—everywhere in the world.

The second is freedom of every person to worship God in his own way—everywhere in the world.

The third is freedom from want—which, translated into world terms, means economic understandings which will secure to every nation a healthy peacetime life for its inhabitants—everywhere in the world.

The fourth is freedom from fear, which, translated into world terms, means a world-wide reduction of **armaments** to such a point and in such a thorough manner that no nation will be in a position to commit an act of physical aggression against any neighbor— anywhere in the world.

armaments: weapons

This nation has placed its **destiny** in the hands, heads and hearts of its millions of free men and women, and its faith in freedom under the guidance of God. Freedom means the supremacy of human rights everywhere. Our support goes to those who struggle to gain those rights and keep them. Our strength is in our unity of purpose.

destiny: future

To that high concept there can be no end save victory.

At first, the United States helped its allies through the Lend-Lease program, which was enacted by Congress in March 1941. This involved sending tanks, trucks, airplanes, and food to its European allies. Then in December 1941, when the Japanese bombed Pearl Harbor, the United States entered World War II.

Source: Diane Ravitch, ed., *The American Reader: Words That Moved a Nation.* New York: HarperCollins Publishers, 1990.

LINEAGE

by Margaret Walker, 1941

People in towns and cities across the United States hunted everywhere for work during the Great Depression. Throughout the farming communities of the South, however, the main problem was how to make a living from one's hard work. Farm prices fell to an all-time low in the 1930s, and farmers received only pennies for their crops. The situation was even harder for African American farmers, who also faced prejudice when they tried to market their crops. African American poet Margaret Walker was born in Birmingham, Alabama, in 1915. In the poem below she compares farm troubles during the Great Depression to those her grandmothers had faced years earlier. How were things different for Walker's ancestors?

My grandmothers were strong.

They followed plows and bent to toil.

They moved through fields **sowing** seed.　　　　**sowing:** planting

They touched earth and grain grew.

They were full of **sturdiness** and singing.　　**sturdiness:** firmness, strength

My grandmothers were strong.

My grandmothers are full of memories.

Smelling of soap and onions and wet clay

With veins rolling roughly over quick hands

They have many clean words to say.

My grandmothers were strong.

Why am I not as they?

Many people in cities in the North and in other parts of our country must have shared the experiences described in this poem. Many had watched their grandparents work hard in the factories and the mines to build better lives for themselves and their families, only to see these gains wiped out by the Great Depression.

Source: Margaret Walker, *For My People*. New Haven, CT: Yale University Press, 1942.

World War II

from the *New York Times*, 1941–1945

The New York Times headlines on this page depict three events of great importance regarding the involvement of the United States in World War II. The bombing of Pearl Harbor, an American naval base in Hawaii, led to the entry of the United States into World War II (bottom). The D-Day invasion—the mass landing of Allied troops on the shores of Normandy, France—marked the beginning of the end for the Axis powers in Europe (middle). The dropping of the first atomic bomb on Hiroshima, Japan, by the United States led to the surrender of Japan, and the end of the war (top). World War II ended on August 14, 1945. The war had lasted six years. The United States had been involved for almost four years.

Source: *New York Times,* December 8, 1941; June 6, 1944; August 7, 1945.

Life in a Japanese-American Prison Camp

by Yuri Tateishi, 1984

Soon after the Japanese attack on Pearl Harbor in 1941, some people feared that Japanese Americans might serve as spies for Japan. In response to this fear, the United States government began a program in 1942 that forced all Japanese Americans who lived on the West Coast to leave their homes. Many Japanese Americans were citizens who had been born in the United States and had never been to Japan. Japanese Americans protested this unfair treatment and claimed they were being mistreated because of prejudice. But the government took away their citizenship rights, and more than 110,000 Japanese Americans were moved to relocation camps for the rest of the war. One of those was Yuri Tateishi (YUR ee ta TAY shee), a 28-year-old woman living in West Los Angeles, California. In 1984 she described the three and a half years she had spent in Manzanar, a relocation camp in Inyo County, California, near the Sierra Nevada mountains. Manzanar, which became the home of 10,000 Japanese Americans, was surrounded by armed guards, searchlight towers, and barbed-wire fences. As you read this oral history by Tateishi (shown above with four of her children), think of what it was like for innocent people to be made to leave their homes and live in relocation camps. How did some Japanese Americans band together at Manzanar to fight for better treatment?

When the **evacuation** came, we were renting a home and had four kids. It was terrible because you had to sell everything. We were just limited to what we could take with us, and so everything was just sold for whatever we could get. Our furniture was rather new at that time because we had just bought a living-room and dining-room set. I just finished paying for a refrigerator when I had to sell that. Of course, we got nothing for it, because we had such a limited time...[and] we had to rush to sell everything. . . .

The day of the evacuation was April 26 [1942]. The day before, we had to sleep on the floor because all the furniture was gone. We all slept on the floor, ate on the floor, and cooked what we could with what few utensils we had. I recall we had to get up very early in the morning, and I think we all walked to the Japanese school because no one had a car then. And everybody was just all over the

evacuation: forced removal

167

place, the whole Japanese community was there, the West **L.A.** community. The Westwood Methodist Church had some hot coffee and doughnuts for us that morning, which helped a lot, and we were loaded in a bus.

Just about the time we were ready to load, my youngest son broke out with measles that morning, and I had him covered up, and then a nurse came to me and said, "May I see your baby?" He was almost three, . . . and she said, "I'm sorry but I'm going to have to take him away." . . . When I thought about how he might wake up and be in a strange place, with strange people, I just really broke down and cried. I cried all morning over it, but there was nothing we could do but leave him. He stayed at the general hospital and joined us at Manzanar in three weeks.

When we got to Manzanar, it was getting dark and we were given numbers first. We went to the **mess hall**, and I remember the first meal we were given in those tin plates and tin cups. It was canned **wieners** and canned spinach. It was all the food we had, and then after finishing that we were taken to our **barracks**. It was dark and **trenches** were here and there. You'd fall in and get up and finally got to the barracks. The floors were boarded, but they were about a quarter to a half inch apart, and the next morning you could see the ground below. What hurt most I think was seeing those hay mattresses. We were used to a regular home atmosphere. [I still remember] seeing those hay mattresses—so **makeshift**, with hay sticking out—a barren room with nothing but those hay mattresses. It was depressing, such a primitive feeling. We were given army blankets and army cots. Our family was large enough that we didn't have to share our barrack with another family but all seven of us were in one room.

mess hall: dining room

wieners: hot dogs
barracks: living places
trenches: deep ditches

makeshift: poorly made

The next morning was very cold. I went out to brush my teeth. There was a faucet at the front of each building, and it was so cold, so painful it was so cold. You felt like a prisoner. You know, you have to stay inside and you have a certain amount of freedom within the camp I suppose, but . . . it's not a comfortable feeling. You had to stay within the **confines** of that camp, not in the sense that you're in a jail or anything, but you're kept inside a barbed-wire fence, and you know you can't go out.

confines: boundaries

And you don't know what your future is, going into a camp with four children. You just have to trust God that you will be taken care of somehow. It's scary—not in the sense that you would be hurt or anything but not knowing what your future will be. You don't know what the education for the children will be or what type of housing or anything like that. Of course, you don't know how you're going to be able to raise the children.

After we had been in Manzanar for about a year . . . someone by the name of Mr. Ueno was treated unfairly and was taken out of the camp to jail, and some of the men felt that they should try to get him released. They didn't think it was right that they should take him, and a few men were chosen. My husband was one of them, and these men went to the **administration** to **negotiate** this man's release, but while they were negotiating a crowd gathered, and it got larger and larger and it just got out of control. The men came out of the meeting and told the crowd to quiet down and go home, but they just wouldn't listen, and that's when the trouble started outside. Well, somebody got shot. The people that were negotiating were taken. They were kept at the jail in **Independence**, and then after that they were transferred to **Lone Pine** and then sent to Utah. They stayed there quite a while, and then they were transferred from one place to another.

When my husband was arrested, someone came and told me, but I didn't try to go see him because there was no chance of seeing him. They had already taken him. I didn't think I'd have a chance; I don't think they ever would have given me the chance. It wasn't that kind of a situation. I hoped that he would be released soon but, again, you really didn't know what was going to happen. It occurred to me that I might not ever see him again. He wrote letters, but they were all **censored**. He came back, I think [about] eight months later.

When I think back on the evacuation, that's something you'd like to erase if you can, but it's a fact; we went through it. I'm unhappy about it, but I don't think I was really bitter. You feel like you can't do anything against the government. They tell you, You go or else. You just had to go.

You hurt. You give up everything that you worked for that far, and I think everybody was at the point of just having gotten out of the Depression and was just getting on his feet. And then all that happens! You have to throw everything away. You feel you were betrayed.

administration: prison camp authorities
negotiate: bargain for

Independence: town near Manzanar
Lone Pine: town near Manzanar

censored: inspected and had words blotted out by the authorities

Source: John Tateishi, *And Justice for All: An Oral History of the Japanese American Detention Camps.* New York: Random House, 1984.

The Butterfly
by Pavel Friedmann, 1942

During World War II over twelve million people died in Nazi concentration camps in Europe. Approximately half of this number were Jews. Prisoners in the concentration camps suffered greatly. Large numbers of those who were not killed outright by the Nazis died from starvation, disease, and overwork. Many of the victims were young children. In Terezín, Czechoslovakia, some of these children recorded their thoughts and feelings in poems and drawings before their deaths. "The Butterfly" was written by a young boy named Pavel Friedmann. What does the butterfly represent to him?

The last, the very last,
So richly, brightly, dazzlingly yellow.
Perhaps if the sun's tears would sing
against a white stone...

Such, such a yellow
Is carried lightly 'way up high.
It went away I'm sure because it wished to
kiss the world goodbye.

For seven weeks I've lived in here,
Penned up inside this **ghetto**
But I have found my people here.
The dandelions call to me
And the white chestnut candles in the court.
Only I never saw another butterfly.

ghetto: area where members of minority groups are forced to live

That butterfly was the last one.
Butterflies don't live in here,
In the ghetto.

Only 100 of the 15,000 children in Terezín survived the war. The writings and drawings of the Terezín children have been published in a book called I Never Saw Another Butterfly, *which takes its title from Pavel Friedmann's poem.*

Source: *I Never Saw Another Butterfly: Children's Drawings and Poems from Terezín Concentration Camp,* 1942-1944. New York: Schocken Books, 1978.

Ich Bin Ein Berliner

by John F. Kennedy, 1963

In 1963 when President John F. Kennedy visited West Berlin, West Germany, he delivered a speech in front of the Berlin Wall, which had been erected by East Germany in 1961 to stop the flow of East Germans to West Germany. What had begun as a simple barbed wire barrier became a massive concrete wall patrolled by armed guards. The Berlin Wall soon became a symbol of the Cold War. What did President Kennedy mean in this excerpt from his speech when he said, "I am a Berliner"?

There are many people in the world who really don't understand, or say they don't, what is the great issue between the free world and the Communist world. Let them come to Berlin. There are some who say that Communism is the wave of the future. Let them come to Berlin. And there are some who say in Europe and elsewhere we can work with the Communists. Let them come to Berlin. And there are even a few who say that it is true that Communism is an evil system, but it permits us to make economic progress. **"Lasst sie nach Berlin kommen."**

Lasst sie nach Berlin kommen: German for "Let them come to Berlin"

Freedom has many difficulties and democracy is not perfect, but we have never had to put a wall up to keep our people in, to prevent them from leaving us. I want to say, on behalf of my countrymen, who live many miles away on the other side of the Atlantic, who are far distant from you, that they take the greatest pride that they have been able to share with you, even from a distance, the story of the last eighteen years. I know of no town, no city, that has been **besieged** for **eighteen years** that still lives with the vitality and the force, and the hope and the determination of the city of West Berlin. While the wall is the most obvious and vivid demonstration of the failures of the Communist system, for all the world to see, we take no satisfaction in it, for it is an offense not only against history but an offense against humanity, separating families, dividing husbands and wives and brothers and sisters, and dividing a people who wish to be joined together.... Freedom is **indivisible**, and when one man is enslaved, all are not free. When all are free, then we can look forward to that day when this city will be joined as one—and this country, and this great continent of Europe—in a peaceful and hopeful glow. When that day finally comes, as it will, the people of West Berlin can take **sober** satisfaction in the fact that they were in the **front lines** for almost two decades.

besieged: surrounded by military forces

eighteen years: since the end of World War II, in 1945

indivisible: not able to be divided

sober: serious

front lines: being as close as possible to an enemy

All free men, wherever they may live, are citizens of Berlin, and, therefore, as a free man, I take pride in the words **"Ich bin ein Berliner."**

Ich bin ein Berliner: German for "I am a citizen of Berlin"

On page 189 you can read an account of the tearing down of the Berlin Wall, 28 years after President Kennedy delivered his speech.

Source: Diane Ravitch, ed., *The American Reader: Words That Moved a Nation.* New York: HarperCollins Publishers, 1990.

My Day

by Eleanor Roosevelt, 1942

Eleanor Roosevelt was a First Lady who took an active role in her husband's Presidency. Throughout the Depression she traveled all over the United States, maintaining the connection between our government and its citizens. During World War II she visited Great Britain, where she praised the spirit of the people who were enduring great hardships, such as the bombing of their cities by Germany and shortages of food and other supplies. Below is a description of this visit that appeared in her popular newspaper column, "My Day." Why do you think Eleanor Roosevelt visited Great Britain?

London, November 18—On Sunday morning, church bells all over Great Britain pealed to celebrate the victory in Africa and also to remind all God-fearing people of their duty to give thanks to Him whose power is greater than that of mere human beings. I had some guests for breakfast and one or two callers before and after the church hour.

I want to thank again the many people whose thought and planning made it possible for me to see so much in such a short time. Our own people in the Embassy, Army, Navy and the Air Force have given me every possible cooperation. Without their thoughtfulness and careful arranging of the many trips, it would have been impossible to accomplish the things I did.

If it were only the spirit of the people of this country, which one feels everywhere here, I should feel grateful for having experienced it. There is something contagious about an enthusiasm which makes you work ten hours a day uncomplainingly, which carries you through three winters of blackout, which makes light of the losses brought about through bombing and which still has the enthusiasm left to welcome new allies. I think that my faith in the goodness and strength of human beings has been greatly enhanced, and that is something for which I am deeply grateful.

Many people felt that Eleanor Roosevelt was an extra set of "eyes and ears" for FDR. Her newspaper column had millions of readers who were interested in her travels and her opinions about issues that were of common concern. After her husband's death in 1945, she served as a delegate to the United Nations and remained active in the fight for equal rights.

Source: Rochelle Chadakoff, ed., *Eleanor Roosevelt's "My Day": Her Acclaimed Columns, 1936–1945*. New York: Pharos Books, 1989.

Faith that Moved a Dump Heap

by Mary McLeod Bethune, 1941

In the early 1900s education opened up new opportunities for many people in the United States. In the South, however, several states denied African Americans the right to attend the same schools as white students. Few public schools for blacks existed so African Americans had to build schools of their own. As the following magazine article written in 1941 by educator Mary McLeod Bethune (1875-1955) shows, building a school required much hard work—especially if the only place available to build was on a garbage dump! How does Bethune's will and determination lead her to succeed? How does she manage to get help from others?

I was born in Maysville, South Carolina, a country town in the midst of rice and cotton fields. . . . Mother worked in the fields at Father's side, cutting rice and cotton, and chopping **fodder**. Each of us children had tasks to perform, according to our **aptitudes**. Some milked the cows, others helped with the washing, ironing, cooking, and house-cleaning. I was my father's champion cotton picker. When I was only nine, I could pick 250 pounds [93 kg] of cotton a day. . . .

fodder: food for animals
aptitudes: abilities

[Back then] it was almost impossible for a Negro child, especially in the South, to get [an] education. There were hundreds of square miles, sometimes entire states, without a single Negro school, and colored children were not allowed in public schools with white children. . . .

A knock on our door changed my life over-night. There stood a young woman, a colored missionary sent by the Northern Presbyterian Church to start a school near by. She asked my parents to send me. Every morning I picked up a little pail of milk and bread, and walked five miles [8 km] to school; every afternoon, five miles [8 km] home. . . .

By the time I was fifteen I had taken every subject taught at our little school and could go no farther. . . . I used to kneel in the cotton fields and pray that the door of opportunity should be opened to me once more. . . . My prayers were answered. A white dressmaker . . . had become interested in the work of our little neighborhood school and had offered to pay for the higher education of some worthy girl. My teacher selected me, and I was sent to Scotia Seminary in Concord, North Carolina. . . . When I was graduated, I . . . [received] another scholarship, and I spent two years at the Moody Bible School, in Chicago. . . .

In 1904 I [went to]. . . Daytona Beach, a beautiful little village, shaded by great oaks and giant pines. . . . I found a shabby four-room cottage, for which the owner wanted a rental of eleven dollars a month. My total **capital** was a dollar and a half, but I talked him into trusting me until the end of the month for the rest. This was in September. A friend let me stay at her home, and I plunged into the job of creating something from nothing. I spoke at churches, and the ministers let me take up collections. . . .

capital: funds

On October 3, 1904, I opened the doors of my school, with an enrollment of five little girls, aged from eight to twelve, whose parents paid me fifty cents' weekly **tuition**. My own child was the only boy in the school. Though I hadn't a penny left, I considered cash money as the smallest part of my resources. I had faith in a loving God, faith in myself, and a desire to serve. . . .

tuition: cost of schooling

We burned logs and used the **charred** splinters as pencils, and mashed elderberries for ink. I begged strangers for a broom, a lamp, a bit of **cretonne** to put around the packing case which served as my desk. I haunted the city dump and the trash piles behind hotels, **retrieving discarded** linen and kitchenware, cracked dishes, broken chairs, pieces of old lumber. Everything was **scoured** and mended. . . . As parents began gradually to leave their children overnight, I had to provide sleeping **accommodations**. I took corn sacks for mattresses. Then I picked Spanish moss from trees, dried and cured it, and used it as a substitute for mattress hair.

charred: burnt

cretonne: cotton cloth

retrieving: finding
discarded: thrown-out
scoured: scrubbed and cleaned
accommodations: places to sleep

The school expanded fast. In less than two years I had 250 pupils. In desperation I hired a large hall next to my original little cottage, and used it as a combined **dormitory** and classroom. I concentrated more and more on girls, as I felt that they especially were **hampered** by lack of educational opportunities. . . .

dormitory: building for students to live in
hampered: kept back

I had many volunteer workers and a few regular teachers, who were paid from fifteen to twenty-five dollars a month and **board**. I was supposed to keep the balance of the funds for my own pocket, but there was never any balance—only a yawning hole. I wore old clothes sent me by **mission boards**, recut and redesigned for me in our dress-making classes. At last I saw that our only solution was to stop renting space, and to buy and build our own college.

board: meals

mission boards: religious organizations

Near by was a field . . . which was used as a dumping ground. I approached the owner, determined to buy it. The price was $250. In a daze, he finally agreed to take five dollars down, and the balance in two years. I promised to be back in a few days with the **initial** payment. He never knew it, but I didn't have five dollars. I raised this sum selling ice cream and sweet-potato pies to the workmen on construction jobs, and I took the owner his money in small change wrapped in my handkerchief.

initial: first

That's how the Bethune-Cookman college campus started. . . . But what use was a plot [of land] without a building?. . . I went to all the carpenters, mechanics, and plasterers in town, pleading with them to contribute a few hours' work in the evening in exchange for sandwiches and tuition for their children and themselves.

Slowly the building rose from its foundations. The name over the entrance still reads Faith Hall.

I had learned already that one of my most important jobs was to be a good beggar! I rang doorbells and tackled cold prospects without a lead. I wrote articles for whoever would print them, distributed leaflets, rode **interminable** miles of dusty roads on my old bicycle; invaded churches, clubs, lodges, **chambers of commerce**. . . .

Strongly **interracial** in my ideas, I looked forward to an advisory board of **trustees** composed of both white and colored people. . . .

Do you wonder I have faith?

I never stop to plan. I take things step by step. For thirty-five years we have never had to close our doors for lack of food or fuel, although often we had to live from day to day. . . .

As the school expanded, whenever I saw a need for some training or service we did not supply, I **schemed** to add it to our **curriculum**. Sometimes that took years. When I came to Florida, there were no hospitals where a Negro could go. A student became **critically** ill . . . so I went to a local hospital and begged a white **physician** to take her in and operate. My pleas were so desperate he finally agreed. A few days after the operation, I visited my pupil.

When I appeared at the front door of the hospital, the nurse ordered me around to the back way. I **thrust** her aside—and found my little girl segregated in a corner of the porch behind the kitchen. Even my toes clenched with rage.

That decided me. I called on three of my faithful friends, asking them to buy a little cottage behind our school as a hospital. They agreed, and we started with two beds.

From this humble start grew a fully equipped twenty-bed hospital—our college **infirmary** and a refuge for the needy throughout the state. It was staffed by white and black physicians and by our own student nurses. . . .

When I [now] walk through the campus, with its stately palms and well-kept lawns, and think back to the dump-heap foundation, I rub my eyes and pinch myself. And I remember my childish visions in the cotton fields.

interminable: endless

chambers of commerce: groups of local business leaders

interracial: believing in whites and blacks working together

trustees: directors

schemed: planned

curriculum: course of study

critically: seriously

physician: doctor

thrust: moved

infirmary: medical clinic

A great speaker and organizer, Mary McLeod Bethune helped register African American women to vote in the 1920s and founded the National Council of Negro Women in 1935. For many years she worked for the federal government, tirelessly fighting for equal rights for African Americans in education, the workplace, and government. Bethune-Cookman College, the school she founded on a "dump heap," remains open today, a testament to her spirit and determination.

Source: Mary McLeod Bethune, "Faith that Moved a Dump Heap," *Who, The Magazine About People,* Volume 1, June 1941.

We Shall Overcome
Freedom Song, 1901

The civil rights movement has inspired a wealth of music and other forms of artistic expression. The song "We Shall Overcome" was originally composed as a Baptist hymn in 1901. Some 45 years later, the song became popular with African American tobacco workers in Charleston, South Carolina. Over the years it has become the anthem of civil rights movements from the United States to China. It was sung with great emotion at the civil rights movement's March on Washington, which took place on August 28, 1963. On that day Martin Luther King, Jr., gave the speech now remembered as "I Have a Dream." What message does the song convey?

2. We'll walk hand in hand, etc.   5. We are not alone, etc.

3. We shall live in peace, etc.   6. We shall build a new world, etc.

4. We shall all be free, etc.   7. We are not afraid, etc.

Many other folk songs carry a message similar to that of "We Shall Overcome." Can you name any?

Source: Kathleen Krull, *Gonna Sing My Head Off!: American Folk Songs for Children*. New York: Alfred K. Knopf, Inc., 1992.

176

I Have a Dream

by Martin Luther King, Jr., 1963

During the first half of the 1900s, segregation existed throughout the South. Discrimination against African Americans also existed in other parts of the United States. In the 1950s, however, African Americans began organizing for an end to segregation laws and for equal rights for all Americans. One of the leaders of this growing civil rights movement, which included both blacks and whites, was Dr. Martin Luther King, Jr. (1929–1968). King was a powerful speaker whose voice stirred people's hearts. On August 28, 1963, King delivered a speech to a crowd of 250,000 people who had gathered at the Lincoln Memorial in Washington, D.C., to urge Congress to pass a strong civil rights law. As you read King's speech, notice how he often uses forceful words and images to get across his ideas. How do these words and images help you to see both the problems King identifies and the goals he hopes the civil rights movement will achieve? How does King urge his listeners to struggle for equal rights?

Five score years ago, a great American, in whose symbolic shadow we stand, signed the **Emancipation Proclamation**. This **momentous decree** came as a great beacon light of hope to millions of Negro slaves who had been **seared** in the flames of withering injustice. It came as a joyous daybreak to end the long night of **captivity**.

But one hundred years later, we must face the tragic fact that the Negro is still not free. One hundred years later, the life of the Negro is still sadly crippled by the **manacles** of segregation and the chains of discrimination. One hundred years later, the Negro lives on a lonely island of poverty in the midst of a vast ocean of material **prosperity**. One hundred years later, the Negro is still **languishing** in the corners of American society and finds himself an **exile** in his own land. So we have come here today to dramatize an **appalling** condition.

In a sense we have come to our nation's capital to cash a check. When the architects of our republic wrote the magnificent words of the Constitution and the Declaration of Independence, they were signing a **promissory note** to which every American was to **fall heir**. This note was a promise that all men would be guaranteed the inalienable rights of life, liberty, and the pursuit of happiness.

five score: 100
Emancipation Proclamation: order signed by Abraham Lincoln in 1863 banning slavery in Confederate states
momentous decree: important order
seared: burned
captivity: enslavement
manacles: chains

prosperity: wealth
languishing: being neglected
exile: stranger
appalling: terrible

promissory note: promise to be repaid later
fall heir: be entitled to

177

It is obvious today that America has **defaulted on** this promissory note insofar as her citizens of color are concerned. Instead of honoring this sacred **obligation**, America has given the Negro people a bad check; a check which has come back marked "**insufficient** funds." But we refuse to believe that the bank of justice is **bankrupt**. We refuse to believe that there are insufficient funds in the great vaults of opportunity of this nation. So we have come to cash this check—a check that will give us upon demand the riches of freedom and the security of justice. We have also come to this **hallowed** spot to remind America of the fierce urgency of now. This is no time to engage in the luxury of cooling off or to take the **tranquilizing** drug of **gradualism**. *Now* is the time to rise from the dark and **desolate** valley of segregation to the sunlit path of racial justice. *Now* is the time to open the doors of opportunity to all of God's children. *Now* is the time to lift our nation from the quicksands of racial injustice to the solid rock of brotherhood.

It would be fatal for the nation to overlook the urgency of the moment and to underestimate the determination of the Negro. This sweltering summer of the Negro's **legitimate** discontent will not pass until there is an **invigorating** autumn of freedom and equality. Nineteen sixty-three is not an end, but a beginning. Those who hope that the Negro needed to blow off steam and will now be content will have a rude awakening if the nation returns to business as usual. There will be neither rest nor **tranquility** in America until the Negro is granted his citizenship rights. The whirlwinds of revolt will continue to shake the foundations of our nation until the bright day of justice emerges.

But there is something that I must say to my people who stand on the warm **threshold** which leads into the palace of justice. In the process of gaining our rightful place we must not be guilty of wrongful deeds. Let us not seek to satisfy our thirst for freedom by drinking from the cup of bitterness and hatred.

We must forever conduct our struggle on the high plane of dignity and discipline. We must not allow our creative protest to **degenerate** into physical violence. Again and again we must rise to the **majestic** heights of meeting physical force with soul force. The marvelous new **militancy** which has engulfed the Negro

defaulted on: failed to pay

obligation: promise

insufficient: not enough

bankrupt: empty

hallowed: sacred

tranquilizing: calming
gradualism: slowness
desolate: barren

legitimate: rightful
invigorating: lively; filled with energy

tranquility: peace

threshold: entrance

degenerate: break down
majestic: grand; glorious
militancy: fighting spirit

community must not lead us to distrust of all white people, for many of our white brothers, as **evidenced** by their presence here today, have come to realize that their **destiny** is tied up with our destiny and their freedom is **inextricably** bound to our freedom. We cannot walk alone.

And as we walk, we must make the pledge that we shall march ahead. We cannot turn back. There are those who are asking the **devotees** of civil rights, "When will you be satisfied?" We can never be satisfied as long as the Negro is the victim of unspeakable horrors of police **brutality**. We can never be satisfied as long as our bodies, heavy with the **fatigue** of travel, cannot gain lodging in the motels of the highways and the hotels of the cities. We cannot be satisfied as long as the Negro's basic **mobility** is from a smaller **ghetto** to a larger one. We can never be satisfied as long as a Negro in Mississippi cannot vote and a Negro in New York believes he has nothing for which to vote. No, no, we are not satisfied, and we will not be satisfied until justice rolls down like waters and righteousness like a mighty stream.

I am not unmindful that some of you have come here out of great **trials and tribulations**. Some of you have come fresh from narrow cells. Some of you have come from areas where your **quest** for freedom left you battered by the storms of **persecution** and staggered by the winds of police brutality. You have been the veterans of creative suffering. Continue to work with the faith that unearned suffering is **redemptive**.

Go back to Mississippi, go back to Alabama, go back to Georgia, go back to Louisiana, go back to the slums and ghettos of our northern cities, knowing that somehow this situation can and will be changed. Let us not **wallow** in the valley of despair.

I say to you today, my friends, that in spite of the difficulties and frustrations of the moment, I still have a dream. It is a dream deeply rooted in the American dream.

I have a dream that one day this nation will rise up and live out the true meaning of its **creed**: "We hold these truths to be self-evident: that all men are created equal."

I have a dream that one day on the red hills of Georgia the sons of former slaves and the sons of former slaveowners will be able to sit down together at the table of brotherhood.

I have a dream that one day even the state of Mississippi, a desert state, sweltering with the heat of injustice and oppression, will be transformed into an **oasis** of freedom and justice.

I have a dream that my four little children will one day live in a nation where they will not be judged by the color of their skin but by the content of their character.

I have a dream today.

I have a dream that one day the state of Alabama, whose governor's lips are presently dripping with the words of **interposition and nullification**, will be transformed into a situation where little

evidenced: shown
destiny: future
inextricably: inseparably

devotees: supporters

brutality: cruel violence
fatigue: tiredness

mobility: movement
ghetto: poor, segregated section of a city

trials and tribulations: sufferings and troubles
quest: search
persecution: unfair treatment

redemptive: of value; worthwhile

wallow: rest; remain helpless

creed: stated belief

oasis: safe place

interposition and nullification: opposition to integration and the federal government black boys and black girls will be able to join hands with little white boys and white girls and walk together as sisters and brothers.

I have a dream today.

I have a dream that one day every valley shall be **exalted**, every hill and mountain shall be made low, the rough places will be made plain, and the crooked places will be made straight, and the glory of the Lord shall be revealed, and all **flesh** shall see it together.

This is our hope. This is the faith with which I return to the South. With this faith we will be able to **hew** out of the mountain of despair a stone of hope. With this faith we will be able to transform the **jangling discords** of our nation into a beautiful symphony of brotherhood. With this faith we will be able to work together, to pray together, to struggle together, to go to jail together, to stand up for freedom together, knowing that we will be free one day.

This will be the day when all of God's children will be able to sing with a new meaning, "My country, 'tis of thee, sweet land of liberty, of thee I sing. Land where my fathers died, land of the pilgrim's pride, from every mountainside, let freedom ring."

And if America is to be a great nation this must become true. So let freedom ring from the **prodigious** hilltops of New Hampshire. Let freedom ring from the mighty mountains of New York. Let freedom ring from the heightening Alleghenies of Pennsylvania!

Let freedom ring from the snowcapped Rockies of Colorado!

Let freedom ring from the **curvaceous** peaks of California!

But not only that; let freedom ring from Stone Mountain of Georgia!

Let freedom ring from Lookout Mountain of Tennessee!

Let freedom ring from every hill and molehill of Mississippi. From every mountainside, let freedom ring.

When we let freedom ring, when we let it ring from every village and every **hamlet**, from every state and every city, we will be able to speed up that day when all of God's children, black men and white men, Jews and Gentiles, Protestants and Catholics, will be able to join hands and sing in the words of the old Negro spiritual, "Free at last! free at last! thank God Almighty, we are free at last!"

exalted: raised

flesh: people

hew: carve

jangling discords: angry sounds and disagreements

prodigious: great

curvaceous: curving

hamlet: small town

Soon after Dr. Martin Luther King, Jr., delivered this speech in 1963, Congress passed two of the strongest civil rights laws in American history. Ongoing work by people in the civil rights movement helped end many segregation laws in the South during the 1960s. King continued leading marches and speaking out for the equality of all people until 1968, when he was murdered. His dream for a better and fairer America lives on.

Source: Martin Luther King, Jr., "I Have a Dream," 1963.

César Chávez

by Consuelo Rodriguez, 1991

César Chávez (1927–1993) fought for many years to end the use of dangerous pesticides that harm farm workers and the environment. In the 1960s Chávez led a major battle to improve the health and lives of migrant farm workers in California. These workers, many of them Mexican Americans, are people who move from harvest to harvest with the seasons to pick crops. Many migrant farm workers lack healthcare, work long hours, and receive very low wages. In 1962 Chávez formed a labor union to fight for better pay and safer working conditions, including protection from pesticides. In 1965 grape pickers in the union went on strike against the grape growers in California. The strike began peacefully, but three years later violence broke out, and some workers feared the strike would fail. Then in 1968 Chávez did something bold to stop the violence and inspire the workers. To find out what Chávez did, read the excerpt below from a biography about the union leader. How do Chávez's ideas and goals compare with those of Martin Luther King, Jr., and the civil rights movement?

On March 10, 1968, 4,000 people filled a county park in Delano, California. Most of them were farm workers: Mexican Americans, Mexicans, Puerto Ricans, Filipinos, blacks, southern whites. Since 1965, they had been on strike against California's grape growers. But they had not come to the park to attend a meeting of their union, the United Farm Workers Organizing Committee (UFWOC). They had come to attend a **mass**. A **makeshift** altar had been set up on a flatbed truck in the center of the park, and a Catholic priest was preparing to offer **Holy Communion**. Rabbis and Protestant ministers were also on hand to participate.

mass: Catholic religious service

makeshift: quickly built

Holy Communion: main part of the mass

The center of attention was a small man bundled in a hooded parka. He was seated on a chair in front of the altar with his wife and children. Though only 41 years old, he had needed 2 men to help him to his seat. His supporters, seeing his weakness and his **gauntness**, were deeply concerned for his life. The man was César Chávez, leader of the farm workers' union, and he had not eaten for 25 days.

gauntness: thinness

Why had Chávez willfully placed himself near death? Why had he **steadfastly** refused to touch food while his weight plunged from 175 to 140 pounds? Even some of those who had worked with him closely were confused and disturbed. They wondered if Chávez was merely trying to call attention to himself, trying in effect to **martyr himself**. Others who shared Chávez's political goals but not his religious faith were put off by the **mystical** element of the **fast** and the involvement of the **clergy**. The grape growers, locked in a bitter struggle with the UFWOC, considered Chávez's fast nothing more than a publicity stunt designed to **elicit** sympathy from the American public. But those who knew Chávez best—those who had worked with him to build a union from the ground up—knew

steadfastly: firmly

martyr himself: sacrifice his life for a cause

mystical: spiritual

fast: not eating

clergy: religious leaders

elicit: bring out

that everything he did was directed toward a single purpose: to better the lot of the American farm worker.

The farm workers had begun their strike in 1965, refusing to labor in the **vineyards** of California's grape growers. Though farm workers had struck in the past, few of the strikes had ever been successful. The growers, with the local politicians and the police on their side, had almost always beaten down the strikers. Chávez, the son of **migrant workers**, knew this history well. He was totally committed to the philosophy of nonviolence, which had been applied successfully in the Deep South by black civil rights **activists**. As the leader of the farm workers, Chávez was determined to use these **tactics** against the grape growers. He saw no other way to win the strike. "If we had used violence," he told the writer Peter Matthiessen, "we would have won contracts long ago, but they wouldn't be lasting, because we wouldn't have won respect."

Chávez emphasized his belief in nonviolence at many union meetings, but he may have expressed himself most **eloquently** in a letter to the American Farm Bureau Federation, a growers' association: "If to build our union required the deliberate taking of life, either the life of a grower or his child or the life of a farm worker or his child then I would choose not to see the union built.... We hate the **agribusiness** system that seeks to keep us enslaved, and we shall overcome and change it not by **retaliation** or bloodshed, but by a determined nonviolent struggle carried on by those masses of farm workers who intend to be free and human."

Chávez's approach yielded dramatic results. The **picketing** of the fields, a nationwide boycott of California grapes, and skillful use of the **mass media** won the farm workers the sympathy of the nation and pressured several large growers into signing contracts with the union. But the growers were a **tenacious** group who had never before given in to a union. They fought back with threats, violence, court orders, and **maneuvers** such as using different labels on their boxes to **evade** the boycott. With pressures on the union mounting, it became harder and harder for Chávez to restrain those members of his union who wanted to destroy the growers' property or beat up strikebreakers. As the violence began to break out, he knew he had to put an end to it. As Chávez described it to journalist Jacques Levy several years later: "I thought I had to bring the Movement to a halt, to do something that would force them and me to deal with the whole question of violence and ourselves. We had to stop long enough to take account of what we were doing....So I stopped eating."...

Finally, [after almost a month,] at the urging of his doctor, Chávez ended his fast. On the flatbed truck, he prepared to receive bread from the Reverend C. Wayne Hartmire, one of the many local clergy who supported the farm workers' cause. It was an emotional moment for the farm workers, intensified still more by

vineyards: grape fields

migrant workers: farm workers who move from harvest to harvest
activists: people who work for a cause
tactics: methods

eloquently: clearly and beautifully

agribusiness: agricultural big business
retaliation: getting even

picketing: marching with signs of protest
mass media: newspapers, television, and radio
tenacious: strong, stubborn
maneuvers: tricks
evade: avoid

the presence of Senator Robert F. Kennedy of New York. Kennedy, having heard that Chávez was ending his fast, had **chartered** a plane in Los Angeles and arrived in Delano to be present. The crowd was so **enthused** at the sight of him that he could barely make his way to the flatbed without being swept off his feet. Five years after the assassination of his brother President John F. Kennedy, Robert Kennedy was considering a bid for the presidency in the 1968 election. He had gained a reputation as a champion of America's poor and had come out in favor of the farm workers' struggle in Delano as early as 1966. During the fast, Kennedy had sent Chávez a telegram of support. Now he had come to take part in the Holy Communion, in this case by means of the *semita*, or poor man's bread, in accordance with the Mexican ritual.

chartered: hired
enthused: excited

In front of the television cameras, Kennedy gave César Chávez a piece of bread. Then, in the Boston accent which his brother had made familiar to the nation years before, he delivered a simple message: "The world must know that the migrant farm worker, the Mexican American, is coming into his own right."...

The next to speak was the Reverend Jim Drake. He had been a friend and ally of Chávez's from the very beginning of the union struggle. Drake read a speech that César Chávez had penned earlier that day:

"Our struggle is not easy. Those who oppose our cause are rich and powerful, and they have many allies in high places.

"We are poor. Our allies are few. But we have something the rich do not own.

"We have our own bodies and spirits and [the] justice of our cause as our weapons.

"When we are honest with outselves, we must admit that our lives are all that really belong to us. So it is how we use our lives that determines what kind of men we are. It is my deepest belief that only by giving our lives do we find life.

"I am convinced that the truest act of courage, the strongest act of manliness, is to sacrifice ourselves for others in a totally nonviolent struggle for justice. To be a man is to suffer for others. God help us to be men!"

César Chávez's fast in 1968 marked a turning point in the farm workers' strike. The violence ended, and more people began to support the union's cause. Finally, in 1970, the farm workers won the strike and gained better wages and health insurance. They also gained protection from the use of pesticides. Chávez and the farm workers' union have played a leading role in alerting Americans to the dangers of pesticides and pollution.

Source: Consuelo Rodrigues, *César Chávez*. New York: Chelsea House Publishers, 1991.

Charlie Pippin

by Candy Dawson Boyd, 1987

United States involvement in the Vietnam War dragged on for many years. More than 58,000 Americans died in the war. The men and women who survived saw many of their friends die in battle. When Vietnam veterans returned home to a county still divided over the war, many tried to forget the fighting and the pain it had caused. The selection below is from Candy Dawson Boyd's novel Charlie Pippin. Charlie is an 11-year-old girl whose father and uncle both fought in the Vietnam War. Charlie's father is a short-tempered man who refuses to talk about the war. When he fails to answer Charlie's questions, she sets out to learn as much about the Vietnam War as possible. Charlie finds out that two of her father's best friends, Fred Hansen and Gerald Moer, were killed in battle. In the following scene Charlie, her uncle Ben, and her aunt Jessie visit the Vietnam Veterans Memorial in Washington, D.C. The names of all the Americans who died in the war are engraved on the walls of this memorial. As you read this excerpt, notice what gift Charlie seeks to bring home to her father. How does she react to the memorial?

The moment Aunt Jessie had parked, Charlie leaped eagerly from the car. Ahead of her, on a mound of winter grass, Charlie saw a tent, a stand, a sign, and flags flapping in the wind. Blown-up photographs of men were hung on wooden racks near the flags. She walked over and read the large sign: VETERAN'S **VIGIL** OF HONOR. Below that were the words *You Are an American. Your voice can make the difference.* Charlie recognized the initials POW MIA. **Prisoners of War. Missing in Action.** Then she saw pamphlets, buttons, and other items about POWs and MIAs at the stand.

vigil: watch

"Uncle Ben, that stands for the soldiers some people believe are in prison in Vietnam or dead, but the Vietnam government won't give us back their bodies. Right?" she asked, snapping two pictures.

Prisoners of War: captured soldiers some believe are still in Vietnam

Missing in Action: soldiers whose whereabouts are unknown

He nodded, "Charlie, please don't take any of me. I don't feel like posing for pictures today."

"Okay, I won't."

"Ben, you want to go on? Charlie and I will wait for you," said Aunt Jessie.

He nodded again. Charlie recognized the distant, **mournful** expression in his eyes. She knew he had friends on the wall, just as Daddy did.

mournful: sad

184

"Sure, Jess. This is something I have to do." He started walking up the mound to a path to the left.

"Charlie, let him alone," Aunt Jessie said.

"No, Aunt Jessie. I have to go, too!" And Charlie ran after her uncle, grabbing his hand. "That's why I came!" Her aunt followed.

There were other people on the long, curved path, some with small children. To her left, Charlie saw a Black family, the father, mother, and two children. One girl was about her age. An older white man huddled around a wooden stand. Charlie waited with her aunt and uncle while the family turned the pages of a book, then moved away. The **elderly** man did the same.

Charlie read the title of the large book, *Directory of Names*. From her research, she knew that in this book were the names of all of the women and men who had died or were listed as missing in action during the Vietnam War. That included the first deaths in 1959 and the last deaths in 1975. It was a thick book with many single-spaced pages.

Uncle Ben took a piece of crumpled paper out of his wallet. It looked as if it had been there a long time. The paper was so creased that he had to unfold it slowly.

Aunt Jessie showed her brother how to locate the names of the friends he was seeking. She reached into her purse and handed him a pen. After searching, his finger leading him, he paused, writing down a panel number and a line number. These would tell him exactly where on the 492-foot-long [150-m] granite wall the names of the men he knew were engraved. Then he wrote down two more sets of numbers before giving Charlie the pen.

Charlie found Fred Hansen by the date of his death. Then Gerald Moer. She copied the numbers.

The pathway **meandered** through a parklike setting. Stark, bare trees lined both sides. There was light snowfall on the ground that crunched beneath her boots. Charlie had expected to see the wall immediately, but instead, the path led down a gradual **incline**. To her left, in the distance, she saw the grand **spire** of the Washington Monument.

At last they reached one end of the wall. Charlie remembered that the Vietnam Memorial wall was made of polished black granite. It was V-shaped, with one arm pointed toward the Washington Monument and the other arm aimed at the Lincoln Memorial. She was at the end of the wall that pointed toward the Washington Monument, which explained why she could see the tall spire. The long wall was divided into one hundred and fifty panels, each forty inches wide. On each panel were carved the names of the dead and missing in action. Charlie had to squat down to read the names on the panels at the end. That was because the panels decreased in height from the center of the wall, where they were almost eleven feet [3.4 m] high, to the ends of the wall, where they were only eight inches [.2 m] high.

As the path proceeded downward, toward the center of the V, the panels got taller, until they towered above Charlie. She had to stare up to see the names at the top. The wall was like a huge wide V built into the earth, opening its arms in welcome, **beckoning** her to enter. The black granite panels were so highly polished that she could see her face in them.

beckoning: signaling

Walking along the path, she saw small American flags stuck into the ground below. And taped to a panel was one red, **shriveled** rose.

shriveled: dried up

The Vietnam Memorial was real. Real. Scary. Beautiful. Each time Charlie looked at a panel she saw her face, Uncle Ben, the naked trees and sky. In front of her, a woman paused. Her fingers ran down the wall, counting the small dots on the side of each panel that marked ten rows. Next to her a man and a little girl **fidgeted**. The child was watching the woman. Charlie heard her ask, "What is Mommy looking for, Papa?" And she heard him reply, "The name of someone she loves."

fidgeted: moved nervously

Uncle Ben stopped, his eyes sweeping the panel numbers and letters. "Rows and rows of names," Charlie heard him mutter, shaking his head. "Rows and rows." From her report, she knew how many names were cut into the stone that had been quarried not far from Bangalore, India—58,007 names.

While Uncle Ben's hand searched, Charlie watched. Then, as if a cold wind had swept over him, she saw his body begin to tremble. His fingers touched the letters of a name. Afraid, Charlie stood there, wishing that her aunt were closer. But Aunt Jessie was talking to the couple with the little girl.

His hand moved again, this time down and to the left. It stopped, and this time he froze. Charlie couldn't see her uncle's face. There were other people around them. He stood there a long time. Finally, she touched his arm. Clearly she saw the two of them and the snow on the ground and the dull, cold sky and the faded red rose. And she saw tears streaming down her uncle's face.

He reached out and held her close, his eyes never leaving the panel. Charlie looked up at him. And she knew that he didn't see her. For a second she thought she was standing there with her father, holding him while he cried.

"Were they your best friends, too, Uncle Ben?" she whispered, thinking of Gerald Moer and Fred Hansen. She had to repeat the question twice before he heard her.

"They were my men," he said. He wiped at his face with his free hand, sniffing. From the way he held his body, Charlie realized that he wanted to stay, so she gently **disengaged** herself. She had work to do.

disengaged: freed

A few panels down she discovered the names she sought: Gerald Moer and Fred Hansen. One name was too high for her to touch, but she could see it. Charlie faced her panel.

"Hi, I'm Charlie, Oscar Pippin's daughter," she whispered. "I came to see you. My daddy is fine. I know he still misses you." She took a deep breath and squeezed back the tears. This was not the time to cry. Then she saw the person she needed, the park ranger.

"Mister," Charlie asked, "please make a rubbing of two names for me."

The white-haired man **ambled** over and took a pencil and two strips of white paper out of his coat pocket. Charlie pointed to the names and repeated them while she laid a piece of white paper over each name. Next, he rubbed the pencil over the raised letters underneath the paper. He handed her the first strip, then started on the second. Charlie stared at the elegant, engraved letters. She thanked the ranger when he handed her the second strip. He moved on to help someone else.

ambled: strolled

With care, Charlie took the **origami flower** out of her pocket and wedged the stem into the slight break in the panel midway between the two names. "For you two to remember me and Daddy," she whispered. "And for us to remember you, Fred Hansen and Gerald Moer." Then Charlie bent her head and said a prayer, letting the tears fall. Moments later, she composed herself and took several photographs, making sure to get their names.

origami flower: flower made of beautifully folded paper

"Charlie, you ready? It's getting cold out here," her aunt called. Charlie looked around for her uncle. He was still where she'd left him. . . .

"So many names," Uncle Ben murmured to himself, staring back.

Aunt Jessie whirled around. "That's most of the men of my generation on that wall! And too many sent home torn up, on drugs, or with their hearts and minds messed up! What good are memorials when so many of them need medical help and jobs today? Tell me, Ben!"

Aunt Jessie's bitterness startled Charlie. Gone was the laughter, replaced by anger and sorrow. What surprised Charlie was that Mama never talked like that. Mama just loved Daddy and tried to hold the family together. For the first time, Charlie wondered if her mother shared any of Aunt Jessie's feelings.

Uncle Ben sighed and kissed his sister's cheek. Then he took her arm. "Calm down, Jess. I came home. So did Oscar. A lot of us survived."

Charlie wanted to point back to the wall and say, "They didn't." She remembered her family's happy Thanksgiving dinner. And she thought that for every name on the wall there had been an empty space at some family's table.

Charlie later gives the rubbings to her father, and he begins to tell her about the Vietnam War. The pain caused by the Vietnam War—and the divisions it caused among the American people—still exist today. The Vietnam Veterans Memorial in Washington, D.C., is a powerful monument to the men and women who served and died in the war.

Source: Candy Dawson Boyd, *Charlie Pippin*. New York: Macmillan Publishing Company, 1987.

Goodbye to All That

by Robert Darnton, 1990

The Berlin Wall, which divided the former capital of Germany into East Berlin and West Berlin, was a tangible symbol of the division between the communist regimes of the East and the democratic governments of the West. Until it was torn down in 1989, the wall was heavily guarded, and many people lost their lives trying to escape from the East into the West. Why do you think people in the East felt it was worth risking their lives to escape? The following excerpt was written by a reporter who was an eyewitness to the tearing down of the Berlin Wall.

The destruction of the wall began in the early evening of Thursday 9 November, soon after the first wave of East Berliners, or "Ostlers" as they are called by the West Berliners here, burst upon the West. One Ostler, a young man with a knapsack on his back, somehow hoisted himself up on the wall directly across from the **Brandenburg Gate**. He **sauntered** along the top of it, swinging his arms casually at his sides, a perfect target for the bullets that had felled many other wall jumpers, like Peter Fechter, a young construction worker, who was shot and left to bleed to death a few feet in front of **Checkpoint Charlie** on 17 August 1962. Now, twenty-seven years later, a new generation of border guards took aim and fired—but only with power hoses and without much conviction. The conqueror of the wall continued his promenade, soaked to the skin, until at last the guards gave up. Then he opened his knapsack and poured the water towards the East, in a gesture that seemed to say, "Goodbye to all that."

A few minutes later, hundreds of people, Ostlers and Westlers alike, were on the wall, embracing, exchanging flowers, drinking wine, helping up new "conquerors"—and chipping at the wall itself. By midnight, under a full moon and the glare of the spotlights from the watchtowers in **no-man's-land**, a thousand figures swarmed over the wall, hammering, chiselling, wearing its surface away like a colony of army ants. At the bottom, "conquerors" threw stones at its base or went at it with pickaxes. Long slits appeared, and the light showed through from the East, as if through the eyes of jack-o'-lanterns. On the top, at the centre of the **tumult**, with the Brandenburg Gate looming in the background, an Ostler conducted the destruction, a sickle in one hand, a hammer in the other.

By Saturday, chunks of the wall were circulating through both Berlins. People exchanged them as souvenirs of what had already taken shape in the **collective consciousness** as a historical event: the end of the Cold War.

Brandenburg Gate: large stone gate that is a famous symbol of Berlin

sauntered: walked casually and without worry

Checkpoint Charlie: most famous border inspection place between East and West Berlin

no-man's-land: usually an area between two opposing armies; in this case, an area that the East German government had cleared of buildings so that its guards could more easily spot and catch people trying to escape

tumult: uproar

collective consciousness: group awareness

Soon after the Berlin Wall was torn down, communist governments in East Germany, Poland, Hungary, Czechoslovakia, and Romania were overthrown. The Cold War was well on its way to being over.

Reaching the Moon

from *The New York Times*, 1969

During the 1960s the United States space program made some spectacular achievements. In 1961 the first American astronauts soared high above the planet Earth. Four years later, astronauts left their spacecraft and walked in space! But the most spectacular feat of all occurred on July 20, 1969, when the astronauts of the Apollo 11 spacecraft reported that "the Eagle has landed." These now-famous words meant that we had landed on the moon! On this page is a report on the moon landing from the front page of the New York Times. On the next page is a poem by Pulitzer Prize winner Archibald MacLeish (1892–1982) that also appears on this page from the New York Times. What is MacLeish's response to the moon landing?

From 1969 to 1972 American astronauts landed on the moon six different times. Since then, the United States space program has focused on building reusable space shuttles and on sending rockets carrying scientific equipment to study other planets. What's next for the space program? Some people talk of sending astronauts to visit the planet Mars. This could happen in your lifetime! Even if it does, people will still remember the first moon landing in 1969 as one of the greatest scientific accomplishments of all time.

Source: *The New York Times*, July 21, 1969.

Voyage to the Moon

by Archibald MacLeish, 1969

Presence among us,

    wanderer in our skies,

dazzle of silver in our leaves and on our
waters silver,

    O

silver **evasion** in our farthest thought—
"the visiting moon"…"the glimpses of the moon"…

and we have touched you!

    From the first of time,
before the first of time, before the
first men tasted time, we thought of you.
You were a wonder to us, **unattainable**,
a longing past the reach of longing,
a light beyond our light, our lives—perhaps
a meaning to us…

    Now
our hands have touched you in your depth of night.

Three days and three nights we journeyed,
steered by farthest stars, climbed outward,
crossed the invisible **tide-rip** where the floating dust
falls one way or the other in the void between,
followed that other down, encountered
cold, faced death—**unfathomable** emptiness…

Then, the fourth day evening, we descended,
made fast, set foot at dawn upon your beaches,
sifted between our fingers your cold sand.

We stand here in the dusk, the cold, the silence…

and here, as at the first of time, we lift our heads.
Over us, more beautiful than the moon, a
moon, a wonder to us, unattainable,
a longing past the reach of longing,
a light beyond our light, our lives—perhaps
a meaning to us…

    O, a meaning!

over us on these silent beaches the bright
earth,
    presence among us.

evasion: something avoided

unattainable: unreachable

tide-rip: imaginary place where the moon's tide-pull begins

unfathomable: cannot be understood

INDEX BY *Category*

INDEX BY *Title*

ACKNOWLEDGMENTS

(continued from copyright page)

"The New Colossus" from THE POETRY OF AMERI-CAN WOMEN FROM 1632 TO 1945 edited by Emily Stipes Watt. © 1977 University of Texas Press, Austin, TX.

"Aztec Poetry from Nahuatl Texts" from 2-RABBIT, 7-WIND retold by Toni de Gerez, © 1971 Toni de Gerez. Viking Press, NY.

"How Raven Made the Tides" from NATIVE AMERICAN STORIES retold by Joseph Bruchac. © 1991 Fulcrum Publishing, Golden, CO.

"Yeh-hsien" from THE ORYX MULTICULTURAL FOLK-TALE SERIES: CINDERELLA by Judy Sierra. © 1992 Oryx Press, Phoenix, AZ.

"Timbuktu" by Leo Africanus as quoted in THE PENE-TRATION OF AFRICA by Robin Hallett. © 1965 Frederick A. Praeger, Inc. NY.

"Michelangelo Buonarotti" by Giorgio Vasari as quoted IN VOICES OF THE PAST: READINGS IN MEDIEVAL AND EARLY MODERN HISTORY edited by Hanscom, Hellerman and Posner. © 1965 Frederick A. Praeger, Inc., © 1967 The Macmillan Company, NY.

"Drawings of Roanoke" from AMERICA THE BEAUTI-FUL NORTH CAROLINA by R. Conrad Stein, ©1990, Childrens Press, Chicago; from THE NORTH CAROLI-NA COLONY by William S. Powell, ©1969, Crowell-Collier Press, London; and from NORTH CAROLINA by Eugenia Burney. ©1975 Thomas Nelson Inc., New York.

"A Pilgrim's Journal of Plymouth Plantation" FROM HOMES IN THE WILDERNESS by William Bradford ©1988 Linnet Books, Hamden, CT.

Excerpt from FATHER JUNIPERO SERRA by Ivy Bolton ©1952 Julian Messner, Inc., New York.

"Paul Revere's Ride" by Henry Wadsworth Longfellow from ANTHOLOGY OF AMERICAN POETRY edited by George Gesner, ©1983 Crown Publishers, Inc. Avenel Books, New York.

"Concord Hymn" by Ralph Waldo Emerson from THE AMERICAN TRADITION IN LITERATURE, ©1981, Random House, New York.

Excerpt from COMMON SENSE: THE RIGHTS OF MAN AND OTHER ESSENTIAL WRITINGS OF THOMAS PAINE, ©1984 Meridian, New York.

Excerpt from JOHNNY TREMAIN by Esther Forbes. ©1943 Esther Forbes Hoskins, © renewed 1971 by Linwood Erskine, Jr., executor of estate. Cornerstone Books.

"Song of Marion's Men" by William Cullen Bryant from ANTHOLOGY OF AMERICAN POETRY edited by George Gesner. ©1983 Crown Publishers, Inc., Avenel Books, New York.

"Washington's Farewell to His Officers" from MEMOIR OF COLONEL BENJAMIN TALLMADGE. ©1968 Arno Press, Inc. The New York Times & Arno Press, NY.

Excerpt from SHH! WE'RE WRITING THE CONSTITU-TION by Jean Fritz. ©1987 G.P. Putnam's Sons, New York.

Excerpt from THE FEDERALIST PAPERS by James Madison, Alexander Hamilton, John Jay. ©1961 NAL Penguin.

Excerpt from JOURNALS OF LEWIS AND CLARK, 1805. ©1964 John Bakeless. New American Library.

"Farewell Address" by Andrew Jackson from THE PRIN-CIPLES OF AMERICAN STATESMANSHIP edited by Francis Newton Thorpe. ©1909. The Tandy-Thomas Company, NY.

"Last Appeal for Aid" by William Travis from DOCU-MENTS OF TEXAS HISTORY. ©1994 State House Press. Austin, TX.

"Follow the Drinking Gourd" words and music by Paul Campbell TRO–©1951 and renewed ©1979 Folkways Music Publishers, Inc., New York, NY.

Excerpt from "The Declaration of Sentiments and Resolutions" as quoted in THE AMERICAN READER. Diane Ravitch, ed. ©1990 HarperCollins Publishers, New York.

"Oppositions to Women's Rights" by the New York Herald, as quoted in A CENTURY OF STRUGGLE by Eleanor Fixler. ©1959, 1968, 1972 Atheneum, New York.

Excerpt from UNCLE TOM'S CABIN by Harriet Beecher Stowe (1852). ©1981 NAL, New York.

From MR. LINCOLN'S CAMERA MAN, MATHEW B. BRADY edited by Roy Meredith. ©1974 Dover Publications, New York.

"The Emancipation Proclamation" by Abraham Lincoln, as quoted in the WORLD BOOK ENCYCLOPEDIA, Vol. 6. ©1993 World Book Inc.

"O Captain! My Captain!" by Walt Whitman from ANTHOLOGY OF AMERICAN POETRY edited by George Gesner. ©1983 Crown Publishers Avenel Books, New York.

TEACHING Strategies

Teachers share a common goal—to help their students become successful learners who can understand, remember, and apply important knowledge and skills. This important goal is best supported when students are offered a variety of ways in which to learn.

The Social Studies Anthology offers you the rich and varied tools that you need to help your students learn. It includes such diverse sources as diaries, poems, songs, stories, legends, plays, and posters — all of which draw students into the sights and sounds of the places and times they are studying.

You may invite students to explore the Anthology selections in many unique ways— rewriting documents in another genre, dramatizing the selection, creating posters or collages, or writing original poems, stories, and songs. We have provided a strategy for teaching each selection in the Anthology. But these strategies, of course, are only suggestions. You should feel free to teach the selections in any way that you feel is best suited for your own classroom.

A Cassette accompanies the Social Studies Anthology and provides additional support in teaching the documents. Sometimes the recordings reproduce the voices of the people who wrote the selections. A Cassette logo lets you know which selections have been recorded.

THE NEW COLOSSUS
by Emma Lazarus, 1883
Page 2 📼

Use with Chapter 1, Lesson 1

Objectives

☐ *Recognize how Lazarus's poem helped make the Statue of Liberty a symbol of the United States' commitment to welcoming immigrants.*

☐ *Create a monument about an ideal that is worth honoring.*

Background Information

The Colossus, a huge statue that stood outside the ancient Greek city of Rhodes, was built to celebrate Rhodes's victory in a war. It was made to look like Helios, the god of the sun.

Creating a Monument

After describing what the Greek Colossus was, play the recording of Lazarus's poem on the cassette and have students read along with it. Then ask the following questions. *How are the Statue of Liberty and the "brazen giant of Greek fame" alike?* (Both were built to commemorate an important concept or event; both are large; both represent mighty powers.) *How are they different?* (The Statue of Liberty is a woman; it was built to serve as a symbol of peace and friendship instead of as a monument to a victory in war.) *According to Lazarus, what important American values does the Statue of Liberty stand for?* (welcoming new immigrants and offering them freedom and opportunity)

After dividing the class into pairs of students, challenge students to design a monument that symbolizes an ideal that is important to them. You might also wish to have them construct models based on their designs. Encourage volunteers to share their designs or models with the class.

SAVE THE EARTH (IT'S NOT TOO LATE)
by Professor Rap, 1991
Pages 3–5 📼

Use with Chapter 2, Lesson 3

Objectives

☐ *Identify some of the many problems that threaten the environment today.*

☐ *Identify ways in which the rap song encourages people to work together to preserve the environment.*

☐ *Write a song about protecting the environment.*

Writing Your Own Song

After students have read the song, play it for them on the cassette. Tell students that in the recording Professor Rap is performing his own song. Lead them in a discussion about the challenge of preserving the environment. Ask students why it is so important to protect the environment and why we should all pitch in to help in this effort.

Ask students the following questions about the song by Professor Rap: *According to the song, what are some of the problems that are destroying the environment?* (garbage, air pollution, pesticides, acid rain) *What are some ways in which people can work together to preserve the environment?* (stop using aerosol cans, start using biodegradable products, clean up litter, recycle goods)

Divide the class into groups of five students. Challenge each group to compose an original song about why the environment must be preserved and what everyone can do to help. Tell students to write the song in any style they choose. Then have each group perform its song for the rest of the class.

NIGHT JOURNEY
by Theodore Roethke, 1941
Pages 6–7 🔊

Use with Chapter 2, Lesson 1

Objectives

☐ *Recognize how the poet uses the image of a moving train to help us to see and feel the diverse geography of the United States.*

☐ *Write a poem about local landforms and places of interest.*

Writing Your Own Poem

Ask for volunteers to read the poem aloud. Then play the poem on the cassette. Encourage students to close their eyes as they listen and to picture the scenery and movement being described. Lead students to understand how the narrator seems to become a part of the train on which he is riding.

Ask students whether they have ever taken a trip across parts of the United States. Have volunteers describe memorable geographical features that they saw along the way. Then tell students that they will write their own poems about geographical features or parks located in their community. Before students begin writing, ask them to close their eyes and form a mental picture of the place that they will write about. Tell them to think about all the things they would see, hear, and feel if they were sitting in that place. Challenge students to write as descriptively as possible. Encourage volunteers to read their poems aloud to the rest of the class.

AN AMERICAN HISTORY TEXTBOOK IN THE 1800s
by Emma Willard, 1869
Page 8

Use with Chapter 1, Lesson 3

Objectives

☐ *Recognize that textbooks have changed over time.*

☐ *Rewrite this lesson from the perspective of a person living in the 2090s.*

Background Information

Remind students that a social studies textbook is an example of a secondary source. Tell them that social studies textbooks, like all other textbooks, change over time. One obvious difference is that Emma Willard's textbook was black and white. Most books today are in color. A more important difference is the inclusion today of women and of Americans from many different backgrounds. In the past, most social studies textbooks focused on the history of European American men. Today social studies textbooks try to tell the stories of all Americans.

Rewriting from Another Perspective

After students have read the selection, ask them in what ways the style is similar to that of textbooks that they have read and also how it differs. Ask students why they think these differences exist. Discuss with students how they think social studies textbooks written 100 years from now will compare and contrast with the textbooks of today.

Divide the class into pairs of students. Challenge members of each pair to work together to rewrite Emma Willard's lesson from the perspective of a person living in the 2090s. Encourage students to consider how new inventions might change textbooks. (Textbooks may be on computers; they may include videotapes, holograms, and so on.) Also ask students to consider how the landscape and climate of the United States may be different 100 years from now. Have volunteers share their version of the textbook with the class.

THE BEAUTIFUL DREAM

Navajo Story Told by Lana Semallie, 1976
Page 10

Use with Chapter 4, Lesson 2

Objectives

☐ *Recognize the importance of oral history and storytelling to the cultures of the Navajo and other Native Americans.*

☐ *Write a story with animals as characters.*

Writing Your Own Story

After students have read the selection, ask students the following questions: *According to the story, what is Coyote's personality like?* (sneaky, greedy, a good talker) *What are Porcupine's personality traits?* (cleverness, intelligence) *Why do you think animals were important characters in Navajo stories?* (because animals were important to the way of life of the Navajo)

Ask students to name tales that they know of that are similar in some way to the Navajo story. (Aesop's fables are a good example, as are African stories about Anansi the spider.) Lead students to understand that stories and legends of many different cultures often feature animals as prominent characters whose actions teach us about such things as the use of cleverness, good versus evil, brains versus brawn, and other lessons.

Then challenge students to write their own story using animals as characters. Encourage them to make sure that their story teaches a lesson, such as how good triumphs over evil. Have volunteers read their stories aloud. Then have the class try to guess the lessons of the stories.

AZTEC POETRY FROM NAHUATL TEXTS

Retold by Toni de Gerez, 1971
Page 11 🔲

Use with Chapter 3, Lesson 2

Objectives

☐ *Gain a greater understanding of Aztec history from the words of this poem.*

☐ *Draw comparisons with Americans' perspectives of their own history.*

Background Information

This poem—actually part of a sacred dance ceremony—is filled with references that were important to most Aztec in the 1500s. Just as Plymouth Rock, George Washington, and the bald eagle are powerful symbols for us of our own country, so were Tollan, Tlapallan, and quetzal birds to the Aztec.

Linking to Today

Provide background information to students before having them listen to the poem on the cassette. Then have students read the poem. Afterward, ask students to share what they think the poem's main theme is. (People are wishing for the "good old days" when the land was like a paradise and important rulers like Quetzalcoatl were still present.) *What was the environment said to be like back then?* (hugely productive, filled with beautiful birds) *Do things seem to have stayed the same for the Aztec?* (No, those things are described in the past tense.)

Challenge students to think of conclusions Americans often draw when they look back on their own history and compare life 500 years ago to now. (The environment was in better shape; "law and order" was stronger; life was harder.) Then ask how fifth graders living 500 years from now might describe our country today. As a class, use these statements to compose a short poem about life in the United States today from the point of view of those looking back on the past, using a style similar to the Aztec poem.

A DAKOTA WINTER COUNT
by Lone Dog, 1801-1870
Pages 12–14

Use with Chapter 4, Lesson 3

Objectives

☐ *Identify the method used by the Dakota to record their history.*

☐ *Recognize that there are many ways to record history and the passage of time.*

☐ *Have students create a winter count for their own family, school, neighborhood, or state.*

Creating Your Own Winter Count

After students have studied the selection on their own, lead them in an examination of the pictographs. Ask volunteers to tell the class why each of the pictured events would have been important to the Dakota community.

Ask students how Americans record important events today. Then challenge students to create winter counts that depict important events in their own family, school, neighborhood, or state. If students are making a winter count for their family, they may wish to use one pictograph to record an important event that occurred in each year of their lives. Remind students to write a guide that explains the meaning of each pictograph. Ask volunteers to show their pictographs to the rest of the class, and have the class guess what event is illustrated. Finally, create a bulletin board display showing students' winter counts.

FOUNDING OF THE IROQUOIS LEAGUE
by Hiawatha, about 1570
Pages 15–16 🔲

Use with Chapter 4, Lesson 4

Objectives

☐ *Identify the peoples that joined together to form the Iroquois League.*

☐ *Recognize the significance of the league's creation.*

☐ *Rewrite Hiawatha's speech from the perspective of a President of the United States.*

Rewriting from Another Perspective

Remind students that the Iroquois Confederacy is also known as the Iroquois League. After students have read Hiawatha's speech, play it for them on the cassette. Ask students why they think Hiawatha believed it was important to create the league in the first place. *What did each Iroquois people stand to gain by joining?* Students should understand that the member peoples were much stronger as a united group than they were individually.

Then ask students to rewrite Hiawatha's speech from another perspective. Tell them to suppose that they are the President of the United States. They must write a speech to the people of the United States telling them why it is important for the states to remain united. After students have finished writing, ask volunteers to read their speeches aloud to the rest of the class.

HOW RAVEN MADE THE TIDES

Retold by Joseph Bruchac, 1991
Pages 17–18

Use with Chapter 4, Lesson 1

Objectives

☐ *Recognize the importance of storytelling in the daily lives of Native Americans.*

☐ *Design a newspaper spread that addresses "newsworthy" aspects of this story.*

Designing a Newspaper Spread

After students have read the selection, ask them the following questions: *Why was life hard for people before the creation of tides?* (They were hungry because they couldn't gather seafood.) *Why weren't there any tides then?* (An old woman refused to let out the tide-line that controlled the waters.) *How did Raven trick the old woman into letting go of the tide-line?* (At first he pretended he was eating clams, which attracted the woman's curiosity.)

Divide students into groups of four. Challenge them to suppose that they are newspaper reporters assigned to cover this life-changing story of the making of tides. Because it is a story with so many points of view to it, students are to do several articles and illustrations that fill page one of their newspaper. Have students brainstorm the kinds of "angles" they can cover, for example, how tides will change the lives of people, an eyewitness account of Raven's struggle with the old woman, short profiles of the old woman and Raven, how clams and crabs view this new development. Remind students that effective news reports cover the 5 Ws: *Who, What, When, Where,* and *Why.*

YEH-HSIEN

Retold by Judy Sierra, 1992
Pages 19–20

Use with Chapter 5, Lesson 1

Objectives

☐ *Recognize similarities and differences between this Chinese folk tale and the European folk tale known as* Cinderella.

☐ *Write an imaginary interview with Yeh-hsien and Cinderella.*

Writing an Interview

After students have read the selection, challenge them to examine how it is similar to and how it is different from the European version of the story of Cinderella. Ask them how such similar stories might have developed in two separate regions of the world. (Versions of the story might have been shared by travelers, or people might have made up the plot independently based on aspects of life that were common in both regions.)

Challenge students to think about what it would be like if Yeh-hsien and Cinderella discussed their stories on a daytime television talk show. *What kinds of questions would the interviewer ask each woman? How might they respond? How would they describe their shared, and unique, experiences?* Divide the class into groups of three and have them write a script for an interview with Yeh-hsien and Cinderella, including both questions and responses. Encourage a few groups to perform their scenarios.

TIMBUKTU
by Leo Africanus, 1526
Page 21

Use with Chapter 5, Lesson 2

Objectives

☐ *Appreciate the cultural and economic achievements of a major West African city during its heyday in the 1500s.*

☐ *Create a tourist advertisement for Timbuktu.*

Creating Graphics

Have volunteers read the selection out loud to the class. Then ask students to summarize what it was like to live in Timbuktu during the early 1500s. *What kinds of jobs did people have?* (traders, farmers, doctors, crafts workers, judges, merchants, soldiers, priests, other professionals) *What kinds of food did they eat?* (corn, cattle, dairy products)

Divide students into pairs. Tell them to brainstorm what they would have liked about living in Timbuktu and why people might have come to visit the city. Then challenge them to create tourist advertisements or brochures for the city based on their ideas. Encourage them to include catchy slogans and illustrations. Have groups share their work with the rest of the class.

MICHELANGELO BUONAROTTI
by Giorgio Vasari, 1550
Page 22

Use with Chapter 5, Lesson 3

Objectives

☐ *Appreciate the dedication and skill of Michelangelo and the values that prevailed during the Renaissance.*

☐ *Do library research on key people of the Renaissance.*

Building Knowledge

After students have read the selection, ask them to help you make a list of words that describe the kind of person Michelangelo seems to have been. (master craftsman, perfectionist, bold, hard on himself and others) Encourage students to explain their choice of terms. Discuss with students how these values in some ways typified the spirit of the Renaissance in Europe.

Invite students to learn more about key people during the Renaissance. Working in small groups, students can choose to learn more about Michelangelo, or they can choose another great artist, a scientist, or a writer who lived and worked during that time. Have them use the library to gather information on their topic. Then have them prepare an oral presentation to the class. Encourage them to use visuals and multimedia resources, if available, in their research or presentation.

AN INDENTURED SERVANT IN VIRGINIA
by Richard Frethorne, 1623
Pages 24–25

Use with Chapter 7, Lesson 3

Objectives

- ❑ *Identify the way in which many Europeans paid for the voyage to the British colonies in North America during the early 1600s.*
- ❑ *Identify hardships experienced by indentured servants in North America.*
- ❑ *Recognize the perspective of an indentured servant concerning his new life in North America.*
- ❑ *Compare his account with the experience of immigrants coming to the United States today.*

Linking to Today

After students have read the selection, discuss with them the hardships faced by Richard Frethorne in Virginia. Students should understand that food, shelter, clothing, and health were constant concerns for all new colonists. Challenge students to think about how immigrants to the United States today might describe life here in their letters to family members back home. Ask students: *In what ways might their letters be different from Frethorne's? In what ways might they be similar?* (There are fewer deadly diseases in the United States today, and food is more plentiful; life continues to be hard for immigrants today, and many are taken advantage of, as Frethorne was; however, for many immigrants life in the United States is still more secure than life in their home countries; language is also a problem for many immigrants today.)

Have students suppose that they are immigrants writing a letter to a family member back home. Their letters should describe the ease or difficulty of finding a job and a place to live and how they are treated by people already living here. Ask volunteers to read their letters to the class.

THE MAYFLOWER COMPACT
Pilgrim Agreement, 1620
Pages 26–27

Use with Chapter 7, Lesson 4

Objectives

- ❑ *Recognize the importance of self-government.*
- ❑ *Understand the reasons that the Mayflower Compact was written.*
- ❑ *Write an imaginary interview with some of the people who sailed on the Mayflower.*

Writing an Interview

Read the original version of the Mayflower Compact aloud to the class. Then have students read the rewritten version to themselves. When they have finished reading, ask students why the Pilgrims thought it was so important to set up a government in their new home. (to keep order and to improve and help preserve the colony) Ask students to think about what life in their community would be like if there were no laws governing how people should treat each other.

Divide the class into groups and challenge students to write an interview with some of the people who sailed on the *Mayflower*. Tell students to be sure their interviews make clear why the Mayflower Compact was written and why the idea of self-government was important to the Pilgrims. For example, the interviewer might ask Miles Standish why laws are needed in the new colony. (Possible answer: Without laws people do not always consider how their behavior affects others in the community.) Remind students that since only men were allowed to sign the compact, their interviews should also include women and children. Have students volunteer to perform their interviews for the class.

REACHING THE AMERICAS
by Christopher Columbus, 1492
Pages 28–30

Use with Chapter 6, Lesson 1

Objectives

❏ *Recognize how the perspective of Columbus differed from that of his crew members as they voyaged westward from Spain.*

❏ *Recognize Columbus's perspective on the Taino, the Native Americans of Guanahaní.*

❏ *Rewrite the story of Columbus's arrival from the perspective of the Taino people.*

Background Information

Tell students that historians estimate that 250,000 Taino lived in the Caribbean region when Columbus arrived in 1492. This number dwindled to 50,000 in 1515 and 500 in 1550. By 1650 all of the Taino were gone. The major causes of death of the Taino were diseases brought from both Europe and Africa and the harsh conditions, including slavery, imposed by European colonists.

Rewriting from Another Perspective

After students have read the selection, have them discuss the different ways in which Columbus and his crew viewed their voyage westward. Ask students: *Why was the crew unhappy and mistrustful of Columbus? How did he respond?* (The members of the crew were afraid that they would never return to Spain; Columbus scolded them and told them that they had to complete their mission.) Then have students describe Columbus's view of the island of Guanahaní and its people. Ask students if they can think of anything in Columbus's diary that may have foreshadowed the harsh treatment of the Taino.

Challenge students to think about how the Taino may have viewed the arrival of Columbus, his ships, and his crew. Tell them to picture what it might have been like to suddenly meet people who look unlike anyone they had ever seen. Have students rewrite the events described in Columbus's journal from the perspective of a Taino observer. Encourage volunteers to share their versions of the journal with the rest of the class.

THE CONQUISTADORS SEARCH FOR GOLD
by an Aztec Eyewitness, 1550s
Pages 31–32

Use with Chapter 6, Lesson 2

Objectives

❏ *Describe the conquistadors' seizure of the royal treasures of the Aztec empire.*

❏ *Understand the perspective of the Aztec official who observed the Spaniards' actions.*

❏ *Rewrite the account in the form of a news report.*

Rewriting in Another Genre

After students have read the Aztec account, ask them to point out ways in which the author revealed his anger about the behavior of the Spanish conquistadors. Have volunteers pick out specific sentences and read them aloud. (Possible answers include: "Their bodies swelled with greed, and their hunger was ravenous; they hungered like pigs for that gold.")

Divide the class into small groups. Have each group rewrite the account in the form of a news report. Encourage students to "interview" other eyewitnesses, such as Moctezuma, a conquistador, and another Aztec citizen. Remind students that an effective news report includes the 5 Ws: *Who, What, When, Where,* and *Why.* Also tell them that a news article should include perspectives or points of view of several different people. Have students volunteer to perform their news reports for the class.

DRAWINGS OF ROANOKE

by John White, 1585
Pages 33–34

Use with Chapter 7, Lesson 1

Objectives

❑ *Recognize the viewpoint of one of the earliest European settlers who came to North America.*

❑ *Write an imaginary journal entry describing Native American village life based on White's drawings.*

Writing a Journal Entry

As students view the illustrations, tell them that John White was one of the earliest Europeans to make detailed drawings of North America. These drawings are as close as we can come to seeing our continent as the English settlers of Roanoke did. Direct students' attention to the map that shows ships off the coast of Roanoke. *Why did White show some ships sinking?* (to warn that sailing off the Outer Banks is dangerous) *What are other ships doing?* (heading inland to explore) *What name does White give to the big chunk of land at the right?* (Weapemeoc) *What does that say about White's view of who controls the land?* (He recognizes that non-English people already live there.)

Now turn students' attention to the pictures of Native American villages. Explain that White tried to include a great deal of information about the daily life of the people living around Roanoke— useful tips for English people preparing to become their new neighbors. Challenge students to suppose that they are viewing such a scene firsthand along with White. Direct them to study all of the drawings on these pages. Then ask them to write a journal entry describing what they are seeing. What do villagers eat, and how do they get their food? What kinds of houses do the people live in? How do they dress? What is one chore that children appear to do? How are animals treated? What is the environment of the area like? Encourage volunteers to read their journal entries to the class.

LIFE ON A NEW ENGLAND FARM

by Ruth Belknap, 1782
Pages 36–37 🔲

Use with Chapter 8, Lesson 1

Objectives

❑ *Identify the many tasks that women colonists had to perform to feed and clothe their families.*

❑ *Recognize the perspective of a woman colonist regarding country and city life.*

❑ *Act out the poem.*

Using Story Theater

After students have read the poem, play it for them on the cassette. Ask students to name the chores that women colonists had to perform in order to feed their families. (milking cows, baking bread, churning butter, feeding hogs, husking corn) Then have them name the chores required to clothe their families. (washing clothes, spinning yarn) Ask students how Ruth Belknap described life in a town. (She thought town life was much easier than living in the country.) Have them discuss whether they think her point of view was accurate.

Then have the class use Story Theater to act out Belknap's poem. Have several students take turns reading aloud parts of the poem while a group of players performs the actions being described. In addition to playing human roles, players should perform as animals and scenery. When the performance is finished, have students discuss whether performing the poem helped them to understand the life that Belknap described. Ask students if they can think of any ways (for example, the addition of dialogue) in which this Story Theater performance could be improved so that it communicates Belknap's ideas more effectively. Have students stage another performance of the poem which includes these improvements.

A PILGRIM'S JOURNAL OF PLYMOUTH PLANTATION
by William Bradford, 1620
Page 38

Use with Chapter 9, Lesson 1

Objectives

☐ *Appreciate the new opportunities, in addition to freedom of religion, that the Pilgrims found upon arrival at Plymouth, such as abundant natural resources.*

☐ *Make an advertisement for Plymouth.*

Background Information

In this journal entry Bradford noted that practically everything the Pilgrims needed to thrive existed in the area. Fresh water, fish, rich soil, fruit trees, herbs, and vegetables addressed the need for food and water. An abundance of trees contained even more riches. Pine trees were valued as firewood, made excellent ship's masts, and supplied pitch and tar for waterproofing. The hardwood from ash and beech trees made strong tool handles and furniture parts, and black walnut was the wood of choice for making charcoal for gunpowder. Last but not least, sassafras was hugely popular among the English as a cure-all drug, and fetched high prices in England.

Creating Graphics

After students have read the selection, ask them why they think Bradford described the area's natural resources so carefully. Remind them to think about what people had to do to meet basic needs and wants before the invention of grocery stores, indoor plumbing, central heating, plastic containers, and so on. As the discussion becomes more detailed, share the background information above. Then divide the class into small groups of "ad agencies." Challenge them to design a poster-sized ad that shows how the area has what it takes to support a fine lifestyle for new colonists. Encourage groups to include as many detailed examples as possible of how the environment will provide for residents' needs and wants. Then have the groups share their work with the class.

PENN'S WOODS
by Navidad O'Neill, 1996
Pages 39–43

Use with Chapter 8, Lesson 2

Objectives

☐ *Recognize how William Penn's Quaker beliefs shaped Pennsylvania's traditions of religious freedom and justice.*

☐ *Perform the play.*

Performing a Play

After students have read the selection, ask them the following questions: *What kind of a leader was William Penn?* (modest, just, fair) *What kinds of laws did he make for Pennsylvania?* (ones protecting religious freedom, trial by jury, free elections) *How did Penn's Quaker beliefs shape those laws?* (Quakers faced persecution in England, so religious freedom was especially important; Quakers believe in "peaceful coexistence with all mankind," which made Penn want to treat Native Americans fairly.) *How did those laws help make Pennsylvania a special place?* (They stressed freedom and fairness for all.)

Choose volunteers to perform the play's speaking roles. Encourage the rest of the class to play nonspeaking parts—for example, other passengers on the ship *Welcome*; the ship's "rails" (to outline the vessel's boundaries), and the local officials who greet the colonists' arrival. If possible, create scenery. Perform the play for a younger class.

POO RICHA D'S ALMANAC
by Benjamin Franklin, 1732–1757
Pages 44–45

Use with Chapter 9, Lesson 4

Objectives

- ☐ *Recognize the importance of almanacs in colonial society.*
- ☐ *Identify values that were important to colonists as reflected in the sayings from Poor Richard's Almanac.*
- ☐ *Compare and contrast colonial sayings with sayings that are popular today.*

Linking to Today

Ask students if they have ever seen a modern almanac. Have students list ways in which people today learn many of the facts that were once recorded in colonial almanacs. (newspapers, television, radio, and so on) Have each student, in turn, read aloud a saying from *Poor Richard's Almanac*. Have students work together to "decipher" the more difficult sayings so that everyone can understand them. Discuss with students what the sayings reveal about colonial values and the ideas that people thought were important.

Challenge students to think of sayings that are popular today in the United States. (Possible examples are "No pain, no gain"; "Do the right thing"; "Just do it"; "You can lead a horse to water, but you can't make it drink.") Ask students how these modern sayings are similar to sayings from colonial times and how they are different. Point out to students that the saying "No pain, no gain" is popular today but was actually written by Benjamin Franklin. Have students work in small groups to write sayings in the style of *Poor Richard's Almanac*. Then combine these sayings in a class almanac.

SHI OF HO RORS
by Olaudah Equiano, 1789
Pages 46–48

Use with Chapter 9, Lesson 1

Objectives

- ☐ *Recognize some of the horrors that enslaved Africans experienced on their forced voyages to the Americas.*
- ☐ *Understand the perspective of a West African boy who was forced to make that journey.*
- ☐ *Write a poem based on the narrative.*

Writing a Poem

After students have read the selection, have volunteers discuss what it might have been like to be kidnapped from your homeland and enslaved. Then ask students to write a poem about Olaudah Equiano's horrifying experience. Challenge them to describe the long and terrible voyage. Ask volunteers to read their poems aloud to the class.

SLAVE SALES
Advertisements, 1700s
Page 49

Use with Chapter 9, Lesson 3

Objectives

☐ *Recognize that during the time of slavery, human beings were bought and sold as if they were objects.*

☐ *Understand that slave sales took place throughout the American colonies in the 1600s and 1700s, and they continued in the South until the 1860s.*

☐ *Write a letter opposing slave-sale advertisements.*

Writing a Response

After students have studied the advertisements, have them discuss how they portray the people who are for sale. Ask students in what ways the advertisements depict human beings as property rather than people. Ask students what they think about people being offered for sale. Have students discuss what it might be like to watch a slave sale.

Divide the class into pairs. Have each pair of students work together to write a letter to the editor of a newspaper. Students should suppose that they live in the 13 English colonies in the 1700s and are writing letters in opposition to the advertisements for slave sales. Encourage students to communicate the idea that the enslaved Africans being sold are people, not property. Have volunteers share their letters with the rest of the class.

FATHER JUNÍPERO SERRA
by Ivy Bolton, 1952
Pages 50–52

Use with Chapter 10, Lesson 1

Objectives

☐ *Recognize the personal courage of Father Serra and his determination to carry out missionary work in California.*

☐ *Write a true story of personal courage.*

Background Information

Father Junípero Serra and Captain Gaspar de Portolá began their northward journey into California in 1769. Along the way Father Serra— a 19-year veteran of missionary work in North America—kept a journal. In it he wrote that he actually experienced temporary relief from his leg wound due to the muleteer's remedy. The wound, however, would never heal. Nevertheless, Father Serra would go on to found the mission of San Diego on his trip with Portolá, and in years to come he would found many more missions, as he walked throughout the region.

Writing Your Own Story

After students have read the selection, have them discuss what Father Serra's goal was for setting out in the first place. (to begin mission work in California) *Why did Father Serra continue his journey despite his serious medical problems?* (He was very committed to his goal.) Encourage students to share examples of other people that they have read about so far in their textbook or anthology who overcame great obstacles to achieve personal goals. (for example, indentured servants and other immigrants, free or enslaved African Americans)

Challenge students to write a story, using real-life or fictional characters, about a person with great courage. Have them include the person's goal, any hardships faced, how those hardships were overcome, and what it was like to achieve the goal. Ask volunteers to read their stories aloud.

THE BOSTON MASSACRE

from the *Boston Gazette and Country Journal*, 1770

Pages 54–55

Use with Chapter 11, Lesson 2

Objectives

- ❏ *Understand a colonial printer's perspective on the Boston Massacre.*
- ❏ *Recognize how the writer's point of view can influence the way in which facts are presented in a newspaper article.*
- ❏ *Rewrite the article from the perspective of a British journalist of the time.*

Background Information

After the event called the Boston Massacre, colonists angrily demanded that the British troops involved be put on trial for murder. The lawyer who defended the British soldiers was John Adams, the famous patriot who later became the second President of the United States. Adams agreed to defend the soldiers because he felt that they had been victimized by an unruly mob of people. The jury found the captain of the British troops innocent, but two of his men were convicted. However, they received only light punishment.

Rewriting from Another Perspective

After students have read the rewritten version of the newspaper article, have them discuss the point of view of its writer. Ask questions such as the following: *What was his opinion about the event that has come to be known as the Boston Massacre?* (that it was an undeserved, terrible tragedy) *How is the writer's opinion expressed in the article?* (through the words he chooses, such as "bloody massacre" and "terrible tragedy"; through the illustration) Ask students why they think that the illustration of four coffins was included.

Challenge students to rewrite the article from the perspective of a British journalist of the time. Ask students to think about how British coverage of the event might have differed from American coverage.

PAUL REVERE'S RIDE

by Henry Wadsworth Longfellow, 1863

Pages 56–60 🔲

Use with Chapter 11, Lesson 3

Objectives

- ❏ *Recognize Paul Revere's contribution to the fight for American independence from Britain.*
- ❏ *Appreciate the personal risks Revere undertook for the American cause.*
- ❏ *Draw a storyboard dramatizing Revere's ride.*

Background Information

Revere set out close to midnight on April 18, 1775, to spread word that British soldiers were marching out of Boston that night. He had to sneak by the British warship *Somerset* at the outset of his journey, and he was stopped by armed British patrols twice that night. However, he escaped each time and even went on to save a trunk full of secret Patriot documents. Longfellow, however, left out the important fact that Revere's ride was just one part of a united effort by American colonists. Others, for example, received the secret church signals. It was one of his colleagues, not Revere, who reached Concord that night. Revere never said, "The British are coming," but rather, "The Regulars [soldiers] are coming," because most colonists at the time still considered *themselves* British.

Drawing Storyboards with Captions

After students have read the poem, play the cassette and have them outline Revere's ride as described by Longfellow. *What kind of man must Revere have been to carry out such a job?* (brave, good horseman, dedicated to the cause) *What challenges might he have faced on that nighttime journey?* (fatigue, cold, darkness, patrols)

Tell students that they are going to make a movie based on the poem. Tell them that their first job is to make a storyboard, which is like a comic strip complete with captions that shows how directors want their movie to look when it is finished. Encourage students to reflect as much of Longfellow's drama as possible in their storyboards. Have students move about the room to view others' renditions, and create a display of the storyboards when completed.

CONCORD HYMN
by Ralph Waldo Emerson, 1837
Page 61 🔲

Use with Chapter 11, Lesson 3

Objectives
- ❑ *Recognize that the Battle of Concord was a major turning point in the birth of the United States.*
- ❑ *Appreciate the legacy of freedom Americans share today as a result of ordinary citizens' sacrifices at Concord.*
- ❑ *Honor the sacrifices that others have made on behalf of an important cause.*

Background Information
On April 19, 1775, Concord's militiamen debated how they should respond to the throng of British soldiers heading toward their town. Their minister, William Emerson, thundered, "Let us stand our ground. If we die, let us die here!" Over 50 years later the minister's grandson, Ralph Waldo Emerson, one of our country's greatest poets, wrote this poem in memory of the men who died during the Battle of Concord.

Building Knowledge
Read the poem together after listening to it on the cassette. Then ask why people gathered in Concord in 1837. (to remember the heroes of the Battle of Concord and to honor the legacy of freedom that they left for their children) Have students name some ceremonies held in their communities. (for example: Veterans Day; Independence Day; Presidents' Day; Martin Luther King, Jr. Day; local ceremonies) *What kinds of things do they honor?* (important events in our history, ideals that our country stands for, people who embodied these ideals or who made important contributions to our country)

Challenge students to think of a person or an event that they think has made a positive impact on the world. Then have them create a program for a ceremony that celebrates both the person or the event and their legacies. These programs might include speeches, songs, dramatizations, and other activities. Encourage students to share their program descriptions with the class.

DECLARATION OF INDEPENDENCE
by Thomas Jefferson, 1776
Pages 62–66

Use with Chapter 12, Lesson 1

Objectives
- ❑ *Recognize why the Declaration of Independence was so important to people in the American colonies.*
- ❑ *Understand why this document continues to be important in the modern world.*

Background Information
Despite the fact that Thomas Jefferson owned slaves, his first draft of the Declaration of Independence included an attack on Britain for its involvement in the slave trade. However, this section was later taken out at the insistence of other members of the Continental Congress. Like Jefferson, many members of the Congress were slave owners. They argued that the declaration would not be approved by the Congress if it included the passage denouncing slavery.

Linking to Today
Have students read the rewritten version of the Declaration of Independence. When they have finished reading it, have them discuss the declaration's historical significance. Ask students how the declaration is similar to the Mayflower Compact. (They both express ideas about the reasons why a government is needed.) *How are these documents different?* (The Mayflower Compact set up a government where none existed; the Declaration of Independence cites the reasons why the existing government was unjust.)

Tell students that for over 200 years people seeking independence in different parts of the world have made reference to the Declaration of Independence. Ask students why they think that the ideas expressed in this document, written in 1776, are still relevant in the twentieth century.

COMMON SENSE
by Thomas Paine, 1776
Pages 67–68

Use with Chapter 12, Lesson 1

Objectives

☐ *Understand the arguments for independence from Britain that Thomas Paine made in* Common Sense.

☐ *Analyze his arguments in a book review.*

Writing a Book Review

Before reading the selection, tell students to be on the lookout for two major arguments Paine made in favor of independence. One involves a comparison to a child growing up, while the other describes how geography supports the idea of American independence. As volunteers read the selection to the class, clarify any of its more complex words and phrasings. Then ask students: *How does Paine use the example of a child growing up to explain how and why the colonies can thrive apart from Britain?* (Just as a child's diet changes as he or she grows up, so must America's relationship with Britain and the rest of the world.) *How, according to him, does geography work in favor of American independence?* (The colonies' distance and size in relation to Britain confirm that they should be independent.)

Remind students that *Common Sense* became a huge bestseller as soon as it was published in 1776. Challenge them to review the book and its point of view for a colonial newspaper. Recall that, like all good book reviews, their work should provide a short summary of the book's "plot" or point of view as well as their opinion regarding whether that point of view is well expressed and worth reading.

JOHNNY TREMAIN
by Esther Forbes, 1943
Pages 69–70

Use with Chapter 12, Lesson 2

Objectives

☐ *Understand the conflicting emotions colonists felt toward Britain on the eve of the Revolutionary War.*

☐ *Compare and contrast the status of the Continental and British armies at the beginning of the Revolutionary War.*

☐ *Rewrite the scene as a newspaper article.*

Rewriting in Another Genre

After students have read the selection, ask them to describe the overall scene taking place in the excerpt. (British troops are moving out toward Lexington, where the Revolutionary War will begin.) *Why is Johnny divided in his feelings about Britain?* (Its heritage of liberty gave birth to the colonists' own struggle; Johnny, like others, still feels British in heritage but feels even more an American.) *Why does "Yankee Doodle" seem to have almost no hope of succeeding against the "great scarlet dragon"?* (The British are much better armed and trained.)

Tell students to suppose that they are colonial news reporters and have just interviewed Johnny Tremain for an article on the dispatch of British soldiers to Lexington. Remind them to address the 5 Ws of journalism: *Who, What, Where, When,* and *Why.* Encourage students to include a comparison of the British and American armies. Have volunteers read their articles to the class.

A PETITION FOR FREEDOM
by African Americans of Massachusetts, 1777
Pages 71–72

Use with Chapter 12, Lesson 2

Objectives

☐ *Recognize the perspective of African Americans on the Declaration of Independence.*

☐ *Compare and contrast the petition with the Declaration of Independence.*

☐ *Write a letter to the editor of a newspaper explaining why the practice of slavery is in conflict with the ideas expressed in the Declaration of Independence.*

Writing a Letter

Have students read through the petition on their own. Afterward, lead them in a line-by-line reading, stopping to define difficult words along the way. Then have students compare the petition with the Declaration of Independence. Ask a volunteer to read aloud the rewritten version of the second paragraph of the Declaration of Independence. Ask students how the ideas expressed in this paragraph conflict with the existence of slavery. (The declaration states that all men are created equal, that liberty and the pursuit of happiness are unalienable rights, and that governments are designed to protect these rights.) Students should understand that the African American writers of the petition agreed with the ideas expressed in the Declaration of Independence but believed that the declaration should apply to all people.

Challenge students to suppose that they are living in 1776. Have each student write a letter to the editor of a newspaper explaining why slavery is wrong, according to the ideas expressed in the Declaration of Independence. Have volunteers read their letters aloud to the class.

SONG OF MARION'S MEN
by William Cullen Bryant, 1831
Pages 73–74

Use with Chapter 12, Lesson 3

Objectives

☐ *Appreciate the battle tactics and bravery of Francis Marion and other Southern patriots.*

☐ *Produce an imaginary television news report on Marion and his soldiers.*

Background Information

In the final years of the Revolutionary War, Francis Marion and his soldiers led devastating attacks against British forces along South Carolina's Santee River. His bold acts made him a hero whose fame was almost as great as George Washington's. Villages named themselves Marion in his honor, and today there are 17 counties throughout the country that still bear his name.

Rewriting in Another Genre

Lead students in reading the poem, asking volunteers to help you explain difficult phrases or words. After listening to it on the cassette, have students discuss why Marion's nickname, "the Swamp Fox," was well chosen, according to Bryant. Encourage them to use lines from the poem to bolster their opinions.

Divide the class into groups, then challenge them to suppose that they are television reporters sent back in time to make "Marion's Men" the "People of the Year" on their news broadcast. Tell them that, as topnotch journalists, their reports should cover the 5 Ws: *Who, What, When, Where,* and *Why.* Also encourage them to include brief visuals ("footage") of the men "in action" and interviews, if possible—all within about three minutes. Have each group deliver their report to the class.

WASHINGTON'S FAREWELL TO HIS OFFICERS

by Benjamin Tallmadge, 1783
Pages 75–76

Use with Chapter 12, Lesson 3

Objectives

❑ *Appreciate the great devotion Americans felt toward George Washington because of his leadership during the Revolutionary War.*

❑ *Create a farewell card for Washington.*

Creating Graphics

Before students read the selection, ask them to describe someone in their lives that they greatly admire. *What makes that person great?* Ask them how they would react if they were told that they would no longer have any contact with their hero or heroine. Now tell them to read the selection.

After students have finished reading, encourage them to share their impressions of what kind of man and leader George Washington was, based on what happened in the selection. Challenge them to suppose that they are to be one of the well-wishers present at Washington's farewell. Ask them to create a good-bye card to him. Have volunteers share their work with the class or use it in a class display.

SHH! WE'RE WRITING THE CONSTITUTION

by Jean Fritz, 1987
Pages 77–81

Use with Chapter 13, Lesson 2

Objectives

❑ *Recognize the serious issues the Constitutional Convention debated, such as how much power should be given to the federal government and how much should be given to the state governments.*

❑ *Conduct a debate on the issues discussed in the selection.*

Background Information

To get a sense of how powerful state rather than national identity was at the time, it is interesting to note that throughout the 1700s and early 1800s Americans often said, "The United States *are…*" rather than "The United States *is…*" It wasn't until after the Civil War that people commonly referred to the country as a single unit, rather than as a union of individual states.

Conducting a Debate

After students have read the selection, ask them to explain why the term "national government" created such a huge debate at the Constitutional Convention. (It implied that the new government would be supreme over the states.) *Why do you think this issue was so important?* (They had fought a war to win the right to rule themselves, and they didn't want to be controlled again by a large, powerful government.) *Why did some representatives dislike the idea of having one person be head of the government?* (It was too much like monarchy.)

Divide the class into an even number of small groups. Have pairs of groups debate each other on one or more of the issues discussed in the selection. Allow the groups time to plan the arguments they will make before holding the debate. Encourage them to anticipate what arguments the other side will make so they can be prepared to counter them. Then allow each side five minutes to make their case and five minutes to refute the opposing side. You might also wish to have the class read and discuss the excerpt from *The Federalist* on page 84 before holding the debate.

TWO VIEWS ON WOMEN'S RIGHTS
by Abigail Adams and John Adams, 1776
Pages 82–83

Use with Chapter 13, Lesson 1

Objectives

☐ *Understand Abigail Adams's perspective on women's rights.*

☐ *Understand John Adams's perspective on women's rights.*

☐ *Compare and contrast these perspectives.*

Background Information

Early American women had very few legal rights. They could not vote, and their educational opportunities were limited. When they got married, women lost the right to own property; anything owned at the time of their marriage became the legal property of their husbands. At the time of the American Revolution, the only people permitted to vote were white men who owned land. Most women, African American and Native American men, and white men who did not own land were barred from voting.

Conducting a Point/Counterpoint

Lead students in a reading of all three letters. Ask volunteers to explain particularly difficult passages. Then have students discuss how the opinions of Abigail Adams and John Adams differed. (Abigail Adams felt that if men truly believed in independence, they would extend equal rights to women; John Adams suggested that if men gave up any control, they would be subject to the rule of women.) Ask students: *Why did these differences exist?* (Abigail Adams knew from experience what it was like to be treated as a second-class citizen.) *Do you think that John Adams was entirely serious in his reply? Why or why not?*

Tell students that all Americans have equal rights under the law today, but that women did not receive the right to vote nationally until 1920. Ask students to suppose that they are living in the late 1700s. Have them suggest reasons that all Americans should be able to vote.

THE FEDERALIST, NUMBER 10
by James Madison, 1787
Page 84

Use with Chapter 13, Lesson 4

Objectives

☐ *Recognize fears people had about what the Constitution might do to the idea of representative government.*

☐ *Determine that James Madison's point of view was that our government would be fairer with a larger number of representatives.*

☐ *Rephrase his argument in modern-day terms.*

Background Information

Once the Constitutional Convention ended, Americans began to fiercely debate the proposed plan of government. New York's Governor George Clinton summed up many people's fears when he charged that the Constitution was "a license for the rich to plunder the poor." Since the Constitution called for just a few people to represent the interests of the entire country, what would stop rich and powerful people from buying the votes of representatives and effectively taking over? Federalists, or supporters of the Constitution, responded to Anti-Federalists' fears in a flurry of newspaper articles. In this excerpt from one article, James Madison argued that republican government works most fairly on a big rather than a small scale, because special-interest groups have a harder time gaining majority control.

Linking to Today

Share background information with the class before helping them read through the document. *In this excerpt what main argument does Madison make against small republics?* (A large number of representatives would help prevent "cabals," or elite or special-interest groups, from taking over.) Challenge students to sum up Madison's point of view in their own words. Tell them that this debate is still going on today, as some politicians push for smaller government or less government control, and greater control by the states. How might this issue apply to a debate over whether classroom-sized or school-sized representation would be fairer to students' interests?

ESCAPE FROM WASHINGTON
by Dolley Madison, 1814
Pages 86–87

Use with Chapter 14, Lesson 3

Objectives

❏ *Recognize Dolley Madison's courage during the War of 1812.*

❏ *Understand why it is useful to read firsthand accounts of historical events.*

❏ *Draw a storyboard dramatizing Dolley Madison's experience.*

Drawing Storyboards with Captions

After students have read Dolley Madison's letter, have them discuss how she reacted to her situation. Lead students to understand that remaining in the President's House for so long required great courage. Have students discuss how reading a firsthand account is different from reading about historical events in a textbook. Ask students: *Why is it useful to read a firsthand account?* (Firsthand accounts present a vivid and memorable portrait of the events being described; they tell us how people felt at the time.) *Why is it important to read explanations of events written after they occurred?* (Accounts of events that are written later are in some ways a more accurate summary of what occurred as they are less influenced by the writer's own point of view.)

Then have students suppose that they are going to make a movie of Dolley Madison's experience. Tell them that the first thing they need to do as filmmakers is to create a storyboard of the action, complete with dialogue. A storyboard is a type of comic strip that shows how film directors want their movie to look before it is shot. Encourage students to make their storyboards as detailed, dramatic, and realistic as possible and to create a working title for their film. Each storyboard should have several different panels showing different events in the order in which they occurred. Have volunteers share their storyboards with the rest of the class.

THE JOURNALS OF LEWIS AND CLARK
by Meriwether Lewis, 1805
Page 88

Use with Chapter 14, Lesson 2

Objectives

❏ *Appreciate the rigors involved in Lewis and Clark's exploration of western North America.*

❏ *Trace their route to the headwaters of the Missouri River.*

Background Information

Meriwether Lewis began his epic journey in July 1803 by traveling overland from Washington, D.C., to Pittsburgh. From there he boarded a boat headed down the Ohio River and picked up William Clark and others at Louisville, Kentucky. The little group continued on to the point where the Mississippi and Ohio rivers converge; from there they headed up the Mississippi to St. Louis, a trading post founded by the French near the place where the Missouri flows into the Mississippi. There they stayed for five months in order to prepare for the hardest part of their journey. In May 1804 the Lewis and Clark expedition to the Pacific Northwest began in earnest.

Tracing a Route

After students have read the selection, ask them why they think Lewis was so careful to note so many directions and mile markings in his journal. (so others might follow in the future) *Why were expedition members so happy to reach the start of the Missouri River?* (One of the expedition's goals was to explore the Missouri, and it had taken them over a year to reach its source.) *What did Lewis and his group do after leaving the Missouri?* (headed further west, connected with another river, which he called the Columbia)

Divide the class into groups of two. Challenge them to trace as much of Lewis's journey as possible from an atlas map. (Note: the group didn't immediately hook up with the present-day Columbia River; they followed the present-day Lemhi, Salmon, and Snake rivers to the Columbia.) Have them note which present-day states the expedition traveled through as well as what the terrain was like along the way.

THE REMOVAL OF THE CHEROKEE
by John G. Burnett, 1890
Pages 89–90

Use with Chapter 14, Lesson 4

Objectives

☐ *Recognize the tragedy of the Trail of Tears, the forced relocation of the Cherokee from the Southeastern United States to Oklahoma.*

☐ *Understand Burnett's feelings about the injustice of the Trail of Tears.*

☐ *Dramatize Burnett's account through Story Theater.*

Using Story Theater

After students have read Burnett's account, have them discuss why they think that Burnett called this "the blackest chapter on the pages of American History." Ask students: *How would you have reacted if you had been a Cherokee? How would you have reacted if you had been a soldier ordered to participate in the removal of the Cherokee?*

Then have the class act out Burnett's account through Story Theater. Have several students take turns reading aloud parts of the account while a group of players performs the actions being described. "Lead roles" include the parts of Chief John Ross, Ross's wife, President Andrew Jackson, and Burnett himself. When the performance is finished, have students discuss how performing the story helped them to understand the tragedy of the Trail of Tears.

FAREWELL ADDRESS
by Andrew Jackson, 1837
Page 91 🎞

Use with Chapter 14, Lesson 4

Objectives

☐ *Identify Andrew Jackson's point of view regarding why he was about to force Native Americans from their lands in the Southeast.*

☐ *Write a response to Jackson's point of view.*

Writing a Response

After reading the selection to the class, have students listen to the speech on the cassette. Then ask them: *What is President Jackson's view of how life in the United States had faired under the Constitution?* (The country had gone through hard times, but it had "preserved unimpaired the liberties of the people.") *Who are some people who hadn't done as well as they could, in his view?* (people in states with Native Americans and Native Americans themselves) *According to Jackson, how would forced removal benefit both groups?* (White settlers would finally be able to prosper; Native Americans would be moved to a safe spot, would be placed under "the paternal care" of the government, and would be "civilized.") *In this view are all Americans equal and equally entitled to life, liberty, and the pursuit of happiness?* (No, Native Americans are considered to have fewer rights and lesser abilities.)

Challenge students to write a letter to President Jackson responding to his point of view regarding Native Americans and their land. Encourage them to use facts from their textbook and anthology to disprove his views that Native Americans are "uncivilized" and would be better off giving their land up to more "deserving" Americans.

THE FACTORY BELL
by an Unknown Factory Girl, 1844
Pages 92–93 🔲

Use with Chapter 15, Lesson 1

Objectives

- ❏ *Recognize how the poem helps us to understand the life of a worker in an early American factory.*
- ❏ *Recognize how the poet uses bells to illustrate the hard life of a factory worker.*
- ❏ *Compare the work of a young woman in an early American factory to the work of young people today.*

Background Information

From the 1820s until the late 1840s, women from New England made up a large portion of the industrial work force in the United States. During the 1840s, however, factory owners began to hire thousands of men and boys from Irish immigrant families who had come to the United States to escape a terrible famine. These men and boys began to do much of the factory work that previously had been done by women. To factory owners, time was money, and workers were forced to work long hours for very little pay.

Linking to Today

After students have read the poem, play it for them on the cassette. Have them discuss why the author may have chosen a bell to symbolize the new industrial way of life. (Life was no longer regulated by the cycles of nature but by clocks and bells.)

Have students discuss how their own lives are shaped by clocks and bells. Then challenge them to write a schedule of a typical day, including the times that they wake up, go to school, have classes, eat meals, do homework, play, and go to bed. Ask volunteers to share their schedules with the rest of the class. Finally, ask students to compare the hours they spend in school and doing homework to the work hours of a worker in an early American factory.

LAST APPEAL FOR AID
by William Travis, 1836
Page 94

Use with Chapter 15, Lesson 3

Objectives

- ❏ *Understand the unequal battle lines that were drawn when Texans sought to defend the Alamo during their war for independence from Mexico.*
- ❏ *Create an imaginary television news report on the Battle of the Alamo.*

Background Information

In February 1836 a force of around 200 Texans led by William Travis barricaded themselves in the Alamo, despite Texas General Sam Houston's order to abandon San Antonio. When Mexico's General Antonio López de Santa Anna surrounded the old fort with about 5,000 men and demanded that the Texans surrender, Travis answered with cannon fire. He also dispatched a secret messenger to the Texas government with this last appeal for aid. No aid ever came. On March 6 Santa Anna's forces stormed the Alamo and, despite huge losses, retook the fort. No Texas soldier survived the fight.

Rewriting in Another Genre

After students have read the selection, ask them to describe in their own words what was happening around the Alamo as Travis wrote this document. *Why was it clear that the Texans were in serious trouble?* (The Mexicans had more firepower and soldiers.) *Why do you think the Texans fought so fiercely despite overwhelming odds against them?* (They felt strongly about their bid for independence.)

Divide the class into small groups. Tell them to suppose that they are television news crews assigned to produce a three-minute report on the showdown brewing at the Alamo. Challenge them to include short "interviews" with soldiers from opposing sides, "live footage" of the two sides facing off, and commentary on what the battle is all about and why it is important. Have each "news crew" perform its report for the class.

ERIE CANAL
Traditional Song, 1800s
Page 95 🔲

Use with Chapter 15, Lesson 2

Objectives

☐ *Identify how the song conveys what it was like to work on the Erie Canal.*

☐ *Compare and contrast transportation via the Erie Canal with transportation today.*

☐ *Trace the route of the Erie Canal.*

Background Information

Although the Erie Canal was a tremendously important trade route in the 1800s, its design was surprisingly simple. The canal was only 4 feet (1m) deep and about 30 feet (9m) wide. Canal boats were towed by mules that were guided along a path running alongside the canal. At best, the boats could travel 4 miles (6 km) per hour. Towns often built bridges across the canal. These bridges were sometimes so low that the people riding on boats were forced to lie flat as they passed underneath.

Tracing a Route

After students have read the lyrics of the song, play it on the cassette. The version on the cassette includes a second verse. Ask students: *How is the transportation of goods today different from the way goods were transported in the past?* (Today goods are transported much more quickly, mostly by trucks, ships, and planes.) Lead students to understand that the transportation of goods continues to be essential to the economic health of the United States.

Divide the class into pairs of students. Have each pair work together to locate the route of the Erie Canal using the maps on pages 413 and R12–R13 of their textbook. Have students write the answers to the following questions: *Where are Albany and Buffalo, and on which two bodies of water are they located?* (Albany is on the Hudson River in eastern New York; Buffalo is on Lake Erie in western New York.) *How did the canal make it possible for goods from Ohio and Michigan to be shipped to New York City?* (Goods were carried east by boat across Lake Erie, through the Erie Canal, and south on the Hudson River.)

SWEET BETSY FROM PIKE
Traditional Song, 1800s
Page 96 🔲

Use with Chapter 15, Lesson 5

Objectives

☐ *Appreciate a popular song sung by "Forty-Niners" and other cross-country travelers.*

☐ *Rewrite the song as a news article that highlights the struggles and dreams of overland travelers.*

Rewriting in Another Genre

Use this activity after students have read the next selection, *Diary of an Overland Journey to California.* After students have read the song, play it for them on the cassette. Afterward, have them compare Ike and Betsy's fictional experience with Sallie Hester's real-life experience on the overland trail. Ask students: *How were these experiences similar?* (traveling along the Platte River; crossing prairies, wide rivers, and tall peaks; physical hardship and setbacks along the way) *Why do you think that "Sweet Betsy from Pike" was so popular among travelers?* (Lead students to understand that adding humor to a story can make difficult real-life experiences easier to bear.)

Have students suppose that they are news reporters assigned to write an article on the struggles and dreams of travelers heading west. Challenge them to rewrite "Sweet Betsy from Pike" as a news article. Remind students that unlike a song, news articles should stick to the facts. Have volunteers share their articles with the class.

DIARY OF AN OVERLAND JOURNEY TO CALIFORNIA
by Sallie Hester, 1849
Pages 97–100

Use with Chapter 15, Lesson 5

Objectives

- ☐ *Recognize how Sallie Hester's diary describes the difficulty of crossing the United States in 1849.*
- ☐ *Identify challenges faced by Sallie Hester and her family during their journey.*
- ☐ *Draw a storyboard of Sallie Hester's trip.*

Drawing Storyboards with Captions

Have students take turns reading parts of the diary aloud. Then have students use the map on page 99 to trace Sallie Hester's journey. Have students discuss what they think would have been the most difficult, most fun, most exciting, and most boring parts of the journey westward. Ask students: *What skills and personal qualities did travelers need in order to survive?* (courage, perseverance, strength, patience) *What forces beyond their control contributed to their success or failure?* (diseases, accidents, lack of water)

Tell students that they will make a video of Sallie Hester's journey. Divide the class into groups of five students. Have each group create a storyboard with captions showing scenes from their video. All of Sallie Hester's diary entries should be illustrated on the storyboards of each group. Encourage students to show how the landscape changed as Sallie Hester traveled west across the United States. Have a spokesperson from each group present its storyboards to the rest of the class.

SLAVERY DEFENDED
by George Fitzhugh, 1857
Page 102 🔊

SLAVERY DENOUNCED
by Frederick Douglass, 1852
Pages 103–104 🔊

Use with Chapter 16, Lesson 1

Objectives

- ☐ *Understand why a former slave and a slave owner had different perspectives on slavery.*
- ☐ *Compare and contrast these perspectives.*

Conducting a Point/Counterpoint

After students have read the two selections, play Douglass's speech on the cassette. The version on the cassette, read by the renowned actor Ossie Davis, varies slightly from the version in the text. Then have students discuss the views of each writer. Ask students: *What accounts for the writers' differences in perspectives on slavery?* (Fitzhugh used captive African Americans to work his plantation; his livelihood depended on slavery and the misconception that blacks were inferior to whites; Douglass had lived through the cruelty of slavery and had firsthand knowledge of its horrors.) *Which of the selections presents an accurate view of slavery?* (Douglass's) *Which of these two men had the best understanding of how it felt to be enslaved?* (Douglass, because he had spent 21 years of his life in slavery)

Ask students how Frederick Douglass might have reacted to George Fitzhugh's defense of slavery. Then have them write a letter responding to Fitzhugh. Tell students to refer to Douglass's own experiences in slavery. Ask volunteers to read their letters aloud to the class.

FOLLOW THE DRINKING GOURD

Spiritual, 1800s
Pages 105–106 📼

Use with Chapter 16, Lesson 2

Objectives

❑ *Appreciate the role of "code songs" such as "Follow the Drinking Gourd" in the lives of enslaved African Americans.*

❑ *Trace a route enslaved people could follow to freedom along the Ohio River.*

Tracing a Route

Play the song for students on the cassette once through. Then play it again and have students follow the lyrics carefully. Ask students: *How do you think the fact that the secret directions were hidden in a song helped more people to learn those directions?* (The words to songs are often easier to remember than straight text; moreover, singing can be a faster way to spread information than whispering from one person to the next.)

Remind students that the "old man" described three rivers as leading toward freedom in the North: the Tombigbee, Tennessee, and Ohio rivers. Divide the class into pairs of students and challenge them to locate these three rivers on an atlas map. Then have them list all the slave and free states that these rivers passed through. Have students analyze how these geographic facts might have affected the flow of human traffic on the Underground Railroad.

DECLARATION OF SENTIMENTS AND RESOLUTIONS

Declaration of the Seneca Falls Convention, 1848
Pages 107–108

Use with Chapter 16, Lesson 2

Objectives

❑ *Understand that American women were denied basic human rights in the 1800s.*

❑ *Appreciate the efforts of women such as Lucretia Mott and Elizabeth Cady Stanton to improve the status of American women.*

❑ *Outline and interpret the main ideas of the declaration.*

Building Knowledge

Divide students into pairs. Have one turn to the Declaration of Independence, on page 62, and the other to the Declaration of Sentiments and Resolutions. Ask students the following questions: *How does the Declaration of Sentiments and Resolutions compare to the Declaration of Independence?* (The Declaration of Sentiments and Resolutions mirrors much of the format and wording of the Declaration of Independence.) *Why do you suppose that the two documents are so similiar?* (The authors of the Declaration of Sentiments and Resolutions felt that, because they were women, they were being denied basic rights, like the colonists were.) *How are the two documents different?* (The Declaration of Independence deals with the subject of independence from Britain and leaves out any reference to women.) Remind students that like the Declaration of Independence, the Declaration of Sentiments and Resolutions contains a list of grievances.

Ask students to read the Declaration of Sentiments and Resolutions silently. Then have each pair create a summary of its points on poster paper. When the groups have finished their work, have them present their findings to the class.

"AIN'T I A WOMAN?"
by Sojourner Truth, 1851
Pages 109–110 📼

Use with Chapter 16, Lesson 2

Objectives

☐ *Understand Sojourner Truth's perspective on women's rights as a woman who was once enslaved.*

☐ *Compare Sojourner Truth's speech to the letters of Abigail Adams.*

Background Information

When Sojourner Truth was born in New York in 1795, she was named Isabella van Hardenbergh. After the end of slavery in New York State in 1827, she changed her name. "My name was Isabell," she said, "but when I left the house of bondage, I left everything behind." She chose the name Sojourner Truth because she felt that God was calling her to sojourn, or "travel up and down the land," to spread the word of truth. She spent the rest of her life traveling around the Northern states giving speeches against slavery and in support of women's rights.

Building Knowledge

After students have read the speech, play it for them on the cassette. Ask them to describe Truth's message in their own words. (Truth was making the point that women had proven that they were equal to men; she asserted that women would take the rights that they deserved.) Ask students why a woman who had once been enslaved might have a different perspective on women's rights than men and women who had always been free. (Enslaved women were forced to engage in physical labor that was harsher than the work of even very poor free men and women. While enslaved, Sojourner Truth had endured hardships that would have been difficult for any person, man or woman.)

Have students reread the letters of Abigail Adams on pages 82–83. Have students write a paragraph comparing and contrasting these letters to the speech by Sojourner Truth. Ask volunteers to read their paragraphs aloud to the rest of the class.

OPPOSITION TO WOMEN'S RIGHTS
from the *New York Herald*, 1850
Page 111

Use with Chapter 16, Lesson 2

Objectives

☐ *Acknowledge the arguments some Americans used in the 1800s to oppose equal rights for women.*

☐ *Write a response to the arguments.*

Writing a Response

Have volunteers read the selection to the class. Then ask students: *According to the writer, what did leaders of the women's movement want?* (to vote, run for office, become doctors or lawyers) *Why, according to the writer, were women unsuited for these things?* (They were too busy having and caring for babies and would be subject to language inappropriate for women.)

Now lead students in a comparison of this source's point of view with the points of view of the two previous anthology selections. *What do they share in common?* (the subject of women's demands for the vote and for equality in other ways as well) *What point of view do the two previous anthology selections share?* (They both support women's rights, including full equality and the right to vote.) Ask students to write a letter to the editor of the *New York Herald* in which they respond to the arguments set forth in this selection. Remind them to refer to points made in the previous two selections. Have volunteers read their letters to the class.

UNCLE TOM'S CABIN
by Harriet Beecher Stowe, 1852
Page 112

Use with Chapter 16, Lesson 3

Objectives

- ☐ *Appreciate the tragedy of slavery as portrayed in one of the most influential abolitionist writings of the time.*
- ☐ *Create a book cover for the novel.*

Creating Graphics

After students have read the selection, ask them to sum up what happens in this excerpt from the book. *What role does Sam play in the attempt to recapture Eliza?* (He makes a loud noise to warn Eliza that Haley is coming after her and, by creating a distraction, gives her time to run away.) *Why does Sam side with Eliza even though he's working for the slave trader Haley?* (As an enslaved person himself, he empathizes with her plight.) *How does the author make you feel about Eliza?* (You're on her side and want her escape to freedom to succeed.) *Why do you suppose this book was such a powerful document for the abolitionist movement?* (It gave slavery a human face and showed how unjust the institution was to enslaved people.)

Divide students into pairs. Challenge them to create a book cover for *Uncle Tom's Cabin* that will revive interest in the book among people today. Remind students that book covers have eye-catching graphics as well as descriptions of the book's plot and explanations of why it is an important publication. Quotes by famous people about the work are also common. Have teams inspect each other's work.

CIVIL WAR PHOTOGRAPHS
by Mathew Brady, 1860–1865
Pages 113–114

Use with Chapter 17, Lesson 1

Objectives

- ☐ *Appreciate the real-life nature of the Civil War that Mathew Brady caught on film.*
- ☐ *Plan an historical photoessay.*

Background Information

Photography had only been in existence for 21 years when the Civil War broke out. In those early years film consisted of large plates of glass that had to be dipped in chemicals and slowly exposed while the liquid was still wet. Although plagued by very poor vision, Mathew Brady became one of the United States' earliest and most successful photographers. When the Civil War broke out, he devoted his wealth and expertise to capturing the war on film. He hired about 20 other photographers to help in this effort—but the country's gain was Brady's loss. Brady was nearly bankrupted by his Civil War project, and he died a poor man in 1896.

Planning a Photoessay

After students have examined the photographs, ask them how the pictures help them get a better feel for what it was like to live and fight during the Civil War. *What kinds of details from the pictures make the war or the time especially real?* (the kind of clothes worn, the kinds of equipment used, the emotions and activities depicted) Encourage students to suppose that they are responsible for photographing an important historical event. Working in small groups, have them choose an event or time period and make a list of the people, places, and events they would need to photograph in order to provide a comprehensive picture of what things were like. Have each group share their lists with the class and obtain feedback on what else they might include or what they might delete.

THE EMANCIPATION PROCLAMATION
by Abraham Lincoln, 1863
Pages 115–116

Use with Chapter 17, Lesson 2

Objectives

☐ *Understand that the Emancipation Proclamation led to the end of slavery in the Southern states.*

☐ *Summarize the document's main points in the form of a newspaper report.*

Rewriting in Another Genre

After students have read the document, have them discuss why it sparked such a major turning point in American history. (It called for the end of slavery.) Ask them: *Did the proclamation immediately free all slaves?* (No, technically it freed just those in states still in rebellion against the United States; an amendment to the Constitution in 1865 would outlaw slavery for good.) *What else did the proclamation do?* (It called for the recruitment of African Americans as Union soldiers.)

Encourage students to suppose that they are newspaper reporters who have just covered Lincoln's delivery of the proclamation. Challenge them to write a short news report about the new document. Remind students that an effective news report includes as many of the 5 Ws as possible—*Who, What, When, Where,* and *Why.* Finally, tell students to add a suitable headline to their story.

DESTRUCTION OF THE SOUTH
by Eliza Frances Andrews, 1864
Page 117

Use with Chapter 17, Lesson 3

Objectives

☐ *Recognize a Southern woman's perspective on the destruction caused by General Sherman's army.*

☐ *Write an essay on Sherman's march and its place in American history.*

Background Information

Eliza Frances Andrews, born in Washington, Georgia, was the daughter of a highly respected judge. In the stormy years before the Civil War, Judge Andrews and his wife supported those who wanted the Southern states to remain with the Union, while Eliza and her brothers sided with the secessionists. Eliza secretly sewed a Confederate flag that was raised when Georgia seceded from the Union. As he watched this celebration, Eliza's father commented, "Poor fools! They may ring their bells now, but they will wring their hands— yes, and their hearts, too—before they are done with it."

Building Knowledge

After students have read the selection, have them share their reactions to the destruction caused by Sherman's march. Ask students how they would react if an enemy army did the same thing to their homes and community. Tell students that some people think that the devastation caused by Sherman's army was necessary in order to end the war and abolish slavery. To this day some people consider Sherman a hero, while others view him as a barbarian.

Have students write an essay, based on the information contained in this selection and in the textbook, about the place of Sherman's march in American history. Help students to recognize how different perspectives on the war can affect people's views of General Sherman. Have volunteers read their essays aloud to the class.

TEACHING FREED PEOPLE
by Charlotte Forten, 1864
Pages 118–119

Use with Chapter 17, Lesson 4

Objectives

☐ *Understand how Charlotte Forten's magazine article makes clear the desire for education among former slaves.*

☐ *Recognize the sacrifices that these people were willing to make for education.*

☐ *Rewrite Forten's article from the perspective of a student in her classroom.*

Rewriting from Another Perspective

After students have read the selection, have them point out examples in the article that indicate how important education was to former slaves. (Children came to school after a hard day's work in the fields and were eager to learn; many adults came to school and made sacrifices so that their children could attend.) Ask students: *How was Forten's class different from classes today?* (Her classes were much bigger; students ranged from little children to grandparents; people made sacrifices to come to school, which was not mandatory as it is today.)

Challenge students to rewrite Forten's magazine article from the perspective of a student in her class. Remind students that until slavery was abolished, African Americans in the South were forbidden to learn how to read and write. Tell students to explain in their article why education is so important and what it means to be able to learn to read and write at last. Have volunteers share their articles with the rest of the class.

O CAPTAIN! MY CAPTAIN!
by Walt Whitman, 1865–1866
Page 120

Use with Chapter 17, Lesson 4

Objectives

☐ *Recognize that many Americans, like Walt Whitman, were saddened by the death of Abraham Lincoln.*

☐ *Conduct an interview of imaginary people living during the time of Lincoln's assassination.*

Background Information

The poet Walt Whitman was a great admirer of Abraham Lincoln and a strong supporter of the Union. After the President was shot, Whitman wrote: "By many has this Union been helped; but, if one name, one man, must be picked out, he most of all, is the conservator of it to the future. He was assassinated—but the Union is not assassinated.... The soldier drops, sinks like a wave, but the ranks of the ocean eternally press on. Death does its work, obliterates a hundred, a thousand—president, general, captain, private—but the Nation is immortal."

Writing an Interview

Have volunteers read the poem aloud. Then play the version on the cassette. Ask students: *What does Whitman mean when he says, "The prize we sought is won"?* (The "prize" is preservation of the Union and the ending of slavery.) *Why is happiness in the poem mixed with great sadness?* (The Union has won the Civil War, and slavery has been abolished, but the leader who helped bring about these goals has been killed.)

Ask each student to assume the role of an American living during the Civil War. For example, they might choose to play a male or female store owner from the North, a plantation owner from the South, or a formerly enslaved African American. Working in pairs, have students interview each other about their reactions to Lincoln's assassination. Ask for volunteers to perform their interviews before the whole class. Help students to conclude that reactions to President Lincoln and to his death were affected by the point of view or position in life of each person.

RESETTLING THE GREAT PLAINS

Poster, 1870s
Page 122

Use with Chapter 18, Lesson 3

Objectives

- ☐ *Understand how the poster shows the role of railroads in attracting homesteaders to the Great Plains.*
- ☐ *Recognize that land belonging to Native Americans of the Plains was resettled after the Native Americans were forcibly removed.*
- ☐ *Create a storyboard for a fictional advertisement of land on the Great Plains.*

Drawing Storyboards with Captions

After students have studied the poster, have them discuss how advertisers tried to attract new settlers. Ask students: *What did the railroads have to gain by persuading people to move west?* (People moving west meant more railroad passengers and more people shipping goods.)

Divide the class into pairs of students. Tell students to suppose that television existed in the 1870s and that railroad owners wanted to broadcast their advertisements on television. Challenge students to design a storyboard with captions that persuade people to go west to the Dakotas aboard the Chicago & Northwestern Railroad. Remind students to make both their images and their words convincing. Have students share their storyboards with the rest of the class. Afterward, ask students to discuss how Native Americans might have reacted to their advertisements.

DON'T FENCE ME IN

by Cole Porter, 1944
Pages 123–124

Use with Chapter 18, Lesson 2

Objectives

- ☐ *Recognize how the songwriter creates a picture of the vastness of the land in the Western and Southwestern regions of the United States.*
- ☐ *Rewrite the song as a feature article in a magazine.*

Background Information

Cole Porter was a famous American songwriter who wrote many tunes and lyrics for successful stage and screen musicals. Two of Porter's best-known songs are "I've Got You Under My Skin" and "I Get a Kick Out of You." His most famous musicals are *Anything Goes* and *Kiss Me, Kate.*

Rewriting in Another Genre

After students have read the lyrics, play the song for them on the cassette. Have students sing along. Ask students to identify those aspects of life in the Western and Southwestern United States that are reflected in the song. Then challenge students to rewrite the song in the form of a feature article in a magazine. Tell them to suppose that they are Wild Cat Kelly and to explain why they love living in the American West and Southwest. Encourage volunteers to read their articles aloud to the class. Then ask students whether they think Porter's vision of the American West and Southwest presents an accurate portrait of what those regions are like today.

EXODUSTERS
Poster, 1877
Page 125

Use with Chapter 18, Lesson 3

Objectives

☐ *Identify reasons that the poster would have been of interest to African Americans who were formerly enslaved.*

☐ *Write a letter from the perspective of a fictional African American who moved to Kansas from the South.*

Writing a Letter

After students have looked at the poster, have them explain why moving to Kansas would have appealed to African Americans living in the South at that time. (Even after the end of slavery, African Americans in the South lived in extreme poverty and faced terrible discrimination.) Have volunteers summarize the contents of the poster. Ask students the following question: *What would have been the advantages of belonging to a group as opposed to moving to Kansas on one's own?* (Resources such as money, oxen, and plows could be pooled; the community government could help resolve conflicts; it would be easier to combat discrimination as a group.)

Have students suppose that they are an Exoduster who has recently moved to Kansas. Tell them to write a letter to a friend back home about their new life on the Plains. Ask them to focus on the struggles and triumphs associated with living in Kansas and how life there is different from life in the South. Also encourage them to comment on whether they would recommend moving to Kansas. Have volunteers read their letters aloud to the class.

GRASSHOPPER SUMMER
by Ann Turner, 1989
Pages 126–129

Use with Chapter 18, Lesson 3

Objectives

☐ *Recognize how the story makes clear the struggles of a family trying to start a new life on the Great Plains.*

☐ *Identify the natural disaster of 1874 that brought great hardship to many homesteading families.*

☐ *Stage a performance of Story Theater dramatizing the story.*

Background Information

Grasshopper Summer is a book based on an actual event. All across the Great Plains, homesteaders remembered 1874 as the year that grasshoppers nearly destroyed the earth. The grasshoppers ate everything in sight: crops, clothes, wooden handles, even parts of leather harnesses. They returned in smaller numbers the following summer, but by then many homesteaders had been forced to leave their farms. Plains farmers would not be disturbed by grasshoppers again until the 1930s, but by then they had an even greater disaster to fight: the dust storms that turned the region into a "Dust Bowl."

Using Story Theater

After students have read the selection, ask them: *How did you react to the story? How did the White family try to save their farm and crops?* (They tried to drive the grasshoppers away with smoke, guns, and shovels.) *Why were they unsuccessful?* (There were too many grasshoppers.) Challenge students to make a Story Theater out of the selection. Have one group of students take turns reading parts of the story aloud. You may wish to assign each of the speaking characters (Billy, Sam the narrator, Pa, Ma, and Mrs. Grant) to a different student. Then have the other students act out the drama being read. Some actors can even play the roles of the two horses and the swarms of grasshoppers. After the Story Theater has been performed, lead students in a discussion of how performing the story gave them a better understanding of the events being described.

BATTLING WITH THE SIOUX
by George Armstrong Custer, 1873
Page 130

Use with Chapter 18, Lesson 4

Objectives

- ☐ *Recognize the viewpoint of an officer who help lead the United States government's campaign to force Native Americans from their lands in the late 1800s.*
- ☐ *Create a mural depicting the battle described by Custer.*

Background Information

George Armstrong Custer first won fame as a military officer during the Civil War. Like many veterans of that conflict, he was posted to fight in the Plains Wars soon after the Civil War ended. By the early 1870s Custer was winning added fame through magazine articles in which he described his battles with Native Americans. This excerpt from one of these articles describes a bloody battle he waged in 1873 against the Lakota Sioux, who were fighting efforts to build a railroad through their land. In it Custer refers to his brother, Colonel Tom Custer, who served with him in the battle. Custer's article wasn't published until July 1876—one month after he and everyone in his company had been killed by Lakota Sioux warriors at the Battle of Little Bighorn.

Creating a Mural

Give students background information before they read the source. After they have read Custer's account, challenge them to retell it in their own words. Encourage them to be as dramatic as Custer himself was. When they have finished, ask them: *from what point of view is the battle described?* (the United States Army's) *How can you tell?* (The action is described from the soldiers' point of view.)

As a class, plan a mural of a scene from this battle. Then have students work in small groups, with each group responsible for a portion of the mural. Have students do any library research necessary to ensure that their depiction is historically accurate and not based on stereotypes. For example, they may wish to research the type of clothes worn by both the Lakota Sioux and the United States Army in battle during the Plains Wars and the types of weapons used by each.

THE BATTLE OF LITTLE BIGHORN
by Two Moon, 1898
Pages 131–133

Use with Chapter 18, Lesson 4

Objectives

- ☐ *Understand a Cheyenne chief's perspective on the Battle of Little Bighorn.*
- ☐ *Understand that the Native Americans fought to protect their homeland.*
- ☐ *Write a television news report that summarizes the battle and includes interviews with Native American survivors.*

Rewriting in Another Genre

After students have read the selection, have them discuss Two Moon's account. Ask students the following questions. *Why did the Lakota Sioux and Cheyenne decide to go to war with the United States Army?* (Native Americans had been killed; their land and horses had been stolen.) *Why do you think that the Native Americans were sorrowful after the battle?* (Many people had been killed; the surviving Native Americans probably realized that their way of life was being destroyed.)

Divide the class into groups of four or five students. Tell them to suppose that they are television news teams sent to interview Native American survivors of the Battle of Little Bighorn. Inform students that their news reports should include a brief explanation of the conflicts leading up to the battle and that they should ask survivors how the battle will affect their lives. Encourage them to use information on Custer that they learned from reading the previous selection. Remind students that most news reports summarize an issue and include interviews with several people, all in about two minutes. Challenge them to keep their reports to about this length. Then have each group perform its report for the class.

FOR SALE BY MAIL
Advertisements from the Sears, Roebuck Catalogue, 1897
Pages 134–135

Use with Chapter 19, Lesson 1

Objectives
- ❑ *Recognize that the technological advances in the late 1800s resulted in the availability of many more products to people all over the country.*
- ❑ *Compare and contrast advertising in the late 1800s with advertising today.*
- ❑ *Create modern advertisements for the Sears products.*

Creating Graphics

Remind students that many of the new products that became available in the late 1800s were due to the abundance of inventions and new technologies during that time. After students have studied the selection, have them discuss how the old advertisements compare and contrast with advertisements today. Then ask students: *How do the Sears advertisements try to persuade people to buy each product?* (They stress quality, fashion, and newness of goods.) *In what ways are today's advertisements different from those shown here?* (Today's advertisements use photographs as well as celebrities, appealing people, and pets to sell products.)

Divide the class into pairs of students. Challenge them to design their own advertisements for the Sears products as if they were being marketed today. Then have students share their advertisements with the rest of the class and explain how they work to persuade people to buy the products.

THE INDUSTRIAL PROBLEM
by Andrew Carnegie, 1903–1911
Pages 136–137

Use with Chapter 19, Lesson 1

Objectives
- ❑ *Recognize the viewpoint of a powerful businessman regarding the relationship between workers and management in the early 1900s.*
- ❑ *Make a political cartoon based on his view.*

Background Information

During the late 1800s Andrew Carnegie aggressively sought to control much of the United States' steel industry. He hired the best experts, bought state-of-the-art machinery—and also ordered his managers to keep workers' wages as trim as possible to stay competitive. In 1892 a conflict over wages at a Carnegie-owned plant in Homestead, Pennsylvania, resulted in bloodshed when Carnegie's manager called in hundreds of armed guards to break the strike. Nine workers and seven armed guards were killed. Nine years later Carnegie sold his entire stake in the steel industry to U.S. Steel—the company he describes in this excerpt—for $250 million, making him one of the world's richest men. Carnegie then devoted the rest of his life to giving that money away to worthy causes and helping to improve relationships between labor and management.

Creating Graphics

After students have read the selection, ask them to describe what Carnegie said U.S. Steel was doing to make relations between workers and management better. (giving company stock to workers; providing pension funds and medical help) *Why, in Carnegie's eyes, were "capital, labor, ability" like a "three-legged stool"?* (All are necessary and equally important in creating or maintaining success in business.) Challenge students to design a political cartoon based on Carnegie's description. Remind students that political cartoonists can use their images both to support or to protest an issue, action, or cause. Have volunteers share their work with the class.

EIGHT HOURS
Words by I. G. Blanchard and Music by Jesse H. Jones, 1866
Page 138 🎦

Use with Chapter 19, Lesson 1

Objectives
- ❏ *Recognize that American workers in the late 1800s worked long hours and had to fight for the eight-hour workday that is so commonplace today.*
- ❏ *Understand how the song expresses the desire for an eight-hour workday among workers in the 1800s.*
- ❏ *Compare the struggles of American workers in the late 1800s with the struggles of working people today.*

Linking to Today
After students have read the song, play it for them on the cassette. Then have students explain the meaning of each stanza in their own words.

Tell students that at the time the song was written, many people worked at least ten hours a day, six days a week. Have students discuss what they think are the main concerns of American working people today. (unemployment, plant closings, insufficient wages, international competition) Ask students: *How do these concerns differ from those of the eight-hour movement?* (They have less to do with working long hours than with working no hours at all.) Challenge students to think of popular present-day songs that address the concerns of American working people.

THE PROMISED LAND
by Mary Antin, 1911
Pages 139–140

Use with Chapter 19, Lesson 2

Objectives
- ❏ *Understand an immigrant child's perspective on life and education in America.*
- ❏ *Link Mary Antin's account to the experience of immigrants today.*

Background Information
When 13-year-old Mary Antin first went to school in Boston, she was put in a kindergarten class because of her limited ability to speak English. Within four months, however, she had moved up to the third grade. Her teacher was so impressed with one of Mary's compositions that she arranged to have it published in a magazine. This is how Antin's writing career was born. When she was 18 years old, Mary Antin had her first book published. Called *From Plotzk to Boston*, it described the long journey she and her family had made from Russia to America. Most of the book was actually written when Mary was only 13 years old.

Linking to Today
After students have read the selection, have them discuss what it is like to come in contact with new things for the first time. Ask students whether they have visited other countries, other parts of the United States, or even gone to the home of a family that has traditions or ways of doing things that are different from their own. Have volunteers share what it was like for them to experience new things or unfamiliar places.

Challenge students to think about aspects of American culture that would be new and interesting to immigrants to the United States today. If there are students in the class who are immigrants, have them share their first impressions of American culture. Then have students think about what would be most difficult for them to adjust to if they and their families moved to a different country.

FROM THE WALLS OF ANGEL ISLAND

Poems by Unknown Chinese Immigrants, 1910–1940

Pages 141–142 🔲

Use with Chapter 19, Lesson 2

Objectives

☐ *Recognize that Chinese immigrants were treated like criminals in the early 1900s.*

☐ *Understand how the poems express the differences between the Chinese immigrants' hopes for a new life in America and the reality that they found.*

☐ *Rewrite the poems as a radio report on the unjust treatment of Chinese immigrants.*

Rewriting in Another Genre

After students have read the poems, play them on the cassette. The first poem is read first in Chinese and then in English. Have students explain the meaning of each poem in their own words. Have them think about the reactions that each poem discusses.

Challenge students to suppose that they are radio news reporters who have been assigned to report on Angel Island and the people detained there. Have them use the poems and the introduction to them as their source materials. Have volunteers deliver their radio reports to the rest of the class.

JANE ADDAMS AND HULL HOUSE

by Navidad O'Neill, 1996

Pages 143–148

Use with Chapter 19, Lesson 2

Objectives

☐ *Identify problems that Chicago's working poor faced in the late 1800s, which Jane Addams worked to better through Hull House.*

☐ *Outline problems that communities face today and what people could do to fight such problems.*

☐ *Perform a play about Addams and Hull House.*

Background Information

Jane Addams grew up in well-off surroundings in Cedarville, a small town in Illinois. After recovering from a long illness that upset her plans to become a doctor, she set off on a trip to Europe with her best friend from college, Ellen Starr. In London they visited Toynbee Hall, a community center in a poor section of the city that provided classes, library books, and other services to nearby families. Addams wrote home that the hall "is so free from 'professional doing good,' so unaffectedly sincere and so productive of good results ... that it seems perfectly ideal." A year after returning home, Addams and Starr began their own community center, or settlement house, in Chicago—Hull House.

Performing a Play

Have volunteers read the play to the class. Afterward, ask students to describe the problems that poor people in Chicago faced before Hull House was opened. (poor garbage service and other health hazards, poor schools and libraries, lack of childcare and parks for working families, children working in factories) *What did Addams do to tackle such problems?* (set up libraries, classes, childcare facilities, and recreational activities at Hull House; worked with city officials to tackle health and sanitation problems and to build playgrounds; worked to end child labor) Encourage students to discuss problems their own communities face and to identify individuals and organizations that work towards solutions to these problems. Challenge them to think of ways in which they themselves might help. Invite volunteers to perform the play for parents, for the school, or for a younger class.

BUILDING THE PANAMA CANAL

by Theodore Roosevelt, 1910

Page 149 🔲

Use with Chapter 19, Lesson 4

Objectives

☐ *Appreciate the magnitude of the task of building the Panama Canal.*

☐ *Make an imaginary supply list of what was needed at the canal worksite.*

Background Information

In 1881 a French team—headed by the man who oversaw the creation of the 105-mile-long Suez Canal—began efforts to construct a canal in Panama. The region's challenging conditions proved too much, however, and in 1887 the prestigious firm went bankrupt and all work came to a halt. In 1906 American engineers picked up where the French left off. As many as 40,000 people worked at the site at one time, their ultimate goal being to carve out a 40-mile-long channel up to 300 feet wide and over 40 feet deep. The canal would also be divided into a series of complex locks that would raise ships as much as 85 feet above sea level. In the end over 240 million cubic yards of earth and rock were removed—or roughly enough dirt to cover all of the island of Manhattan 10 feet deep—at a cost of over $300 million.

Rewriting in Another Genre

After students have read the selection, play the speech for them on the cassette. Then ask them the reasons why President Roosevelt was proud of the Panama Canal's completion. (Others had tried to do it but failed, and the work was done efficiently.) Challenge students to list all the things managers would have had to keep track of at the canal site. (for example, food, clean water, medical care for 40,000 people; accountants to keep track of incoming and outgoing goods; equipment and parts for the work itself; transport to the site) Lead students in a discussion of how the exercise has given them added admiration for the makers of the Panama Canal.

EXPLOSION OF THE *MAINE*

from the *New York Journal*, 1898

Page 150

Use with Chapter 19, Lesson 3

Objectives

☐ *Identify the consequences of the explosion of the Maine.*

☐ *Recognize the power of newspapers to influence public opinion.*

☐ *Determine the credibility of the newspaper report about the explosion of the Maine.*

Determining the Credibility of the Document

After students have read the newspaper article, have them discuss how the *New York Journal* presents the facts of the *Maine* explosion. Ask students: *Do the publishers of the newspaper seem to have an open mind about the cause of the explosion?* (No, the explosion is portrayed as "the work of an enemy," probably the Spanish.)

Challenge students to imagine that they are detectives. Ask them: *How would you determine whether the* Journal *reports about the Maine were credible? What other sources could you check to learn more facts about the explosion?* (For a start, they might talk to Spanish and Cuban officials—the *Journal* mentions only the views of United States officials; they might also question survivors and eyewitnesses.)

Ask students: *Might newspapers today print stories like the* Journal's *if a similar disaster happened? Why or why not?* (Most newspapers try to back up their stories with solid facts and evidence; however, sometimes newspapers do not adequately check their facts.) *Why don't all newspapers print basically the same story when they are covering the same event?* (Newspapers are written by people who have different points of view and different ways of interpreting events.) *Why is this important to remember?* (Newspaper articles should be read critically; many have points of view, just like people.)

OVER THERE
by George M. Cohan, 1917
Pages 152–153 🔲

Use with Chapter 20, Lesson 1

Objectives

- ❏ *Examine the main perspective on American involvement in World War I through a song that was popular during the war.*
- ❏ *Write song lyrics that express a point of view.*

Background Information

In the first year of World War I, more than one million people were killed. As Americans learned of the bloodshed overseas, most came to believe that the United States should not become involved. Antiwar songs such as "I Didn't Raise My Boy to Be a Soldier" became big hits. But in 1917, after German submarines sank American ships, the United States declared war on Germany. Songwriter George M. Cohan was one of many Americans who now favored going to war. Cohan said that "Over There" began as a bugle call in his mind. The song became a rallying cry for the one million Americans who served in World War I. More than 50,000 Americans died in the war.

Writing Song Lyrics

After students have read the song, play it on the cassette. Then ask students what point of view is expressed in this song. (It stresses the pride of fighting for a good cause.) Tell students that most wars produce songs by people who are either in favor of the war or who are against it. Have students discuss why people use songs in this way. Then have them write song lyrics that express their point of view on an issue of importance to them. Invite volunteers to read their lyrics aloud to the class.

THE GREAT MIGRATION
by Jacob Lawrence, 1992
Pages 154–155

Use with Chapter 20, Lesson 1

Objectives

- ❏ *Recognize the impact that the Great Migration had on the history of the United States as well as on the lives of individuals who made the journey northward.*
- ❏ *Make a collage about one's own community.*

Creating Graphics

After students have read the selection, ask them to summarize what the Great Migration was. (a mass movement of African Americans from the South to the North, begun around the time of World War I) *How did the Great Migration affect Jacob Lawrence's own life?* (It resulted in his parents meeting and his being born in New Jersey.) *How does he attempt to fit his own life "into a much larger story—the history of African-Americans in this country"?* (by painting scenes from African American history and from the daily lives of African Americans)

Ask students to name big events that are shaping life in the United States today. (increasing popularity of computers and the Internet, ongoing fight against crime and violence in communities, and so on.) Ask them to think about how such events play a role in their own lives. Challenge students to make their own paintings of a historical event that affected their own families or communities. Remind them that all of our lives also fit "into a much larger story"—the ongoing history of our country.

LET AMERICA BE AMERICA AGAIN

by Langston Hughes, 1936
Pages 156–158 🔲

Use with Chapter 20, Lesson 2

Objectives

- ☐ *Recognize the perspective of a poet from the Harlem Renaissance on America's past, present, and future.*
- ☐ *Recognize the struggles that Americans have undergone in order to make their country a land of liberty and justice for all.*
- ☐ *Create an illustrated time line of American history that highlights some of these struggles.*

Creating a Time Line

After students have read the poem, play it on the cassette. Ask students: *In whose voice does Langston Hughes speak in his poem?* (Native Americans, African Americans, immigrants, farmers, factory workers) *How does the poem express both anger and hope?* (The poem expresses anger that although the United States is built on the idea of freedom, many Americans throughout history have been denied freedom and equality; the poem also expresses the hope that America may one day be "the land where every man is free.")

Divide the class into groups of four students and give each group a long piece of paper. Remind them that Hughes's poem refers to many events in American history. Challenge students to design illustrated time lines that highlight the events mentioned by Hughes as well as other events that represent the ongoing struggle for liberty, justice, and equality in the United States. Encourage students to title their projects and to refer to their textbooks for dates and information. Then have each group present its time line to the rest of the class. Post the time lines around the classroom.

THE TRIAL OF SUSAN B. ANTHONY

Trial Transcript, 1873
Pages 159–161

Use with Chapter 20, Lesson 2

Objectives

- ☐ *Recognize that it was not legal for most women to vote in the United States before 1920.*
- ☐ *Understand how the trial transcript shows Susan B. Anthony's perspective on the rights of American women.*
- ☐ *Dramatize the transcript of the trial.*

Background Information

In the 1840s women began accelerating the struggle for the right to vote on both the state and national levels. In 1869 and 1870 they won their first victories when the territories of both Wyoming and Utah legalized voting for women. Subsequently women attracted attention to their cause by voting illegally in other states and in national elections. However, their votes were usually disregarded, and some women were arrested for breaking the law. Susan B. Anthony was one of these women.

Dramatizing the Trial

Have students read the introduction. Then read the trial transcript aloud to the class, stopping to define difficult words. Afterward, have students share their reactions to the case. Ask them in what ways Susan B. Anthony was treated unfairly. Have them discuss the main points in Anthony's powerful argument. Divide the class into groups. Have each group act out the trial, using the transcript. Encourage students to capture the spirit of Susan B. Anthony's conflict with the judge. Although only two students from each group will actually play out the scene, others should serve as directors or acting coaches. Have each group present its dramatization to the class.

DUST STORM DISASTER
by Woody Guthrie, 1935
Pages 162–163 🔲

Use with Chapter 20, Lesson 3

Objectives

- ☐ *Recognize how the song makes clear the effects that the Dust Bowl had on the lives of farmers.*
- ☐ *Trace the route of the storm described in the song.*

Background Information

Woodrow Wilson Guthrie was born in Okemah, Oklahoma, in 1912. His childhood was one of great hardship. When he was a boy, his father went bankrupt, and the Guthrie house burned down. These experiences helped Woody Guthrie to understand the daily struggles most Americans faced in order to survive, particularly during the 1930s. At the age of 15, Guthrie left high school and set out to travel around the country. During the travels that occupied most of his life, he wrote more than 1,000 songs. Most of them had to do with the struggles of workers and farmers trying to feed and clothe their families.

Tracing the Route

After students have read the lyrics, play the song for them on the cassette. Ask students if the song helps them to understand the devastating effects of the Dust Bowl. Ask students: *What did the storm force many farmers to do?* (leave their farms forever) Have students work in groups to make a map of the United States, showing the places affected by the dust storm in Guthrie's song. Then ask students to count the number of states that were affected by the storm. Have students imagine the number of lives touched by this disaster.

THE FOUR FREEDOMS
by Franklin Delano Roosevelt, 1941
Page 164 🔲

Use with Chapter 20, Lesson 4

Objectives

- ☐ *Appreciate Franklin Roosevelt's summary of the ideals of freedom Americans prized in the past and continue to value today.*
- ☐ *Recognize how the speech echoes the ideals of freedom set forth in earlier, classic American documents.*

Linking Past, Present, and Future

After students have read the selection, play the speech for them on the cassette. Then ask them to summarize what Roosevelt's speech is all about. (It makes the possibility of Americans fighting in World War II all about protecting freedom—freedom of speech and religion, and freedom from need and fear—throughout the world.) *What other classic American documents talk in a similar manner about the value of freedom?* (Declaration of Independence, Constitution, Bill of Rights, Declaration of Sentiments and Resolutions, Emancipation Proclamation, and others)

Ask students: *How does Roosevelt's Four Freedoms speech take Americans' love of freedom one step further?* (It gives it a global dimension—"Freedom means the supremacy of human rights everywhere.") Finally, lead students in a discussion of how the United States in recent years has viewed this concept and acted upon this view.

LINEAGE

by Margaret Walker, 1941
Page 165

Use with Chapter 20, Lesson 3

Objectives

❏ *Recognize how Margaret Walker conveys in a poem her perspective on the Great Depression and the ways it tested her spirit.*

❏ *Write a poem about a personal hardship experienced by each student.*

Writing Your Own Poem

After students have read the poem, play it for them on the cassette. Have them discuss why the poet may have felt weak in comparison to her grandmothers. Ask students: *How might the hard times of the Depression have affected the poet?* (During the Depression even those desperate for work could not find jobs; farm prices fell so low that farmers could not buy the things necessary to keep their farms running; Margaret Walker may have thought there was no way for her to improve her life.) Then have students discuss how poetry helps people to express their reactions to situations.

Ask students why hard times can affect the way people think about themselves. Challenge students to think about something with which they have struggled. Have them write a poem about that struggle and its outcome. Have volunteers read their poems to the class.

WORLD WAR II

from the *New York Times*, 1941–1945
Page 166

Use with Chapter 20, Lesson 4

Objectives

❏ *Appreciate the magnitude of three turning points in World War II history: Pearl Harbor, D-Day, and Hiroshima.*

❏ *Write newspaper articles to accompany the headlines.*

Rewriting in Another Genre

After students have viewed the headlines, ask them why the bombing of Pearl Harbor, the D-Day invasion, and the dropping of the atomic bomb on Hiroshima were such important events in World War II history. (The first got the United States into war; the second marked the beginning of the end for Germany; the third brought a final end to the war.) *How do the headlines themselves reflect the great importance of the events?* (All are in capital letters and take up three lines.)

Divide the class into groups of three. Challenge them to write brief newspaper articles for the three headlines. Remind them to address the *5 Ws* of journalism: *Who, What, Where, When*, and *Why*. Also encourage them to include "photographs," maps, or charts, if possible, as well as their byline.

LIFE IN A JAPANESE AMERICAN RELOCATION CAMP
by Yuri Tateishi, 1984
Pages 167–169

Use with Chapter 20, Lesson 4

Objectives

❏ *Identify with the experience of a Japanese American family while they were in a relocation camp in California during World War II.*

❏ *Recognize that the Constitutional rights of Japanese Americans were violated when they were placed in relocation camps.*

❏ *Dramatize part of Yuri Tateishi's story.*

Dramatizing the Story

After students have read the selection, ask them how they might have reacted if they had been in Yuri Tateishi's place. Divide the class into groups of four or five students. Challenge each group to dramatize a part of Yuri Tateishi's story. Have each group choose a passage or section and write a script based on it. Encourage them to try to dramatize some of the reactions that they mentioned in the discussion. Then have them rehearse the scene several times. Encourage each group to perform its scene before the class. Ask students whether acting out the scenes helped them to understand what the Tateishis and other Japanese Americans experienced during World War II.

THE BUTTERFLY
by Pavel Friedmann, 1942
Page 170 🔊

Use with Chapter 20, Lesson 4

Objectives

❏ *Understand the incredible horrors of the Holocaust through the poetry of one of its victims.*

❏ *Paint a picture with accompanying text about the Holocaust or about one's fears and hopes for the future.*

Background Information

As Nazi forces conquered their way across Europe, they forced hundreds of thousands of Jews into fenced-off, prisonlike areas called ghettos. One of those ghettos was Terezín, a city in Czechoslovakia. Hunger, cold, and overcrowding; child labor; carts pulled by people rather than horses; and executions by Nazi guards all became a daily part of life for the city's 15,000 children. One of them was Pavel Friedmann. But the worst was yet to come. Most residents were eventually killed by the Nazis. Only 100 children from Terezín survived to see World War II's end.

Creating Paintings

Share the background information above with students before reading the poem aloud. Then have students read the poem while it is played on the cassette. Ask students what they think butterflies stood for in Pavel's mind. (freedom, beauty, nature) *Why did the last butterfly leave Terezín, in Pavel's opinion?* ("It wished to kiss the world goodbye.") *What do you think he meant by "Butterflies don't live in here, in the ghetto"?* (No one in the ghetto was free.) Point out that the painting on the page was also done by one of the children of Terezín.

Have volunteers share their knowledge of and reactions to the horrors of the Holocaust. Then ask them to create paintings based on their reactions or knowledge. Alternatively, you might wish to have students do paintings about their own view of the future. Let those who wish compose poems or prose to accompany their paintings. Have volunteers share their artwork and writing with the class.

ICH BIN EIN BERLINER
by John F. Kennedy, 1963
Page 171 📼

Use with Chapter 20, Lesson 5

Objectives

❑ *Recognize how the Berlin Wall became a symbol of the Cold War.*

❑ *Create a political cartoon about the Cold War.*

Creating Graphics

Before students read the selection, tell them to pay special attention to the contrasts that Kennedy makes between communism and democracy. *Why, in his view, is the wall a symbol of communism's failure? Why is Kennedy so proud to call himself a Berliner?* After students have finished reading, play the speech on the cassette. Then ask them what answers they found to the previous questions. (Communists had to build the wall to keep people from leaving their area, reflecting the failure of their system; West Berlin symbolized the freedom found in democracies everywhere—freedom denied in communist countries.) Next have students describe Kennedy's predictions of what would happen to the wall in the future. (It would come down.) *What kind of a symbol would the wall be then, in Kennedy's view?* (a symbol of freedom everywhere)

Divide students into pairs. Challenge them to make a political cartoon about the Berlin Wall or the Cold War in general. For ideas, they may wish to study the images Kennedy creates in his speech. Have groups view each other's work.

MY DAY
by Eleanor Roosevelt, 1942
Page 172

Use with Chapter 20, Lesson 4

Objectives

❑ *Recognize Eleanor Roosevelt's appreciation of the spirit of cooperation that enabled people to weather the hard times of World War II.*

❑ *Create a poster that celebrates that spirit.*

Background Information

In November 1942 Eleanor Roosevelt and her newspaper column became a major source of information on the effect of the war on Britain. During her visit to the bomb-ravaged nation, Roosevelt described staying at Buckingham Palace, which itself had been hit by bombs and was subject to strict rationing of food, water, and clothing. She also described the joy many British felt upon the arrival of American troops in North Africa, where they were to aid British forces already fighting there. On November 18 the British received word of a major Allied victory in North Africa. Roosevelt duly described Britain's reaction, and her own, to the news.

Creating Posters

Share background information with students and ask them to read the selection. When they have finished, ask them to describe "the spirit of the people" of Britain that Roosevelt is so grateful for. (one of hard work without complaint, sacrifice) *Why is it so amazing that this spirit existed in Britain at the time?* (They had been under siege and attack for three winters.) Remind students that the war would continue for more than two years after the date of Roosevelt's article.

Challenge pairs of students to create a poster that illustrates how the spirit Roosevelt described enabled the Allies to make it through the war. Encourage them to include people they have read about in their textbook or other anthology selections—American factory workers, WACs, soldiers at D-Day, survivors of the Holocaust and of American relocation camps, and so on. Compile the posters into a bulletin board or hallway display.

FAITH THAT MOVED A DUMP HEAP
by Mary McLeod Bethune, 1941
Pages 173–175

Use with Chapter 21, Lesson 1

Objectives

- ❏ Recognize the great demand for education among African Americans in the early 1900s.
- ❏ Understand the reasons for Mary McLeod Bethune's determination to build a school and hospital for African American children.
- ❏ Create a storyboard biography of Mary McLeod Bethune's life.

Drawing Storyboards with Captions

After students have read the selection, lead them in a discussion of Mary McLeod Bethune's amazing achievement. Ask students the following questions: *What did it take to make the school a reality?* (vision, hard work, and creativity) *Who worked with Mary McLeod Bethune to make her school a success?* (students, parents, volunteers such as builders and doctors, teachers, people attending church services who donated money)

Have students suppose that they are filmmakers who have been hired to make a film about Mary McLeod Bethune's life and the creation of Bethune-Cookman College. Divide the class into "production crews" made up of four or five students. Then have the members of each crew work together to design a storyboard with captions showing Bethune's amazing achievements. Remind students to make their storyboards as accurate as possible, based on Bethune's article, and have them create working titles for their "movies." Have each group share its work with the class.

WE SHALL OVERCOME
Freedom Song, 1901
Page 176

Use with Chapter 21, Lesson 1

Objectives

- ❏ Appreciate the song's powerful vision of freedom and unity, which became a centerpiece of the civil rights movement.
- ❏ Make a drawing that expresses the themes of the song.

Background Information

Although it is not known for sure precisely when this song was written or who its authors were, by the early 1900s it was recognized as a hymn called "I'll Be All Right" or "I'll Overcome Someday." After World War II it became a theme song for African Americans fighting discrimination in the South, and by the 1960s it had become the theme song of the civil rights movement.

Creating Drawings

Ask students whether they have ever sung this song before. Have volunteers share where they were and why they were singing the song. Then play the cassette version for students and sing the song together as a class. Ask students why the song's simple words have become so powerful. Then have students work on making a drawing that artfully expresses the meaning and mood of the music. Encourage them to draw images or cut out pictures from magazines to enhance their work. Decorate the classroom or a hallway with their artwork.

I HAVE A DREAM
by Martin Luther King, Jr., 1963
Pages 177–180 🔲

Use with Chapter 21, Lesson 1

Objectives

- ❏ *Identify the vision of the civil rights movement that is described by its leader, Dr. Martin Luther King, Jr.*
- ❏ *Understand King's desire to achieve equal rights through nonviolent protest.*
- ❏ *Write a speech about your vision for America's future.*

Writing Your Own Speech

After students have read the speech, play it on the cassette. Tell them that the recording is an excerpt from King's actual speech. Tell them also that when speaking, King sometimes departed from the written text, so that the version on the cassette varies slightly from the version in the text. Discuss with students why the speech is so powerful. Ask students how King uses images to make his message clear. Have students skim the speech and point out the images that he uses. Then ask them to describe King's dream for America. (King dreamed of a country where people were not judged by their color but

by their character, a place where black people and white people could join hands as sisters and brothers.) Ask students: *What did King urge his listeners to avoid in their struggle for equal rights?* (King said that the "creative protest" should not break down into physical violence.) *What did King mean when he talked of meeting physical force with soul force?* (that nonviolence was more powerful than violence and would triumph in the end). Ask students how and why King refers to Abraham Lincoln. Have students compare the beginning of King's speech to the beginning of Lincoln's Gettysburg Address, which appears in their textbooks on pages 484–485.

Finally, challenge students to think about what they hope will come true for America in the future. Tell them to think about how people should work to achieve these goals. Then have each student write a speech, telling of his or her hopes for America and encouraging other people to take part in making that hope come true. Have volunteers deliver their speeches to the class.

CÉSAR CHÁVEZ
by Consuelo Rodriguez, 1991
Pages 181–183

Use with Chapter 21, Lesson 2

Objectives

- ❏ *Recognize César Chávez's role in improving the lives of migrant farmworkers and protecting the environment.*
- ❏ *Understand Chávez's commitment to the principle of nonviolent protest.*
- ❏ *Write an interview with César Chávez.*

Writing an Interview

After students have read the selection, have them discuss the ideas that were important to César Chávez. Ask students: *What beliefs shaped his life?* (commitment to win fair treatment for farmworkers, faith in the Catholic Church, commitment to nonviolence) *Why did Chávez go without food?* (He wanted to stop union members from acting violently.) Ask students what they would want to ask César Chávez if he visited their class. Challenge students to work in pairs to write a list of questions and then write the answers that Chávez might give. Then have volunteers perform their interviews for the class.

244

CHARLIE PIPPIN
by Candy Dawson Boyd, 1987
Pages 184–188

Use with Chapter 21, Lesson 2

Objectives

- ☐ *Recognize the Vietnam War's long-term effects on American society.*
- ☐ *Understand the perspective of an American girl who is trying to learn about the war that changed her father's life.*
- ☐ *Present a dramatized reading of the story.*

Background Information

The Vietnam Veterans Memorial is located in Washington, D.C. On its shiny, black granite walls are carved the names of more than 58,000 Americans who were killed or missing in action during the Vietnam War. Every day thousands of visitors are moved by this silent tribute. The memorial was designed by a 21-year-old student named Maya Ying Lin. It opened in 1982.

Using Story Theater

After students have read the selection, have them discuss why the Vietnam Veterans Memorial held such special meaning for Charlie, her aunt, and her uncle. Ask students: *Why was it difficult for Charlie's aunt and uncle to visit the memorial?* (It brought back painful memories of lost friends and anger about the war itself.) *What makes Charlie realize that the effects of the war are still present in today's society?* (She realizes that for every name on the memorial, there is an empty space at some family's Thanksgiving dinner table.)

Divide the class into groups of five students. Challenge each group to prepare a Story Theater of the selection. While one group member reads the excerpt aloud, other members should act out what is being read. Encourage actors to think about what is in the minds of their characters. Monitor the progress of each group. Then ask volunteers to perform their Story Theater for the class.

GOODBYE TO ALL THAT
by Robert Darnton, 1990
Page 189

Use with Chapter 21, Lesson 3

Objectives

- ☐ *Appreciate the human drama involved in the final collapse of the Cold War's most powerful symbol, the Berlin Wall.*
- ☐ *Rewrite the account in the form of a television news report.*

Rewriting in Another Genre

After students have read the selection, ask them to contrast what happened when Peter Fechter tried to scale the Wall in 1962 with what happened when the knapsack-toting man got on the wall in 1990. (Fechter was shot and left to die; the other man was sprayed with a hose.) *Why do you suppose so many people wanted to get on the wall that night in 1990?* (For so many years it had been strictly off-limits, a symbol of fear.)

Divide the class into small groups. Have each group rewrite the account in the form of a television news story. Encourage the "news teams" to show "live footage" and "interviews" as well as a summary of why the night's events are such a turning point in Cold War history. All reports should be about three minutes long. Have all "news teams" perform their reports for the rest of the class.

REACHING THE MOON/VOYAGE TO THE MOON

from the *New York Times*, 1969
Pages 190–191 🔲

Use with Chapter 21, Lesson 4

Objectives

❏ *Recognize how the front page of the newspaper expresses the significance of American astronauts landing on the moon.*

❏ *Understand how Americans perceived the event at the time.*

❏ *Write a story about the first landing on the planet Mars.*

Writing Your Own Story

After students have studied the selection, play the NASA recordings and *Voyage to the Moon* on the cassette. Have students discuss why the moon landing was such an amazing event. Ask students: *How would you have reacted to being the first person ever to set foot on the moon? Why was the moon landing important to scientists?* (Scientists had much to learn about the moon and space exploration.) *What reactions to the moon landing did Archibald MacLeish express in his poem?* (excitement, awe, wonder)

Have students suppose that they have been sent forward in time to experience the first landing on the planet Mars. Tell them that they may choose to be any person (for example, an astronaut, the President, an American watching the event at home). Then have students write a story about the Mars landing from the point of view of their character. Encourage them to describe why the event is important to them. Have volunteers share their stories with the class.